SK277 Human Biology
Science: Level 2

Control and Communication

This publication forms part of an Open University course SK277. The complete list of texts which make up this course can be found at the back (where applicable). Details of this and other Open University courses can be obtained from the Student Registration and Enquiry Service, The Open University, PO Box 197, Milton Keynes MK7 6BJ, United Kingdom: tel. +44 (0)870 333 4340, email general-enquiries@open.ac.uk

Alternatively, you may visit the Open University website at http://www.open.ac.uk where you can learn more about the wide range of courses and packs offered at all levels by The Open University.

To purchase a selection of Open University course materials visit http://www.ouw.co.uk, or contact Open University Worldwide, Michael Young Building, Walton Hall, Milton Keynes MK7 6AA, United Kingdom for a brochure. tel. +44 (0)1908 858785; fax +44 (0)1908 858787; email ouwenq@open.ac.uk

The Open University
Walton Hall, Milton Keynes
MK7 6AA

First published 2004. Second edition 2006.

Edited and designed by The Open University.

Typeset by The Open University

Printed and bound in the United Kingdom by The University Press, Cambridge.

ISBN 0 7492 1441 4

2.1

THE COURSE TEAM

Course Team Chair and Academic Editor

Heather McLannahan

Course Managers

Alastair Ewing

Colin Walker

Course Team Assistants

Catherine Eden

Rebecca Efthimiou

Course Team Authors

Patricia Ash

Pete Clifton

Paul Gabbott

Nicolette Habgood

Tim Halliday

Heather McLannahan

Kerry Murphy

Daniel Nettle

Payam Rezaie

Other Contributors

Vickie Arrowsmith

Leslie Baillie

Production and Presentation Manager

John Owen

Project Manager

Judith Pickering

Editors

Rebecca Graham

Gillian Riley

Bina Sharma

Margaret Swithenby

Design

Sarah Hofton

Jenny Nockles

Illustration

Steve Best

Pam Owen

CD-ROM Production

Phil Butcher

Will Rawes

External Course Assessor

Dinah Gould

Picture Researcher

Lydia Eaton

Indexer

Jane Henley

Course Website

Patrina Law

Louise Olney

SK277 *Human Biology* makes use of material originally produced for SK220 *Human Biology and Health* by the following individuals: Janet Bunker, Melanie Clements, Basiro Davey, Brian Goodwin, Linda Jones, Jeanne Katz, Heather McLannahan, Hilary MacQueen, Jill Saffrey, Moyra Sidell, Michael Stewart, Margaret Swithenby and Frederick Toates.

Cover image: © Alan Schein Photography/CORBIS

CONTENTS

CHAPTER 1   THE NERVOUS SYSTEM   7

Learning Outcomes   7

1.1   An introduction to the nervous system   7

1.2   Imaging the nervous system   8

1.3   The general structure of the nervous system   10

1.4   The brain   13

1.5   The cranial nerves   21

1.6   Does the left brain know what the right brain is doing?   22

1.7   The neuroanatomy of laughter   23

1.8   Organization of the nerves of the body   25

1.9   Cells of the nervous system; the action potential and
       neurotransmission   30

1.10   Overview of sensory and motor systems   37

1.11   When things go wrong   43

Questions for Chapter 1   49

References and Further Reading   50

CHAPTER 2   THE SPECIAL SENSES   51

Learning Outcomes   51

2.1   Overview and introduction to the special senses   51

2.2   The visual system   62

2.3   Central visual pathways and visual areas   68

2.4   Colour vision and colour blindness   68

2.5   Causes of impaired vision   70

2.6   The auditory system   73

2.7   The vestibular system and equilibrium   78

2.8   Causes of impaired hearing   78

2.9   Conclusion   82

Questions for Chapter 2   82

References and Further Reading   83

CHAPTER 3   THE ENDOCRINE SYSTEM   85

Learning Outcomes   85

3.1   An introduction to the endocrine system   85

3.2   The role of the endocrine system   89

3.3   The organization of the endocrine system   93

3.4   The hypothalamic-pituitary axis   98

3.5   The function of the hypothalamic-anterior pituitary axis   101

3.6   Endocrine tissues that are outside the
      hypothalamic-pituitary axis   112

3.7   Regulation of blood glucose levels   115

3.8   Cytokines and growth factors   121

3.9   The life of a hormone   123

3.10 Conclusion   129

Questions for Chapter 3   130

References and Further Reading   132

CHAPTER 4   BODY ORGANIZATION AND GROWTH   133

Learning Outcomes   133

4.1   Introduction   133

4.2   The pros and cons of standing on our own two feet   135

4.3   The skeleton   137

4.4   Growth in the musculo-skeletal system   144

4.5   Changes in body shape and posture   155

4.6   Joints   158

4.7   Muscles   163

4.8   Muscles and movement   166

4.9   Conclusion   171

Questions for Chapter 4   171

References   172

CONCLUSION   173

ANSWERS TO QUESTIONS   175

ACKNOWLEDGEMENTS   181

INDEX   182

CHAPTER I

THE NERVOUS SYSTEM

Learning Outcomes

After completing this chapter, you should be able to:

1.1 Describe the basic structural components of the nervous system and understand the functional significance of their interconnections.

1.2 Distinguish between the central and peripheral nervous system, and between sympathetic and parasympathetic pathways.

1.3 Describe the cellular components of the nervous system and explain their roles.

1.4 Explain how neurons transmit information by means of action potentials, give examples of neurotransmitters and outline the sequence of events that occur at a synapse and how these may be modulated.

1.5 Describe how physiological malfunctions of the nervous system affect normal behaviour and outline diagnosis and treatment regimens for both disease and accident-induced causes.

1.1 An introduction to the nervous system

Do we really use only 10% of our brains? The idea has certain appeal, does it not? However, this does beg the question: what do we do with the other 90%? Despite such claims you may have come across in advertisements, misquoted in books and journals, or talked about with friends, all 100% of our faculties (when functioning well of course!) are at our disposal. The most misconstrued phrases of our times may be 'scientists tell us' or 'scientists now know' such and such a fact, and the worst misconceptions are probably those that everyone claims to be fact, and yet are unsubstantiated. This is one of those instances of our collective ignorance, which has fuelled much of present-day notions that we can tap into and develop 'psychic and intuitive powers'. So let us put away our crystal balls, and move forward into the 21st century.

You may be wondering where this popular myth originated – this is still unclear. It may have originated around the beginning of the 19th century when phrenologists claimed that they could deduce individual human character traits (such as love of children or an exceptional flair for mathematics) from the patterns and sizes of bumps on the skull. In contrast, Marie-Jean-Pierre Flourens (1794–1867) argued that although specific regions of the brain possessed separate functions, these areas also functioned globally and in concert. In the 1920s to 1930s, Karl Lashley attempted to determine where memories were stored in the brain by removing large areas of the **cerebral cortex** in trained rats. (*Cortex* means bark in Latin, as in the outer layer of a tree, and the cortex is the outer layer of the brain; see, for example, Figure 1.6.) His results showed that a loss of tissue, irrespective of the precise area, affected performance, and indicated that memory was not confined to one singular area of the cerebral cortex. So the idea that we only use 10% of our brain seems to have emerged around the time that the functions of the brain were beginning to be mapped. We now know that damage to even small areas of the brain (for example in stroke; see Book 3, Chapter 2) can sometimes have dramatic influences on behaviour or cause drastic neurological disturbance. Note that a loss of 10–20% of neurons (nerve cells), in Alzheimer's disease, produces significant reduction in brain function, even though the structure of the brain itself is relatively well preserved. Albert Einstein has also been credited with giving the 10% response as a sardonic answer to a journalist when asked to explain why he was smarter than other people, and his comment has been misconstrued ever since! Others have attempted to rationalize the myth by suggesting it refers to the conscious versus the subconscious mind (i.e. the conscious mind is used 10–20% of the time, and the remaining 80–90% must therefore belong to the subconscious). Without venturing into philosophical domains, this notion is clearly at odds with research into brain functioning.

Today, research into the neurosciences (the study of the nervous system) is prospering. Neuroscience research is also at the forefront of media interest and the public eye, mounting the pressure for new treatments to be developed for such ailments as Alzheimer's disease or Parkinson's disease, not only to improve the quality of life but also to reduce the burden on National Health Services. In the last two decades, we have made considerable technological advances in imaging the complexity and functions of the human nervous system. Our understanding of the functions of the nervous system and inner workings of the mind (cognitive processing or 'higher mental functions') has flourished rapidly as a consequence.

1.2 Imaging the nervous system

Recent advances in our understanding of the relationship between structure and function of the human nervous system have largely been developed through new techniques that image the brain. Examples are **computerized tomography (CT) scanning** in which cross-sectional images of the brain are created from a series of X-ray beams directed through the head (Figure 1.1a). In a similar manner, **computerized angiography** allows us to detect the blood vessels of the brain by directing a series of X-rays at the head, after injecting a specific radio-opaque dye into the bloodstream. The structure of the brain and cerebral blood vessels (arteries and veins) can be readily seen using these techniques but they do not tell us about their function.

Imaging the brain using **positron emission tomography (PET)** gives us functional information on the activity of the brain (Figure 1.1b). The technique relies on the detection of radioactively labelled material that is injected into a patient's bloodstream and transported around the body. It can be detected in the part of the brain which is metabolically active at a given time.

Magnetic resonance imaging (MRI) provides much more clarity of detail in structural anatomy, and does not require the use of X-rays or radioactive material (Figure 1.1c). This technique uses a magnetic field to detect areas of brain activity. Some patients with metal devices such as pacemakers are not able to have an MRI scan because the device interferes with the magnetic field. An MRI scanner is shown in Figure 1.2.

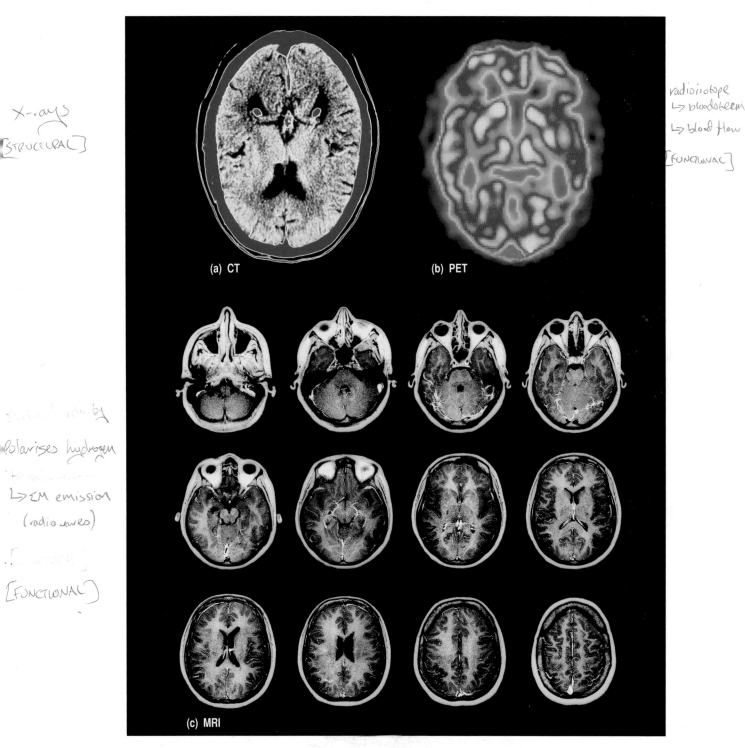

(a) CT

(b) PET

(c) MRI

Handwritten annotations (left margin):
X-rays
[STRUCTURAL]

electrical activity
Polarises hydrogen
↳ EM emission
(radio waves)
[FUNCTIONAL]

Handwritten annotations (right margin):
radioisotope
↳ bloodstream
↳ blood flow
[FUNCTIONAL]

Figure 1.1   CT, PET, and MRI images of the normal human brain. (a) Coloured computed tomography (CT or CAT) horizontal scan through a healthy brain from a 70-year-old man. The front of the brain is to the bottom. The *cerebral hemispheres* are indicated in orange. The *ventricles* are shown in black. Blue-coloured circles on the ventricles either side of the brain's midline represent the *choroid plexi* that produce cerebrospinal fluid. (These terms will be explained later in this chapter.) (b) Positron emission tomography (PET) horizontal scan of a normal human brain. Brain activity is indicated as low (blue colour code) to high (yellow colour code) on the figure. (c) Coloured magnetic resonance imaging (MRI) scans through the human brain – the sequence of scans (from left to right) passes from the base of the brain (at the base of the nose, top left), up to a level near the top of the brain (bottom right). The eyes and nose (blue/white) appear in the first six scans.

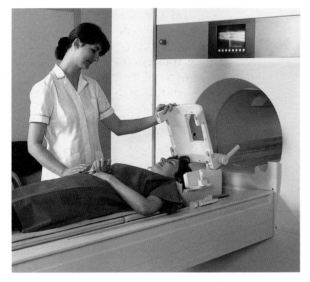

Figure 1.2 An MRI scanning machine.

● Consider Figure 1.2. Can you think under what circumstances people may be unable to have an MRI scan?

● In addition to those people with metal devices, very large people and those who suffer from claustrophobia (fear of confined spaces) would have difficulties, as the patient must lie very still inside a narrow space for the duration of the imaging.

However, advances in technology have meant that a wider machine is now available that can accommodate very large individuals and is also suitable for people with claustrophobia.

Functional MRI (fMRI) is a more recent technique that is used to detect changes in blood flow to specific brain areas, whilst at the same time providing a detailed anatomical view of the brain.

These techniques not only allow us to understand the anatomical basis of cognitive function, but they can detect areas of the brain that are affected in neurological and psychiatric disorders, and are very useful tools that help us to develop new strategies to treat such disturbances. In the majority of circumstances, present-day neurologists can identify damage (lesions) within the brain based on the patient's clinical symptoms and deficits, and confirm this with detailed imaging, for example using fMRI.

In the following sections, we will focus on the structural and functional anatomy of the nervous system and discover how the various components within our nervous system operate and integrate with each other. Towards the end of this chapter, we shall discuss examples of what happens when things go wrong with the system.

1.3 The general structure of the nervous system

1.3.1 The main divisions: central and peripheral nervous systems

Figure 1.3 shows the nervous system is made up of the brain, spinal cord (neural tissue located in the middle of the backbone) and peripheral nervous system. The brain and spinal cord together constitute what is termed the **central nervous system (CNS)** and all of the nervous system that is outside of the brain or spinal cord is termed the **peripheral nervous system (PNS)**.

Within the nervous system a neuron that conveys information *to* the CNS (brain and spinal cord) is called a **sensory** (or afferent) **neuron** and one that carries information away *from* the CNS to activate muscles and glands, is called a **motor** (or efferent) **neuron**. The term **nerve** refers to a collection of axons (the long process that extends from the neuron's cell body as shown in Figure 1.3c) in

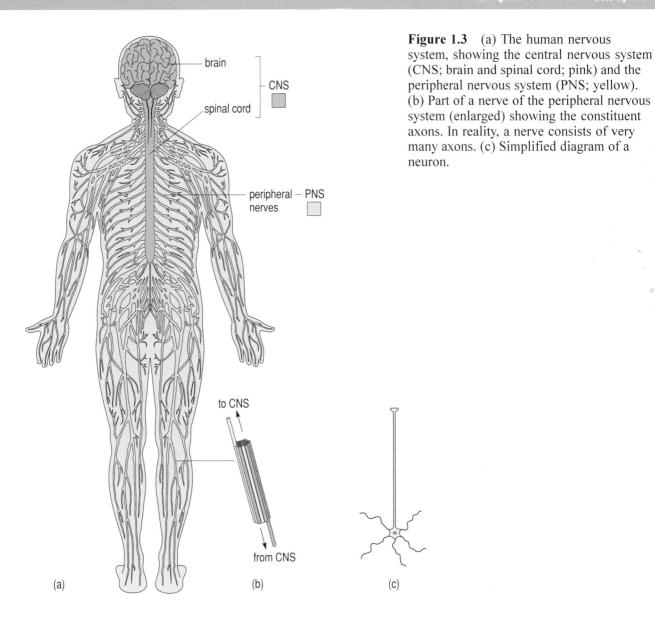

Figure 1.3 (a) The human nervous system, showing the central nervous system (CNS; brain and spinal cord; pink) and the peripheral nervous system (PNS; yellow). (b) Part of a nerve of the peripheral nervous system (enlarged) showing the constituent axons. In reality, a nerve consists of very many axons. (c) Simplified diagram of a neuron.

the PNS, all physically located alongside each other and extending over the same distance, like a bundle of wires in a cable of a telephone system (Figure 1.3b). The individual axons within a nerve will convey information as brief pulses of electrical activity, known as nerve impulses, either to or from the CNS. In Figure 1.3b the pale yellow axons carry information to the CNS and are called **afferent fibres**, and the deep yellow axons carry information from the CNS and are called **efferent fibres**. A nerve will usually be composed of a mixture of these two sorts of axons. Many neurons are neither sensory nor motor but are located as **interneurons** somewhere between them, deep in the brain or spinal cord. Our perceiving, feeling, thinking and acting, is the result of the activity of millions of neurons in the brain integrating incoming information with memories of previous experiences.

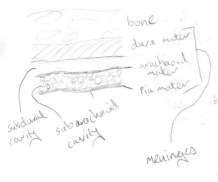

1.3.2 The CNS environment: meninges and cerebrospinal fluid

The brain is enclosed within the skull and covered by three protective sheets of tissue (collectively termed the **meninges**) that extend down the spinal cord and are known as the dura, arachnoid and pia mater. Of these, the pia mater is the membrane that lies closest to the surface of the brain (Figure 1.4). Bacterial or viral infection of these meninges leads to inflammation called *meningitis*. Rupture of blood vessels located below either the dura or arachnoid mater occurs in some types of stroke (cerebrovascular accident; see Book 3, Chapter 2) or following traumatic injury to the head (see Section 1.11.2).

Figure 1.4 Diagram showing a cross-section through the skull and meninges covering the brain and their corresponding spaces. The falx cerebri is a partition between the two cerebral hemispheres.

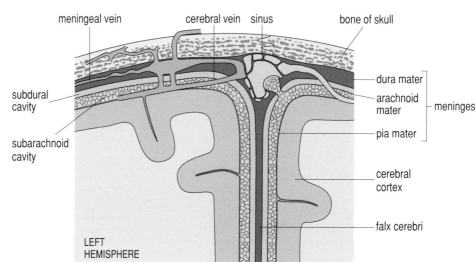

The brain itself contains fluid-filled spaces known as **ventricles**, as illustrated in Figures 1.1 and 1.5. The fluid they contain is called **cerebrospinal fluid (CSF)** which is similar in its constituents to blood plasma (Book 1, Section 2.3.3). One significant feature of the ventricles is that in some pathological conditions they become enlarged (as a consequence of an accumulation of CSF), causing cell death and a reduction in neural tissue, which can result in behavioural disturbances. Production of up to half a litre of CSF per day is maintained by the *choroid plexus* (a rich network of blood vessels projecting into the cavities of the lateral ventricles; see Figure 1.1a). The subarachnoid cavity is also filled with CSF, and major blood vessels can be found here as well as in the meninges. CSF is reabsorbed into veins in the meninges. The CSF helps to maintain a constant environment within the brain and can protect the brain from mechanical injury through reducing the impact of injury sustained to the head.

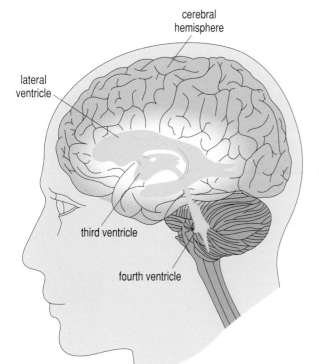

Figure 1.5 Schematic view into the brain to show the arrangement of the ventricles.

Summary of Sections 1.1 to 1.3

1 A variety of imaging techniques are used in modern medicine to visualize the anatomy and gain insight into the function of the human nervous system – these include CT, PET and MRI.

2 The central nervous system (CNS) consists of the brain and spinal cord, and the remainder of the nervous system constitutes the peripheral nervous system (PNS).

3 Sensory neurons convey information to the CNS whereas motor neurons (innervating muscles and glandular tissue) carry information from the CNS. Interneurons are the class of neuron that are neither sensory nor motor; they convey information between other neurons.

4 The meninges form an outer covering on the surface of the brain and spinal cord.

5 The ventricles are fluid-filled spaces containing cerebrospinal fluid (CSF) that help to maintain a constant environment within the brain and also help to cushion the brain during trauma.

1.4 The brain

The brain is not a homogenous lump of tissue; it has a clearly defined structure and some parts look very different to others. An early understanding of brain function was gained from diseases (such as stroke) and head injuries where there was partial loss of mental functions. So it is not surprising that early scientists anticipated that there would be **localization of function** (i.e. that different areas would be specialized to carry out different functions). Modern brain imaging techniques (including PET and functional MRI) have clearly assigned functions to the vast majority of our brain. A complex activity such as a set of tasks, or patterns of thought and laughter (see Section 1.7) will typically engage multiple parts of the brain. However, the fact that we use all of our faculties does not imply that all of our neurons are active all of the time. Just as you would use a specific set of muscles for a particular movement, so you may use a number of specific parts of your brain to deal with a specific task.

ABLETION?

LEFT HEMISPHERE

On average, the human brain weighs around 1.4 kg, approximately 2–5% of the total body weight (by comparison, the adult human spinal cord weighs around 35 g) yet, on average, it consumes up to one-fifth of the oxygen and glucose used by your entire body. Contrary to popular misconceptions, neither the size nor the gender of a brain gives any indication of intelligence – Albert Einstein's brain actually weighed 1.23 kg! (Anderson and Harvey, 1996) We will now take a 'tour of the brain', showing some of its main landmarks and outlining functions.

1.4.1 Cerebral hemispheres

The **cerebral hemispheres** dominate the brain and are separated into left and right hemispheres. Separation is not complete because there is a bundle of myelinated axons (the **corpus callosum**) that link the two hemispheres, thereby allowing communication between them (Figure 1.6).

● What is myelin and what is its function?

○ It is the fat-rich electrically insulating layer that surrounds many axons (Book 1, Section 2.3.2).

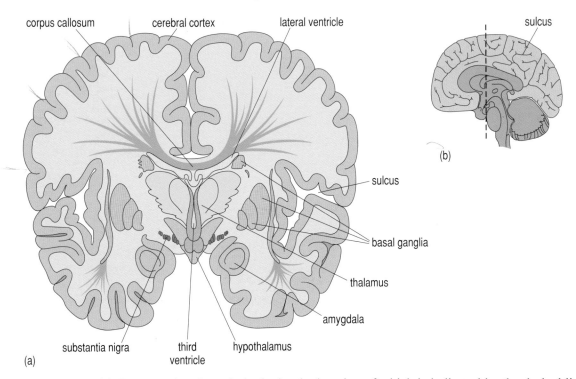

Figure 1.6 (a) Cross-section through the brain, the location of which is indicated by the dashed line in (b).

The cerebral hemispheres appear wrinkled because their outer layer, the cerebral cortex, is folded, as shown in Figure 1.6a, thus allowing a large amount of tissue to be packed into the skull. Spread out, the cerebral cortex would occupy the area of one page of a broadsheet newspaper (approx. $0.22\,\mathrm{m^2}$) and it is estimated that it contains at least 15 billion neurons, each making connections with thousands of other neurons. These huge numbers represent very considerable processing power. It was therefore unexpected when, in 1981, the British neurologist, John Lorber, described a group of young patients referred to him for minor neurological problems (Lorber, 1981). The patients were all of average and above average intelligence, but astonishingly CT scans revealed that the cerebral cortex in these patients was very much thinned, having been compressed by the slow progressive build-up of cerebrospinal fluid in the ventricles. This occurs if reabsorption or the flow of CSF is blocked or there is excessive production of CSF. In consequence the ventricles dilate and intracranial pressure is raised. This condition known as *hydrocephalus* is commonly called water on the brain (from the Greek *hydro* meaning water, *cephalus* meaning head). Lorber documented over 600 cases and categorized

HYDROCEPHALUS

them as follows: (i) those with nearly normal brains, (ii) those with 50–70%, (iii) 70–90% and (iv) 95% of the cranium (skull) filled with CSF. The last group (fewer than 60 cases) had profound disabilities, whereas the remainder possessed IQs greater than 100 (where 80–120 is the range given for 'normal' IQ). One of the least severely affected patients, a 26-year-old man, in fact had an IQ of 126, and achieved a first class honours degree in mathematics at Sheffield University, despite his cortex being only 1 mm thick (instead of the usual 4–5 mm). The fact that some of these patients could function with a fraction of this tissue demonstrates the capacity of the brain, in some instances, to adapt to slowly progressing neurological disturbance, to compensate for injury and to reassign functions.

● What methods could be used to investigate which areas of the brain are active in this capacity?

● Functional mapping of the brain, using PET and fMRI techniques.

Imaging studies suggest that whilst there are strong tendencies for certain regions of the brain to assume specialized tasks (as we shall describe next), our capacity to learn and reason depends on coordination between different regions of our brain.

Areas of the cerebral cortex and their functions

One of the earliest methods that considered the architecture of the cerebral cortex (brain mapping) was that devised by Korbinian Brodmann in 1909, and this is still in use today (Figure 1.7). Brodmann assigned numbers to 52 specific parts of the brain which equated to some extent with their functional organization. More simply, we can divide each hemisphere into four lobes (Figure 1.8), that have both anatomical and functional meaning. Anatomically there are folds, (**sulcus**; plural, sulci) that have essentially the same position in any brain, although marked variations can exist between individuals. The location of a fold can provide landmarks for describing brain regions.

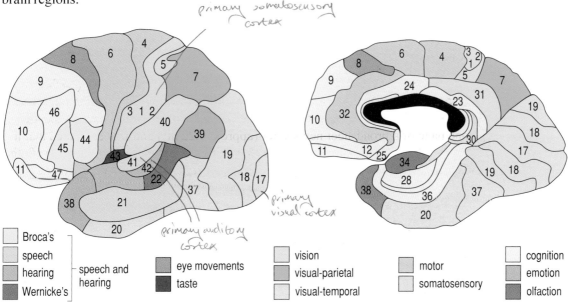

Figure 1.7 Brodmann areas in the human brain with an emphasis on vision and language. The external surface of the left cerebral hemisphere is shown on the left and a section through the brain on the right.

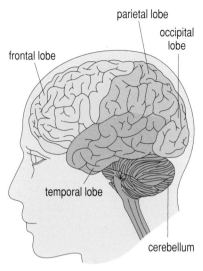

parietal lobe

occipital lobe

frontal lobe

temporal lobe

cerebellum

Figure 1.8 A view of the brain showing the four lobes which make up the cerebral hemisphere.

[Handwritten notes in margin:]

ABLETION

FRONTAL   PARIETAL   TEMPORAL   OCCIPITAL   (CEREBELLUM)

Frontal lobes - planning
↳ cortical association areas
- primary motor cortex (skeletal)
- (Restrained) behaviour

• cognitive processing
↳ processing perception
↳ learning
↳ reasoning

• social/emotional responses

• EPILEPSY (partial seizures)

Of the four lobes: **frontal**, **temporal**, **parietal** and **occipital**, the frontal lobes are the largest. The earliest account of their function is dramatic and derives from information gleaned from the injuries suffered to the brain of a 25-year-old US railroad construction worker back in the mid-19th century. Phineas Gage was a foreman, who was reported to be well-liked and regarded as an honest, trustworthy, hard-working and dependable individual prior to his accident. The tragedy occurred one day while Gage was packing explosive charge into drilled holes with a tamping iron which was about an inch wide and around three and a half feet long (it weighed close to 61 kg!). A chance spark accidentally ignited the charge that propelled the iron rod clear through his skull, and over 30 yards from where he stood (it entered under his left cheek bone, damaging part of his frontal lobes, and exited through the top of his skull).

Miraculously, following a 10-week stay in hospital, Gage recovered from this accident with little intellectual impairment, but his *personality* had been dramatically transformed. He became vulgar, irresponsible, impatient, capricious and offensive, and this eventually led to his dismissal from work. The concept that Gage's personality had been altered as a result of damage to the *frontal lobes* (which must therefore be responsible for the restraint and well-mannered behaviour that the majority of people possess) was proposed by the doctor who was treating him at the time – John Harlow (Harlow, 1868). Patients who suffer from traumatic damage or degenerative diseases that affect the frontal lobes demonstrate strikingly similar alterations in their behaviour but have no insight into their own condition.

In fact, as you can see in Figure 1.7, there are a number of distinct areas within the frontal lobes having varied functions. Measurements show that there is an increased blood flow to the frontal lobes when one is engaged in tasks involving planning.

● What is the significance of this increased blood flow?

○ Neurons in the frontal lobe will be particularly active and will require a large supply of glucose and oxygen brought to them via the blood.

These areas of the frontal lobes that are active in planning are known as *cortical association areas*. Association areas integrate information from different areas of the cortex and perform cognitive processes; so they might integrate incoming sensory information with ongoing performance and memory and as a consequence a new plan of action might be put into effect.

Although much of the frontal lobe is occupied with association cortex there is also an area that is called the **primary motor cortex**. (This is shown as area 4 on Figure 1.7.) This area sends commands to the skeletal muscles (i.e. muscles associated with the skeleton, see Chapter 4).

The brain has primary sensory areas too. These are the cortical areas that receive input from the senses and begin the task of processing the information that will ultimately result in our perceptions. We will be discussing them in the next chapter but for now use Figure 1.7 to locate the:

primary visual cortex (area 17 in the occipital lobe)

primary auditory cortex (areas 41 and 42 in the temporal lobe)

primary somatosensory cortex (areas 1, 2 and 3 on the parietal lobe)

Deeper structures of the cerebral hemispheres

Figure 1.9 shows some of the deeper structures of the cerebral hemispheres. The **amygdala** is concerned with attaching emotional significance to sensory information, and therefore has a role in memory as well as motivation. Together with the **hippocampus** (a banana-shaped structure) and some other brain regions it is part of what is sometimes called the **limbic system**. These limbic structures are interconnected and some neuroscientists and psychologists believe that they are the 'emotion system'. Others would disagree and instead subscribe to the view held by the neuroanatomist Per Brodal that use of the term *limbic system* involves 'substituting magical naming for understanding'. The hippocampus and amygdala lie within the middle of the temporal lobes, and electrical stimulation of such regions can evoke feelings of fear, hunger or lust (see Box 1.1). The hippocampus also plays a central role in memory (particularly in short-term processing and storage of memory, and consolidation into long-term memory).

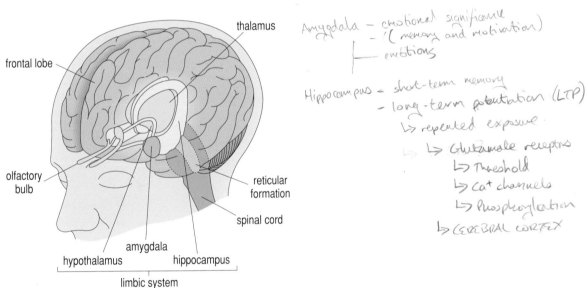

Figure 1.9   Diagram of the brain showing some of its deeper structures.

The **basal ganglia** (Figure 1.6) are made up of three large collections of neuronal cell bodies or nuclei. In relation to brain anatomy, the term **nucleus** (plural, nuclei) is used to denote any **histologically** identifiable (i.e. identifiable by tissue type) mass of neuronal cell bodies in the brain or spinal cord. Although the basal ganglia neither receive direct sensory information nor directly influence motor output they have a role in learning motor skills and they play a crucial role in the control of movement, particularly its initiation. Disorders of the basal ganglia are seen as disorders of movement, ranging from an excess of involuntary movement (as in Huntington's disease), to an inadequacy of voluntary movements, as in Parkinson's disease.

Box 1.1   Surgery and electrical stimulation of the brain

Given that brain tissue is delicate you may wonder about the ethics of electrical stimulation of brain regions. However, it is often carried out prior to the removal of brain tissue. An important phenomenon to note is that the brain, despite being able to detect pain located anywhere within the body, does not have receptors within its own tissue that detect damage and is therefore not itself capable of 'feeling' pain or touch. This means that the surgeon can stimulate the brain and the patient can report their sensations and feelings. There are some people who have epilepsy that does not respond to medication. If they are afflicted with several seizures daily, normal life becomes impossible and drastic measures are needed. One type of seizure involves a specific part of the brain becoming constantly active (*focal or partial seizure*) and electrical stimulation can locate the focus of the seizure. These foci are often in the temporal lobe, which is where the limbic structures lie, and this is how the limbic functions first came to be ascribed. Once the problem area is located the dysfunctional tissue can be destroyed. Another type of epilepsy involves the whole brain in excessive activity (*generalized seizure*) and for these patients, when medication fails, a *callotomy* is performed. This is a procedure which severs the corpus callosum.

● What is the function of the corpus callosum?

● The corpus callosum connects the two hemispheres (Figure 1.6).

Despite being crude, this successfully prevents the spread of seizure from one hemisphere to the other. For most of these '**split-brain**' patients life is much improved. Their abilities to walk, to read and converse and carry out everyday activities return to normal. However, quite subtle differences are discovered soon afterwards as is described in Section 1.6.

The Canadian brain surgeon Wilder Penfield operated on hundreds of patients with epilepsy during the 1950s and found that areas in the temporal lobes evoked specific memories when stimulated. He also found areas of the cortex that when stimulated produced responses in muscles and in this way he mapped the motor cortex (see Section 1.10 for details). Other cortical areas gave rise to sensations from different body areas so it was he who also mapped the somatosensory cortex (Section 1.10).

1.4.2 Thalamus and hypothalamus

These two structures are shown in Figures 1.6 and 1.9. The **thalamus** is a structure made up of several large collections of neuronal cell bodies.

● What do we call large collections of cell bodies?

● Nuclei.

Handwritten margin notes:

TEMPORAL LOBE? (EPILEPSY)
• Memories – Memories
• EPILEPSY (Partial seizures)

THALAMUS
- sorts/processes sensory info
- Gateway to cerebral cortex
  ↳ control of movement

PNS → sensory → THALAMUS → CEREBRAL CORTEX

The thalamus sorts and interprets sensory information received from the peripheral nervous system and relays these to the appropriate region of the cerebral cortex. It also links the cerebral cortex with other parts of the brain; for example, it has links with the basal ganglia and thus it too has a role in the control of movement.

Immediately below the thalamus lies the **hypothalamus** (*hypo* means 'lower than', so this structure lies below the thalamus), which controls activities such as heart rate, respiration and fat metabolism. The hypothalamus exerts other important *homeostatic* functions such as regulating body temperature, appetite and water balance (see Book 1, Section 2.4). It acts as an important bridge between the nervous and endocrine systems through the production and regulation of various hormones (see Chapter 3). For instance, regions of the hypothalamus that are sensitive to the presence of hormones such as testosterone in the bloodstream seem to play a crucial role in organizing our sexual inclinations and desires. Because of this and its connections with the amygdala and hippocampus, the hypothalamus is deemed to be part of the limbic system.

1.4.3 The brainstem

From Figure 1.10 you can see that the **brainstem** is made up of midbrain, pons and **medulla**. The brainstem is concerned with the basic activities necessary for life. In particular you will come across the role of the medulla in the regulation of breathing and blood circulation (Book 3) and of structures within the pons that regulate sleep (Book 4). In Book 1, mention was made of the vomiting and swallowing centres in the brainstem, both of which are in the medulla.

BRAINSTEM :
Legally dead (coma)

• MIDBRAIN

• MEDULLA
* – breathing*
* – circulation*
* – vomiting centre*
* – swallowing centre*
* – Auditory processing*

• Pons
* – sleep*

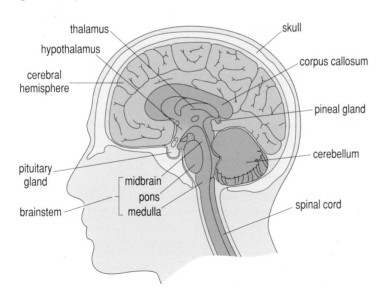

thalamus
hypothalamus
cerebral hemisphere
pituitary gland
brainstem
skull
corpus callosum
pineal gland
cerebellum
spinal cord
midbrain
pons
medulla

Figure 1.10   Section through the brain showing the right cerebral hemisphere and some other important regions.

When all activity in the brainstem ceases a patient is legally declared dead. This may seem a rather obvious statement but it becomes of great importance where an individual is in a state of prolonged and deep unconsciousness (**coma**) but being maintained on a life-support system.

CEREBELLUM:

- Motor feedback/assessment

- Exproprioception?

- Movement termination

- ATAXIA

- Learning motor skills

- Drunken movements

1.4.4 Cerebellum

In Figures 1.8 and 1.10 you can see a brain region called the **cerebellum**. In humans this structure weighs around 150 g. It receives sensory information from, amongst other places, the muscles and it exerts an influence on descending motor pathways (i.e. the neurons that connect the primary motor cortex to the motor neurons).

● What is the function of the primary motor cortex?

◐ The motor cortex sends commands to the skeletal muscles.

● What do you suppose is the function of the cerebellum?

◐ The cerebellum is likely to be primarily involved in control of movement.

Its role concerns the organization of posture, balance and locomotion, although it has little involvement in the *initiation* of behaviour. If one wants an analogy, then perhaps it is best described as something like an aircraft's 'on-board computer', performing computations on the position of the body, the state of the muscles and the plans for action. It is the site where comparisons are made between movements actually performed and the movements required to achieve a goal. During a movement, the cerebellum, informed of progress, can make revisions in the programme according to how well things are going. In other words, the cerebellum is a location where commands to action appear to be compared with what has been achieved, the latter being based upon feedback from various sensory sources. Disparity will trigger signals to the motor system that result in a modification of behaviour. The cerebellum also has a role in terminating actions by triggering appropriate muscle contraction in order to bring a movement to an end, i.e. a braking effect.

ATAXIA
↳ deficiency in smooth coordinated movements.

Since patients with lesions to the cerebellum are deficient in performing normal, smooth and effective, goal-directed movements, a condition termed **ataxia**, damage to the cerebellum can result in a response that overshoots the target. The patient then needs to make a conscious decision to bring, say, the hand back to the target. Therefore, an action such as reaching out to pick up an object can be characterized by a jerky movement with an oscillation of the hand around its target. The walk of patients with damage to this region is commonly awkward and they can appear to be drunk. They have difficulty in modifying behaviour in the light of experience, demonstrating that the cerebellum is involved in learning motor skills. However, unlike patients with Parkinson's disease, they do not have difficulty in initiating movement. This suggests that the cerebellum is not involved in the initiation of behaviour, but in its smooth execution once started, and in the learning of skills based upon deviations of actual movements from that intended. It is particularly sensitive to the effects of alcohol; the swaying, uncoordinated gait of a drunkard is a cliché, but an accurate one. Chronic alcohol abuse leads to permanent damage and problems with balance and walking. (You might recall that mention was made of Wernicke–Korsakoff syndrome in connection with alcohol abuse in Book 1.)

1.5 The cranial nerves

The **cranial nerves** are not part of the brain but they are visible on the under surface of the brain (Figure 1.11) so it seems appropriate to end our tour of the brain here. Table 1.1 gives a summary of their functions and is for reference only.

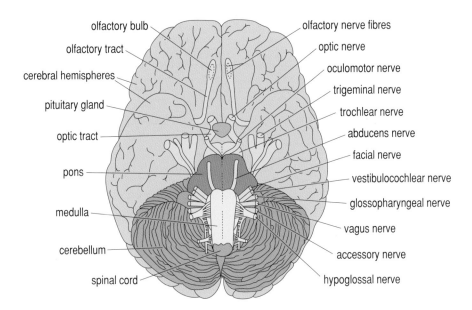

olfactory bulb
olfactory tract
cerebral hemispheres
pituitary gland
optic tract
pons
medulla
cerebellum
spinal cord

olfactory nerve fibres
optic nerve
oculomotor nerve
trigeminal nerve
trochlear nerve
abducens nerve
facial nerve
vestibulocochlear nerve
glossopharyngeal nerve
vagus nerve
accessory nerve
hypoglossal nerve

Figure 1.11 The cranial nerves.

Table 1.1 Summary of the functions of the cranial nerves.

Name	Function
olfactory	sense of smell
optic	vision
oculomotor	control of eye muscles, pupil muscles
trigeminal	sensory input from head, control of jaw muscles
trochlear	control of eye muscles
abducens	control of eye muscles
facial	sensory input from tongue, control of muscles of facial expression
vestibulocochlear (vestibular and auditory nerves)	sense of balance (vestibular nerve) and hearing (auditory nerve)
glossopharyngeal	sensory input from tongue, control of throat muscles
vagus	sensory input from external ear, tongue and internal organs; control of muscles in throat and larynx; innervation of heart and internal organs
accessory	control of muscles in the ear
hypoglossal	control of tongue muscles

1.6 Does the left brain know what the right brain is doing?

Having toured the brain and seen the split between the two hemispheres you may be wondering whether the two halves carry out different functions or duplicate their efforts. Is this a 'back up' system? Is this where the 10% myth gained credence? In fact, many brain functions are *lateralized.* That is, they exist in one hemisphere of the brain. Each hemisphere seems to be specialized for certain behaviours. In very simplistic terms, calculative, mathematical and logical processing (reading, writing and arithmetic) are predominant functions of the left hemisphere, and the right brain governs pattern (e.g. face) recognition, visual imagery and musical abilities (form, geometry and music). However the two hemispheres do communicate and coordinate their activities.

● How do the two hemispheres communicate?

○ The two hemispheres are connected by the corpus callosum and you might have noticed on Figure 1.6 that there are other pathways that link the two hemispheres.

The right hemisphere controls muscles on the *left side* and also receives sensory information from the left side of the body. The left hemisphere exerts motor control on and receives sensory input from the *right side* (although there are also some ipsilateral, i.e. same side, pathways to and from each hemisphere). Damage to one cerebral hemisphere (for example, in stroke) will therefore have direct impact on the opposite side of the body.

A problem that is often a consequence of stroke is loss of speech. The *left hemisphere* is dominant for language in the majority of people. The language areas associated with the left hemisphere (Broca's area and Wernicke's area – Figure 1.7) bear the names of the neurologists who discovered their functions in the 19th century – Paul Broca and Karl Wernicke. These neurologists independently found that patients who had suffered damage to particular areas on the left (but not the right) hemisphere demonstrated speech and language difficulties. However, as this left-brain-language link is not true for all individuals it is important to know what the individual situation is when surgery is required (e.g. see Box 1.1). From the 1960s onwards, brain lateralization has been gauged using selective anaesthesia prior to surgery. An anaesthetic (a substance that blocks feeling or awareness) is injected into the left carotid artery (which supplies the left hemisphere) or the right carotid (which supplies the right hemisphere). This method selectively sedates either of the hemispheres.

● If an anaesthetic is injected into the left carotid artery and the patient still responds verbally to the surgeon's questions, what can you say about their localization of language?

○ This person is one of the tiny minority with right-brain localization of language.

For a person with language dominance in the left hemisphere the anaesthetic would have resulted in their being unable to speak.

LEFT HEMISPHERE:

– Right motor control
– Mathematical processing
– Language dominance
  ↳ Broca's area
  ↳ Wernicke's area

RIGHT HEMISPHERE:

–

In certain patients with epilepsy (see Box 1.1) who are resistant to conventional drug treatments, one surgical option that has been commonly used for therapy is to cut the corpus callosum connecting the two hemispheres (Figure 1.6). Despite being crude, this successfully prevents the spread of seizure from one hemisphere to the other and the patients show no side-effects. However, quite subtle differences were discovered when Roger Sperry and Michael Gazzaniga examined these split-brain patients in the 1960s. All patients had language lateralized to the left hemisphere. If the patient was given an object (that they couldn't see) in their left hand, they could not name it, but this was overcome when the object was transferred to their right hand.

Callosectomy?

● Explain this observation.

◐ The left hemisphere receives sensory information from the right hand (see above). So the language centres in the left hemisphere can use this information to describe the object. However, when the object is in the left hand the sensory information goes to the right hemisphere and, as the corpus callosum has been cut, the information is not passed to the left (language) centres.

In further experiments using a tachistoscope, an instrument that allows you to present a visual image to one hemisphere only, similar results were obtained. When asked to identify an object presented as an image to the right hemisphere they would respond verbally that there was no object. There was no difficulty identifying and naming the same object when it was presented to the left hemisphere. The experiences of these patients provide valuable insights into hemispheric lateralization and emphasizes how important it is that the left brain knows what the right brain is doing.

Also shows that language areas of the cortex linked to consciousness.

↳ BLINDSIGHT

In the next section we take a look at a complex example of the way that the different parts of the brain work together.

1.7 The neuroanatomy of laughter

Have you ever wondered why we laugh? What is the physiological basis of laughter, or in more scientific terms, *gelotology*? We develop the ability to laugh within the first few months after birth, before we can even speak, and our ability to smile is shared by our closest cousins – primates (e.g. chimpanzees). Laughter is the physiological response to humour, and is closely associated with speech. It is both social and contagious. Studies into the phenomenon indicate that laughter causes a change in our blood pressure and heart rate, alters breathing, reduces levels of certain neurochemicals, relaxes muscular tension, boosts the immune system, helps us to cope with stress, and can even relieve pain. It is thus not surprising perhaps, that our brains process and interpret humour and laughter through complex pathways, involving much the same skills as are necessary for solving problems. Three key areas of the brain take part in the process of laughter – the frontal lobe (cognitive processing, i.e. the processing of information with regards to perception, learning and reasoning), supplementary motor area (governing movement), and the nucleus accumbens (associated with processing the emotional significance of stimuli and also involved in addictive behaviour).

β-endorphins

LAUGHTER
↳ Frontal lobe
* ↳ perception/reasoning*
↳ supplementary motor area
* ↳ movement*
↳ nucleus accumbens
* ↳ (basal ganglia?)*
* ↳ emotional significance*
* ↳ reward centres.*

A study of an adolescent girl (A.K.) with intractable epileptic seizures that failed to respond well to drugs has given insights into the workings of laughter. (Fried et al., 1998). In the course of surgical treatment, mild electrical stimulation was applied to

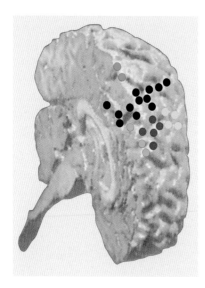

Figure 1.12   Three-dimensional reconstruction from MRI scans showing the areas of the left hemisphere where electrical stimulation produced laughter in patient A.K.

AK – epilepsy
↳ stimulation (artificial)
↳ laughter

discrete sites on the cortical surface of her left frontal lobe. Surprisingly, the surgeons found that stimulation of a region on the frontal lobe consistently produced laughter, accompanied by a sensation of mirth in this patient (Figure 1.12).

The duration and intensity of the laughter increased with the level of stimulus current (ranging from a smile at one end of the scale to contagious laughter at the other). Smiling and laughter appear therefore, to involve similar mechanisms, and there is coordination between motor, limbic (mood/emotion) and cognitive centres of the brain. However, interestingly, a different explanation was offered by the girl for the cause of the merriment on each separate occasion, and she always attributed her behaviour to external stimuli.

Brain "rationalizes" laughter (creating cause)

● What do her explanations tell us?

○ That the electrical stimulation results in a response of laughter, but not the 'reason' which she offers.

It has also been found that the brain produces a regular electrical pattern when responding to humorous material. Within four-tenths of a second following exposure to something funny (like a joke), an electrical wave moves through the cerebral cortex. The cortex of the left hemisphere analyses the structure and content of the joke, the frontal lobes (involved in social and emotional responses) become active, and the cortex of the right hemisphere is next involved in intellectual analysis so that we can understand the joke (Shammi and Stuss, 1999). Brainwave activity then spreads to the sensory processing area of the occipital lobe. Laughter is produced via a circuit that involves multiple brain areas. Bearing in mind that we are not all the same, and that differences in our age, personality, intelligence, mental state, mood and cultural upbringing all influence the way we respond to humorous stimuli, most of us can still recognize when a situation is meant to be funny! Nevertheless, it is our brain that makes the final decision on what should be deemed funny and when, for us. Do note, however, that there is also a type of epilepsy with gelastic (laughter) seizures – unfortunately causing people to laugh for no apparent reason.

Summary of Sections 1.4 to 1.7

1   Different regions of the brain can be associated with different functions, e.g. the visual cortex processes visual information, the motor cortex sends commands to skeletal muscles.

2   Some brain regions have specialized functions that are not directly related to motor or sensory processing – an example is the frontal lobes (which govern behaviour, reasoning, strategic planning and action).

3   The limbic system allows integration of cognition and emotions such as fear, hunger, and lust; the basal ganglia and the cerebellum influence movement.

4   The thalamus is a link in motor and sensory pathways that has a processing role, it is not just a relay station; the hypothalamus has many important homeostatic functions and provides a link between the endocrine and nervous systems.

5   Many brain functions are lateralized but the two cerebral hemispheres communicate and coordinate their activities mainly via the corpus callosum.

1.8 Organization of the nerves of the body

1.8.1 The spinal cord

Figure 1.13 shows a section of the spinal cord. From this section you can clearly see the protection that is provided for the neural tissue by the associated bony vertebra. Whilst Figure 1.11 shows how the cranial nerves feed into the brain, Figure 1.3 shows that the peripheral nerves feed into the spinal cord and Figure 1.13 gives more detail of this.

Figure 1.13 shows that the spinal cord can be divided into **grey matter** and **white matter**. Myelin is a whitish, fatty substance so areas where it is abundant are called white matter. The areas of grey matter get their colour from densely packed cell bodies.

The dorsal root ganglion contains the cell bodies of sensory neurons. (A **ganglion** – plural, ganglia – is a collection of cell bodies of neurons in the **peripheral nervous system**. The term 'dorsal' refers to the back, so in Figure 1.13 the person whose spinal cord is represented should be imagined to be facing you.)

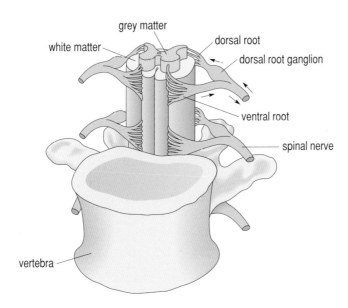

grey matter
white matter
dorsal root
dorsal root ganglion
ventral root
spinal nerve
vertebra

Figure 1.13 A part of the spinal cord and an associated vertebra, shown in section. The arrows show the direction of passage of nerve impulses.

The cell bodies of motor neurons are located within the spinal cord itself so that there is no 'ganglionic' structure comparable to the dorsal root ganglion within the ventral root.

Dorsal root nerve
↳ sensory
↳ afferent
Ventral root
↳ motor?
↳ efferent

● Will the cell bodies of the motor neurons be found in the white matter or the grey matter?

● They will be in the grey matter.

The dorsal root and ventral root converge to form a spinal nerve. The spinal cord, together with the spinal nerves, is organized on a segmental basis. Each segment of spinal cord corresponds to a spinal nerve. This can be seen in Figure 1.14a which shows also the corresponding segmentation of the vertebrae.

Figure 1.14   (a) Each segment of the spinal cord receives sensory information and sends motor output through a corresponding set of spinal nerves. These are named with the prefix letters C, T, L, S and Col which refer to the cervical (neck), thoracic (chest), lumbar (lower back), sacral (hip) and coccygeal (tail) regions of the vertebral column. Both vertebrae and spinal nerves are numbered sequentially corresponding to their position. Note that the first set of cervical nerves C1 is situated above the first vertebrae C1 and does not have a dermatome. This anatomical feature means that the numbering of spinal nerves and the vertebrae that encase the segments of the spinal cord they connect to do not correspond. For example, the spinal nerve C8 receiving information from the hand connects to the segment of the spinal cord encased within the cervical vertebrae C7. (b) The dermatomes (explained in Section 1.10) are areas of skin that correspond to the segmented structure of the spinal cord. Each dorsal root ganglion receives sensory information from the area of the skin forming its corresponding dermatome. Note: the face is innervated by the trigeminal nerve, one of the cranial nerves (see Table 1.1).

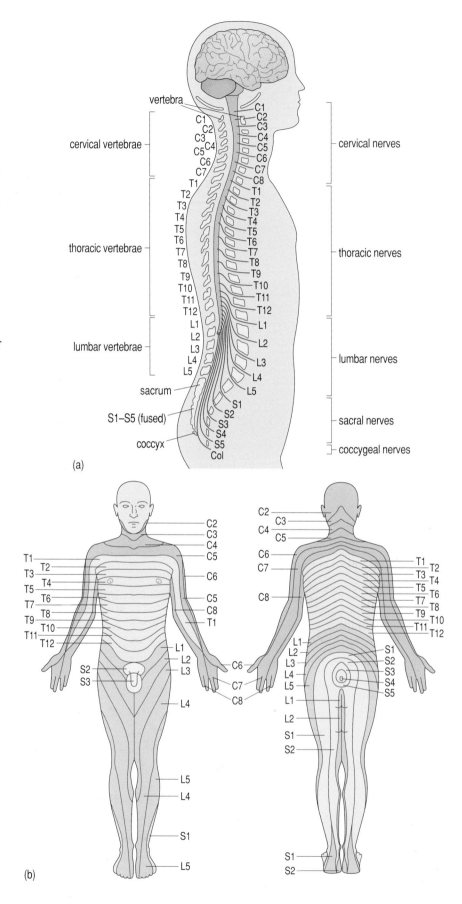

1.8.2 The peripheral nervous system (PNS)

The PNS (Figure 1.3) is subdivided into two functional branches; somatic and autonomic. The *somatic* (or voluntary) *nervous system* controls the skeletal muscles and it provides sensory information from the body and from the outside world. For example, consider the situation shown in Figure 1.15. A person steps on a drawing pin which causes damage to the skin of the foot. The damage triggers activity in neuron 1, which is a special type of neuron, termed a **nociceptor** (pronounced *no-see-septor*, from the Latin *noxius* meaning harm). The nociceptive sensory neuron (neuron 1) forms connections in the spinal cord with two further neurons. One of these (neuron 2) projects up to the brain. The information conveyed by this pathway will terminate in the brain and it is through such information that we have the conscious experience of pain. The other connection is with an interneuron (neuron 3) which then connects to a motor neuron (neuron 4).

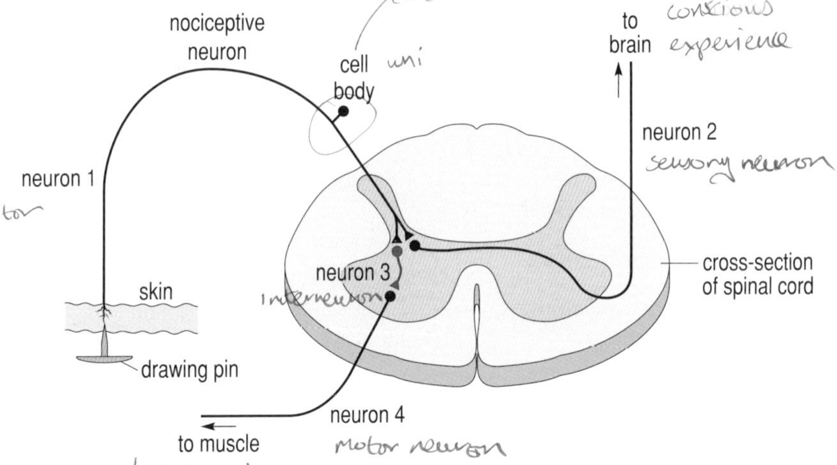

[handwritten margin notes:]
FUNCTIONAL NOMENCLATURE

SOMATIC NERVOUS SYSTEM:
- skeletal muscle movement
- Sensory info
  ↳ perception
  ↳ exproprioception
- Nociceptors (harm response)
- 1-neuron pathways

Figure 1.15 Pathways involved in the detection of tissue damage and the resulting effector action.

[handwritten annotations on figure: Dorsal root ganglion; conscious experience; uni; sensory neuron; nociceptor; interneuron; motor neuron; movement/withdrawl]

[handwritten margin note:]
In practice many nociceptors would be activated, also interneurons, and lots of motor neurons would be required for effective withdrawl.

- Look at the four neurons shown in Figure 1.15. Are they within the central or the peripheral nervous system?

- Neurons 2 and 3 are entirely within the CNS (i.e. the spinal cord). Most of neuron 1, including the cell body, is in the peripheral nervous system but part of it, after entering the spinal cord is within the CNS. The cell body of neuron 4 is in the CNS but most of this neuron lies in the peripheral nervous system where, ultimately it innervates the muscle.

The activity of **motor neurons** like neuron 4 controls the state of contraction of the muscles determining the position of the foot. Activation of this pathway causes the muscles to withdraw the foot from the offending object. Thus there is both a local **reflex** elicited through neurons 1, 3 and 4 and a central processing of information by the brain (conveyed by neuron 2).

[handwritten margin note:]
Can be inhibited at synapse (by IPSP) - through neuron 5?

- What is the significance of these two pathways for effecting action to terminate harmful events?

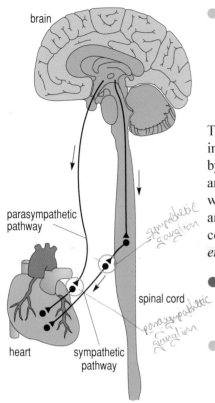

brain

parasympathetic pathway

heart

sympathetic pathway

spinal cord

sympathetic ganglion

parasympathetic ganglion

Figure 1.16 The neural influences on the heart. The ANS pathways span the distance from the CNS to the heart. The green circles represent autonomic ganglia.

ANS: (2-neuron pathways)
• enteric – e.g. in stomach
• sympathetic – mostly excitory
   e.g. incr. heart BPM
• parasymp – mostly inhibitory
   e.g. slow heart rate

- The local reflex pathway offers a local solution at a relatively high speed. Clearly, speed is essential in such a situation. However, the brain also needs to be informed of what has happened, even though this information would reach it only after the local action has already been initiated. Also if the local withdrawal reflex fails, e.g. if the drawing pin remains in the foot, other solutions are indicated. For instance, you can pull the pin out of the foot.

There are a separate range of activities that are involuntary, where muscles are involved but not skeletal muscles. There is the beating of the heart, brought about by contraction of the cardiac muscle, and the peristaltic activity of the stomach and intestines, the production of saliva and the constriction of blood vessels, all of which involve the activity of smooth muscle. These activities proceed without any intervention of our conscious will, whether we are asleep or awake, and are controlled by the **autonomic nervous system (ANS)**. The ANS is subdivided into *enteric*, *sympathetic* and *parasympathetic* nervous systems.

- The sympathetic and parasympathetic nervous systems often exert opposing influences on the structure or organ they innervate, for example the heart. Can you think why this would be necessary?

- In order to maintain **homeostasis** within the body. Their effects are regulated via feedback mechanisms (each system exerts influence over the other to maintain balance).

Figure 1.16 shows a simple representation of the neural influence on the heart. To speed up the heart rate there must be an increase in sympathetic activity and a decrease in parasympathetic activity. Conversely, a reduction in sympathetic activity, and an increase in parasympathetic activity serves to slow down the heart rate.

- Do you notice any difference between pathways of the autonomic system (Figure 1.16) and that of the somatic system (Figure 1.15) from where they leave the CNS (brain/spinal cord)?

- Two neurons are shown in the autonomic pathways.

This important distinction between the ANS and the somatic nervous system is shown in Figure 1.17. In the **somatic nervous system**, single motor neurons whose cell bodies are in the spinal cord (Figure 1.15) link the CNS to the skeletal muscles. In the case of the **autonomic nervous system**, combinations of *two* neurons span the distance from the CNS to the organ that is the site of action. There is an *autonomic ganglion* which houses the cell bodies of the second neuron. In the **sympathetic system**, the ganglia are mostly situated close to the spinal cord itself, as indicated in Figure 1.16, whereas the **parasympathetic** ganglia lie close to the organ.

Generally speaking, these two branches exert opposite effects.

- How do these two systems exert these opposite effects on heart rate?

- Sympathetic activity causes the heart to increase its pumping activity and parasympathetic activity will tend to reduce it.

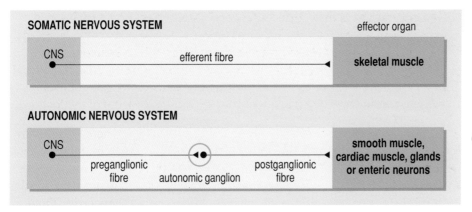

Figure 1.17 A distinction between the somatic nervous system and the autonomic nervous system. (Enteric neurons are in the wall of the gut and effect action upon smooth muscle.)

This is achieved by different types of **neurotransmitter** (chemical messengers which neurons use to communicate with each other) being released by the two branches. Sympathetic neurons release **noradrenalin** (in USA this is called norepinephrine), parasympathetic neurons release **acetylcholine (ACh)** at their target organs. The significance of the division into sympathetic and parasympathetic branches is that one or other branch of the system can dominate according to circumstances. At times of emergency when the body is activated, such as in 'fight or flight', the sympathetic branch will tend to be excited and the parasympathetic will be inhibited. Conversely, at times of rest, the parasympathetic branch will tend to dominate over the sympathetic.

This 'fight or flight' reaction, or 'adrenalin rush' is probably what the ANS is best known for, because this is one of the few occasions that we become aware of ANS activity. Imagine the scenario where you are in an unfamiliar tropical country and you suddenly experience a pain in your foot, not from a drawing pin this time, but from an unknown source. Your reflex works as it should (i.e. withdrawal of your foot from the pain source), but you may also experience stomach-churning terror. Have you been bitten by a very exotic and deadly insect? Will you need immediate medical aid to survive? Your pulse rate increases, hands become cold and clammy and you feel a chill sweat running down the back of your neck. What is happening to the internal environment in your body?

As well as its effect on the heart, the ANS controls the activity of endocrine and exocrine glands. For instance, it triggers the secretion of sweat from glands distributed over the surface of the body, which will cool the body (useful if you are about to run away from danger). And what about the churning stomach? This is a consequence of activity in the enteric nervous system. The enteric nervous system refers to the collection of neurons located within the wall of the gut, that effect action upon smooth muscle (Book 1, Section 4.2.1).

The previous sections have looked at the organization and some of the functions of the nervous system. The next section introduces the actual mechanisms of neurotransmission (how neurons communicate with each other) and how this can be modulated.

Summary of Section 1.8

1   The cranial nerves of the peripheral nervous system (PNS) feed into the brain and the spinal nerves feed into the spinal cord.

2   The peripheral nervous system is divided into the somatic nervous system and the autonomic nervous system (ANS).

3   The somatic nervous system conveys sensory information to the CNS and effects voluntary actions via skeletal muscles, whereas the ANS controls the involuntary, internal state of the organs of the body

4   The classical division of the ANS is into sympathetic and parasympathetic branches, which generally exert opposite effects on a target tissue. There is a separate division of the ANS called the enteric nervous system, which exerts control over the smooth muscles of the gut.

1.9 Cells of the nervous system; the action potential and neurotransmission

There are approximately 100 billion neurons in the human brain alone (around 50–80 000 neurons per cubic millimetre). The individual neurons which make up the nervous system come in a wide variety of different shapes and sizes. Some examples are shown in Figure 1.18. The cell body contains the nucleus of the cell. There are often extensions from the cell body, called **dendrites**, where information is received. The structure referred to as an axon or nerve fibre, which extends from the cell body, carries information away from the cell body. Figure 1.18a shows a neuron with its cell body at one end; a motor neuron would have this structure and the one that reaches from your spinal cord to your big toe has a very long axon.

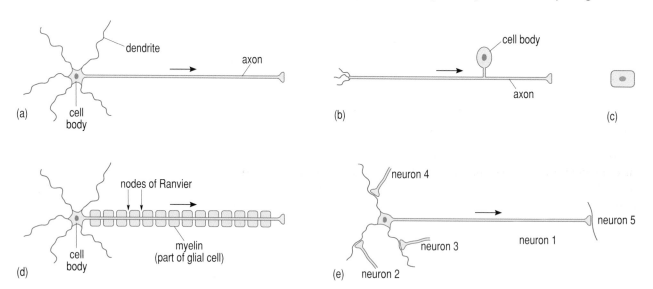

Figure 1.18   Some different types of neuron found in the nervous system: (a) with the cell body to one end of a long process (the axon); (b) with cell body to the side of the axon; (c) with no processes; (d) as for (a) but with an insulating coating, called myelin, around the axon; (e) a neuron showing the inputs and outputs. Information is carried along the length of the axon when the neuron is carrying out its function of communication. The neuron shown in (e) has input from neurons 2, 3 and 4 and, can in turn influence neuron 5.

- The neuron shown in Figure 1.18b has the cell body positioned to the side of the long axon. Use Figure 1.15 to identify a neuron with this structure.

- The nociceptive neuron 1 has this structure.

Figure 1.18c shows a very small neuron without an associated process; neurons of this type transmit information over very short distances. However, the brain and spinal cord do not consist only of neurons.

There are other classes of cells collectively termed **glial cells** (astrocytes, oligodendrocytes, Schwann cells and microglia) which far outnumber neurons. In addition to these, there are also the **endothelial cells** that line the lumen of blood vessels (arteries, veins and capillaries) which supply the brain (see Book 3, Chapter 2).

The word 'glia' is derived from the Greek word meaning 'glue', as these cells were originally thought to literally glue the rest of the brain and keep it in place! Glial cells assist in the development and maintenance of the nervous system (it is uncertain whether they can also help neurons with information processing). Some help to regulate the chemical composition of the nervous system. Astrocytes, small star-shaped cells, are particularly important for maintaining the integrity of a barrier between the circulating blood and the brain. They do this by promoting formation of high-resistance or 'tight' junctions (see Book 1, Section 2.8) between endothelial cells. Microglia are found throughout the white and grey matter and they defend the nervous system from infection and injury. **Oligodendrocytes** are responsible for forming the lipid-rich insulating sheath around certain types of neurons in the central nervous system (Figure 1.18d).

- What is the name of this lipid-rich sheath?

- Myelin.

Schwann cells are responsible for the myelination of neurons in the peripheral nervous system. Myelin speeds up the rate at which information is transmitted along axons (this is discussed further below). The speed of a reaction to a stimulus, e.g. removal of the hand from a hot object, is often of crucial importance. Loss of myelin from nerve fibres (demyelination) is a characteristic pathological disturbance of multiple sclerosis.

Neurons normally convey information by means of brief pulses of electricity, introduced earlier as nerve impulses but more correctly known as **action potentials**. These arise at one end of the axon of the neuron and are transmitted along the length of the axon. Neurons transmit such information at speeds of between 0.2 and 100 metres per second ($m\,s^{-1}$) and in doing so are said to be showing activity or 'firing'. Figure 1.19 shows a schematic three-dimensional representation of the junction between two neurons, called a **synapse**. Note that neurons may also form a synapse with muscle fibres – in this case the synapse between a neuron and a muscle fibre is termed a **neuromuscular junction**. The synapse consists of a presynaptic terminal, a postsynaptic membrane and a gap separating these, called a **synaptic cleft** (around 20–40 nanometres (nm) wide, where 1 nm is one millionth of a millimetre). The next section introduces the mechanisms of neurotransmission.

Figure 1.19   Three-dimensional representation of a synapse between two neurons.

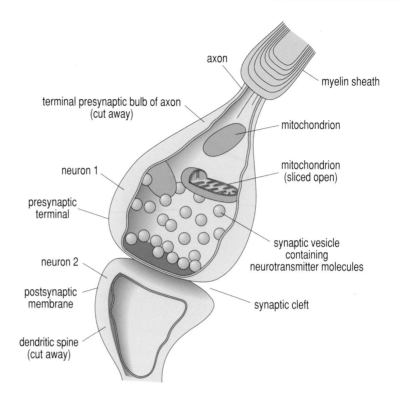

1.9.1 The resting potential and the action potential

Neurons, like all cells of the body, have a cell membrane which forms a barrier between the inside of the cell and the matrix that surrounds the cell. This barrier is permeable to some substances but not to others (it is 'semipermeable'; see Book 1, Section 2.5.1). Recall that the fluid on the inside of the cell (*intracellular fluid*) is of a different ionic composition to that of the fluid on the outside of the cell (*extracellular fluid*).

● What is the consequence of this difference in ionic composition?

○ There are more sodium ions outside the cell and more potassium ions inside the cell (Figure 1.20a). This difference results in a difference in electrical charge across the membrane (the membrane potential).

The differences in ion concentrations between the inside and the outside of cells are normally well maintained. When a neuron is not transmitting an action potential, there is a small potential difference across its cell membrane: the inside is electrically negative with respect to the outside. This is the **resting membrane potential** (–70 millivolts (mV)) (indicated on the graph in Figure 1.20b). Neurons communicate with each other by electrochemical means. That is to say, via chemicals which give rise to an electrical signal.

● How do you suppose the neuronal membrane varies its permeability to ions?

○ By opening channels such as those shown in Figure 2.10 of Book 1.

A neuron receives signals either from other neurons (typically a neuron receives input from thousands of other neurons) or from sensory events around it (either the

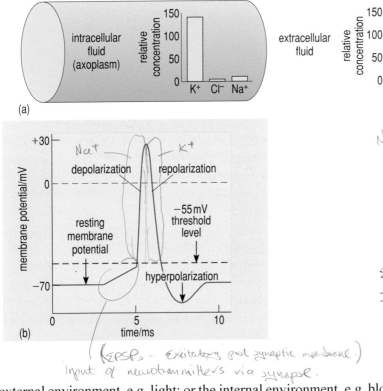

(a)

(b)

Handwritten annotations in figure:

Na+ K+

depolarization   repolarization

resting membrane potential

−55 mV threshold level

hyperpolarization

(EPSPs – Excitatory post synaptic membrane.)
Input of neurotransmitters via synapse.

Na+ K+ ATPase pump
⤷ maintains resting potential
⤷ restores resting potential

EPSPs – depolarizations
IPSPs – hyperpolarization
⤷ diminish effectiveness of EPSPs
⤷ ie needs greater EPSP to reach threshold.

Figure 1.20 (a) The concentration of some major ions on the inside and outside of the axon of a neuron. Note that there are many other ions and molecules present but not shown here. (b) The resting membrane potential and action potential in a neuron.

external environment, e.g. light; or the internal environment, e.g. blood sugar level). If the excitatory strength of incoming signals is sufficiently strong it will cause the opening of **ion channels** that allow sodium ions (Na^+) to cross the membrane.

● Look at Figure 1.20a and say in which direction the Na^+ will pass and why.

○ Na^+ will enter the cell driven by both the sodium concentration gradient and the membrane electrical (potential) gradient.

● What effect will the entry of Na^+ have on the membrane potential?

○ The positive ions will make the potential less negative.

Movement of sodium ions into the neuron makes the membrane potential (in the area where the ions are moving) less negative, and if the change in value reaches a critical level, known as the threshold level (around −55 mV) yet more ion channels, of a type known as **voltage-dependent sodium channels**, open and more Na^+ enters the cell. This causes a rapid alteration in electrical potential until the membrane loses its potential (**depolarization**) and, momentarily, the membrane potential becomes positive (around +20 to +30 mV). However, it abruptly peaks and then drops back to a negative value (repolarization). The reason for this being that the Na^+ ion channels suddenly close at around the same time as **potassium ion (K^+) channels** open.

Handwritten margin notes:

voltage-dependent sodium channels.

delayed voltage-dependent potassium channels.

● Look at Figure 1.20a again and explain why the opening of K^+ channels brings about a restoration of the negative membrane potential.

○ The K^+ concentration gradient will drive K^+ out of the cell. As they carry their positive ionic charge out of the cell they leave the inside of the membrane with less positive charge, i.e. it becomes relatively more negative.

We can use devices to record these electrical changes at the cell membrane. Figure 1.20b shows the graph we obtain when these values are plotted against time. The characteristic spike that is generated once the threshold value is reached is the *action potential.* A neuron will not generate an action potential unless the critical threshold (−55 mV) for firing has been reached.

The passage of information along an axon has been likened to the lighting of a firecracker. The generation of an action potential at one end of the axon is a consequence of the neurochemical changes that have just been described. These changes influence the adjoining section of membrane and trigger similar changes there – and so on, along the length of the axon. Each section of the membrane generates its own action potential so the signal does not decrease in strength as it travels along the axon.

After each action potential has occurred, there is a *refractory period*, when a second action potential cannot be generated on precisely the same region of the membrane. This is a phase of hyperpolarization (the movement of positive ions out of the cell) when the inside of the membrane becomes more negative with respect to the outside as more potassium ions exit (Figure 1.20b). This period prevents an indefinite number of action potentials moving backwards and forwards along the axon. Consequently, action potentials normally travel in only one direction along an axon.

A series of action potentials can move along the neuron in rapid succession. Their speed, however, is increased if the diameter of the axon is large or if it is coated by myelin. Myelinated axons have faster transmission because there are gaps or 'nodes' located along the myelin coating of the fibre (called nodes of Ranvier; see Figure 1.18d). In a simplistic sense, this arrangement allows the electrical signal to 'jump' from node to node because the exposed axonal membranes at these sites lack a myelin coat. This phenomenon is referred to as **saltatory conduction** and it increases the conduction speed compared with unmyelinated axons of the same diameter. Information is coded by the frequency of firing of action potentials (the number of spikes over a given period of time) rather than the size of the action potential itself (which is constant).

1.9.2 Synapses, neurotransmitters and synaptic transmission

An action potential that arrives at the terminal of a neuron (presynaptic terminal) cannot cross over the gap of the synaptic cleft (Figure 1.19). This barrier is overcome by the release of neurotransmitters (chemical messengers) from the terminal that are able to cross over the gap. Some common examples of neurotransmitters include noradrenalin (norepinephrine), adrenalin (epinephrine), dopamine, acetylcholine, serotonin, the amino acids – gamma-aminobutyric acid (GABA for short) and glutamate. Dopamine, serotonin, noradrenalin and adrenalin are collectively called monoamine neurotransmitters because they are all derived from the same molecule: tyrosine. (Tyrosine is an amino acid and its structure is shown in Table 3.8 of Book 1.) We have already encountered noradrenalin and acetylcholine (they are important in the functioning of the sympathetic and parasympathetic nervous system, respectively).

refractory period: hyperpolarisation/ hyperpolarisation means a greater EPSP is needed to reach threshold (-55 mV)

GABA - involved in epilepsy (pp.45)

Monoamine neurotransmitters
⤷ tyrosine derived
⤷ Dopamine, serotonin, adrenaline, noradrenaline

Neurotransmitter molecules are typically made in the cell body, transported to the terminal in membrane-bound 'packages' called **synaptic vesicles** and stored there until released. Individual neurons do not produce all of the types of transmitters mentioned above. Instead, different types of neurons can be characterized through their production, storage and release of a single transmitter. For example, a neuron that synthesizes, stores and releases dopamine is termed a dopaminergic neuron. The word ending '-ergic' defines the transmitter that characterizes the particular neuron.

Returning to Figure 1.19, an action potential that arrives at the presynaptic terminal (neuron 1) causes an influx of **calcium ions**. This influx of calcium triggers the release of neurotransmitter into the synaptic cleft by the fusion of the vesicles with the cell membrane.

● What do we call this process?

● Exocytosis (Book 1, Section 2.5.2).

The neurotransmitter molecules diffuse rapidly across the synaptic cleft and become attached to specific receptors (protein binding sites) on the postsynaptic membrane (of neuron 2, or indeed the muscle if this is a neuromuscular junction). The outcome of a neurotransmitter binding to its receptor, can be one of *excitation* or *inhibition* (i.e. excitation means that the postsynaptic neuron is more likely to fire, inhibition means that it is less likely to fire). Activity at the neuromuscular junction always causes the muscle to be excited and contract. Now look at Figure 1.21. Let us say synapse 1 is excitatory and synapse 2 inhibitory. Note that the neurotransmitters stored at the terminals of the two incoming neurons are represented by different shapes. These correspond to the different receptor types at the surface of the receiving neuron. For example, the neurotransmitter represented by a triangular shape (neuron B) might be GABA (GABA is an inhibitory neurotransmitter) with its corresponding receptors located on a dendrite of neuron C whereas the transmitter represented by a square shape (neuron A) might be glutamate which is always excitatory. In reality there are thousands of synapses onto a neuron, not all active at the same time. The extent of the activity and whether the balance is to excite or inhibit activity in the neuron is the basis for the complex computations that take place in our brains.

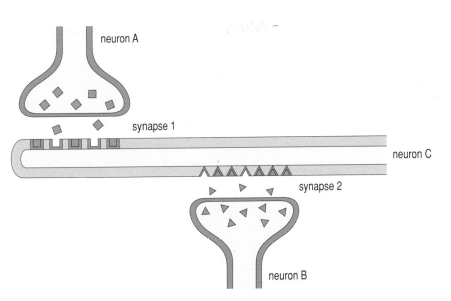

Figure 1.21 Excitatory and inhibitory synapses. In both excitation and inhibition there is a specific lock-and-key fit between neurotransmitter and its receptor. (*Note*: this diagram is schematic – in reality, neurotransmitter molecules are stored in membrane-bound vesicles at the neuron terminal.)

[Handwritten margin notes:]
Rough endoplasmic reticulum
↓
Golgi apparatus
↓
(Microtubules)
↓
presynaptic membrane

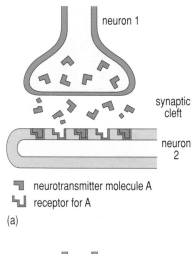

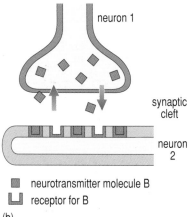

Figure 1.22 Removal of transmitter from the synaptic cleft. (a) Removal by enzymatic destruction. Note the breakdown of neurotransmitter molecules into smaller molecules. (These then diffuse away from the synaptic region.) (b) Removal by reuptake across the membrane of the first neuron.

Agonist ⎤ SYNAPTIC EFFICACY
Antagonist ⎦

The actions of neurotransmitters do not go on indefinitely. Instead, they are usually inactivated when the stimulus has stopped through one or more of the following mechanisms:

- diffusion away from the synaptic cleft;

- deactivation by an enzyme that breaks down the chemical structure of the neurotransmitter into components which cannot bind to the receptor (e.g. acetylcholine is deactivated by the enzyme acetylcholinesterase) (Figure 1.22a);

- reuptake into the terminal of the neuron that produced them (dopamine and serotonin are taken up in this manner) (Figure 1.22b).

We also know that glial cells (astrocytes in particular) have the ability to remove neurotransmitters from the synaptic cleft.

Abnormalities in the quantities of acetylcholine and serotonin released by certain *specific* neurons in the brain appear to play a role in a variety of different disorders such as depression and Alzheimer's disease. It is also known that drugs such as lysergic acid diethylamide (LSD), heroin and cocaine, and even the more socially accepted ones, such as nicotine and alcohol, exert their effects via their action at synapses. So synapses hold an important key to understanding much of human behaviour. It is possible to mimic the effect of a natural neurotransmitter by administering a drug that occupies the same receptors and has a similar effect upon these receptors as does the natural transmitter. Such a substance is termed an **agonist**. Conversely, a substance that blocks the natural transmitter's occupation and action, but does not itself exert any effect on the second cell, is called an **antagonist**. In medicine, drugs acting as specific agonists or antagonists are used to modulate the strength of synaptic transmission (*synaptic efficacy*) at certain types of synapses.

Psychoactive drugs and neurotoxins may alter such properties as the release or reuptake of a neurotransmitter, or the availability of its receptor binding sites on the target cell. A drug such as cocaine acts partly by blocking the reuptake of dopamine. Hence for a while after the drug reaches the synapse there is an abnormally high concentration of dopamine in the synaptic cleft and receptors are abnormally occupied by dopamine, as represented in Figure 1.23. For reasons that are not entirely understood, the high occupation of dopamine receptors can induce euphoria. In time, the high levels of dopamine in the synaptic cleft will tend to be eliminated and this will correspond to a loss of the euphoric feeling.

Antidepressant drugs also commonly target the process of reuptake of a neurotransmitter. A class of drugs that target the neurotransmitter serotonin have been developed specifically to treat obsessional neurosis (e.g. abnormal intrusive thoughts and excessive hand washing and checking). These drugs act by blocking the reuptake of serotonin, but they are not without unwanted side-effects (these may include nausea, dizziness, dryness of the mouth or diarrhoea, amongst others).

● Why do you suppose there are side-effects to these drugs?

● There are many different places in the brain where serotonin is used as a neurotransmitter. (We said above that there were certain specific neurons using serotonin in depression.) Unfortunately it is rarely possible to target just the site where there is a particular problem.

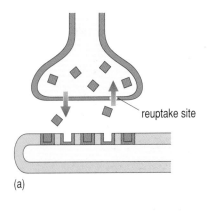

(a)

Summary of Section 1.9

1   The nervous system is made up of different types of neurons, glial cells (astrocytes, oligodendrocytes, Schwann cells, microglia) and endothelial cells of blood vessels.

2   Information is carried along the axon of a neuron in the form of action potential frequency.

3   An action potential is generated by the transitory rapid flow of sodium and potassium ions across the neuron cell membrane causing localized changes in voltage across the membrane.

4   Action potentials normally move in one direction along axons.

5   Information is carried across the gap between neurons (synapse) and across the gap between a neuron and a muscle (neuromuscular junction) by means of neurotransmitter molecules.

6   Neurotransmitter is stored at the terminal of a neuron and released in response to the arrival of an action potential.

7   A neuron is characterized by the neurotransmitter that it synthesizes, stores, and releases at a synapse.

8   The postsynaptic membrane has receptors that bind the neurotransmitter but the neurotransmitter is normally removed from the synaptic cleft shortly after release.

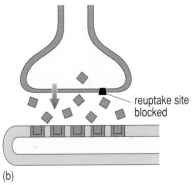

(b)

Figure 1.23   Blocking of reuptake boosts levels of transmitter at the synapse: (a) normal situation with reuptake proceeding normally; (b) reuptake blocked.

The effect of a neurotransmitter can be one of excitation or inhibition, depending upon the properties of the combination of neurotransmitter and its receptor.

1.10 Overview of sensory and motor systems

At the start of this chapter we looked at some of the functions carried out by different brain regions without any particular regard to ongoing behaviour. It is much easier to take this reductionist view when trying to unravel the complexities of this most complex body system but we will end by trying to link different components of the nervous system together.

Recall the nociceptive sensory pathway first shown in Figure 1.15 which conveyed information concerning tissue damage to the brain. Figure 1.24 takes this route further and we can now see the destination of neuron 2 after it crosses from one side of the spinal cord and ascends in the white matter.

Figure 1.24 Pathway that conveys information from a noxious stimulus to the brain.

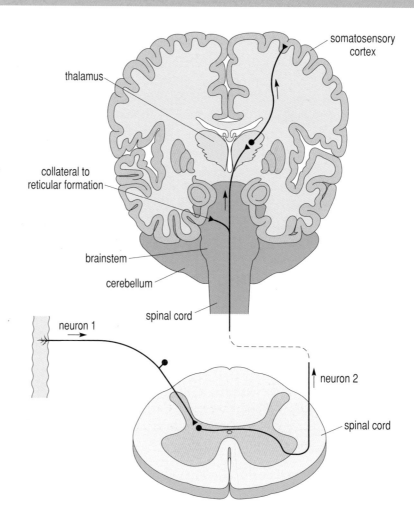

RETICULAR FORMATION:

• Alertness
• State of wakefulness/sleep.
• collateral ~ ~ ~
    ↳ NOCICEPTIVE response

● Why is the white matter so called?

○ It is called white matter because the many neurons that travel up to the brain (like neuron 2) are myelinated and myelin is whitish in colour.

● Look at Figure 1.24 and describe what happens to neuron 2 when it enters the brainstem.

○ The neuron branches and then terminates in the **thalamus**. The branch is termed a *collateral* and it terminates in a region of the brainstem called the *reticular formation* (an area of the brain also shown in Figure 1.9 that is concerned with states of waking, alertness and sleep).

The collateral branch stimulates the reticular formation which in turn arouses large parts of the brain. This link could well underlie the emotional connotation of pain. You will doubtless have noted that pain is a very effective means of keeping you awake!

● Recall the function of the thalamus.

○ The thalamus is a relay station but it also processes sensory information.

- From Figure 1.24 say what connection neuron 2 makes in the thalamus.

- Neuron 2 forms a synapse that connects it with a further neuron that conveys information to the somatosensory cortex.

[handwritten note: SOMATOSENSORY CORTEX: • analyses info from body]

The **somatosensory cortex** (Brodmann's areas 1, 2 and 3 on Figure 1.7) analyses information from the body (*soma* is Greek for body). But how does it know where neuron 2's information originated? Each region of the body (and indeed each organ) feeds into a specific spinal or cranial nerve. For example, the eye connects to the brain via the optic nerve (Table 1.1) and a given spinal nerve conveys information from a given part of the body termed a *dermatome*. Figure 1.14b shows how the sensory surface of the body is divided into dermatomes. The nociceptor (neuron 1) in our scenario recorded damage caused by a drawing pin in the foot so the nociceptor axon would be found in one of the sacral nerves (Figure 1.14a). The information from neuron 2 fetches up in a very specific area of the somatosensory cortex as is shown in Figure 1.25a. Recording sensations evoked by stimulation of the somatosensory cortex (Box 1.1) has enabled us to plot the body across the surface of the somatosensory cortex. The resulting bizarre form is termed a *sensory homunculus*.

- What do you notice about the areas devoted to the different regions of the body?

- Some areas of the body (e.g. the fingers) correspond to rather large areas of somatosensory cortex whereas other areas (e.g. the hips and trunk) have a disproportionately smaller area.

This matches the sensitivity of resolution of detail in these areas. The fingers have a fine resolution, enabling them to discriminate detail whereas the trunk is rather coarse with respect to discriminatory detail.

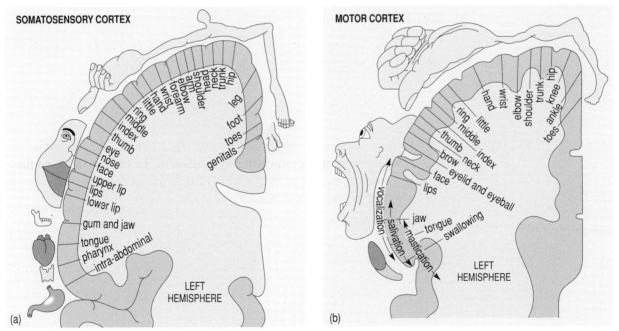

Figure 1.25 (a) Map of the somatosensory cortex showing the corresponding sensory homunculus. (b) Map of the motor cortex showing the corresponding motor homunculus.

Figure 1.26 Brain regions and some of the pathways involved in motor control.

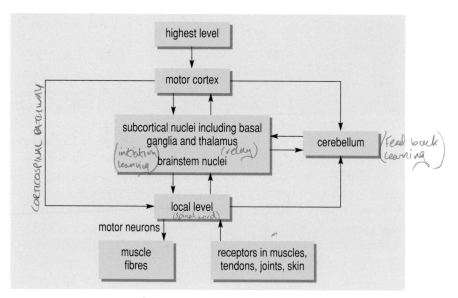

So the brain locates the stimulus, and let us assume that the local reflex of withdrawing from the pin did not work, the object is still in the foot. Now what? It may be possible to assess the situation further by looking at the foot, at the same time regions of the brain will be thinking, reasoning and planning action based on past experience. Figure 1.26 summarizes the most important brain regions and pathways involved in motor control. The thinking and planning that is going on is represented in Figure 1.26 as 'highest level'.

The control of movement by the brain is complex and involves large amounts of information being transmitted between different brain regions. The term 'local level' refers to the organization at the level of the spinal cord where the motor neuron cell bodies are located. This is the level at which the reflex withdrawal from noxious stimuli such as the drawing pin, occur. In some cases, the descending pathways, consisting of neurons carrying information down the spinal cord, from the motor cortex to the muscles, will terminate on the cell bodies of motor neurons. More usually they will terminate at local interneurons which in turn activate the motor neurons (both arrangements are illustrated in Figure 1.27).

When we say a region of the cortex 'has control over' certain muscles, we mean the following: activity in neurons in a defined location in the motor cortex triggers activity along pathways that ultimately reach the motor neurons in the spinal cord which control the action of a particular part of the body. If the region of motor cortex is stimulated electrically by means of electrodes, a response will be triggered in a specific part of the body. Figure 1.25b shows the map of the primary motor cortex and the associated *motor homunculus*.

Exactly where in the brain the initial commands to move arise is an interesting question. Motor control involves various brain regions, including parts of the cortex that are outside the motor cortex. From the 'highest level', where intentions originate information is conveyed to the motor cortex where specific actions are instigated. The premotor cortex and the supplementary motor cortex (Brodmann's areas 6 and 8 on Figure 1.7) are also involved in the preplanning of motor actions.

● Which other areas are involved in movement control?

● The basal ganglia and the cerebellum.

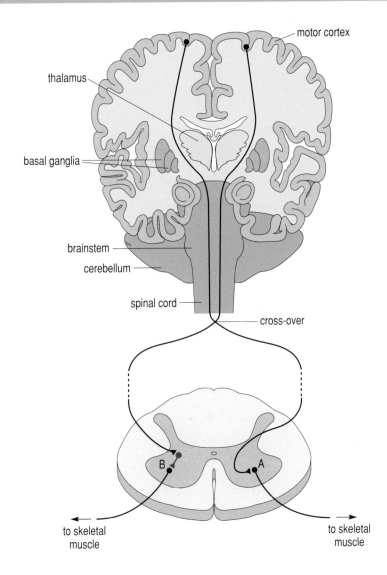

motor cortex

thalamus

basal ganglia

brainstem

cerebellum

spinal cord

cross-over

B   A

to skeletal
muscle

to skeletal
muscle

Figure 1.27   A section through the brain and spinal cord to show the corticospinal pathway and two motor neurons (A and B) that innervate muscles. For clarity only one interneuron (in red) is shown.

● Recall their main contributions to movement control.

● The basal ganglia are particularly concerned with the initiation of movement and the learning of motor skills. The cerebellum refines ongoing movement as well as being required to enable motor skills to be learned.

A structure below the basal ganglia, extending down to the brainstem, termed the *substantia nigra* (Figure 1.6) connects with regions of the basal ganglia. A group of dopaminergic neurons, whose cell bodies are in the substantia nigra, project into the basal ganglia. The disorder known as Parkinson's disease arises as a result of a degeneration of these dopaminergic neurons. Individuals with Parkinson's disease have difficulty initiating movement.

Ultimately, commands are sent from the primary motor cortex in descending pathways that terminate in specific regions of the spinal cord (Figure 1.27). Here they contact motor neurons that innervate muscles that will, for example, move the foot to reveal the offending drawing pin. Other descending pathways terminate in the brainstem, where they contact cranial nerves such as the oculomotor nerve (Table 1.1) which is one of the nerves that controls eye movement. By means of

[handwritten note:]
SUBSTANTIA NIGRA:
• connects to basal ganglia
• dopinergic neuronal nuclei
• Parkinson's disease
  ↳ inadequacy of voluntary mov.
  ↳ initiating mov.-probs

41

EPSPs

such descending pathways, not only can behaviour be initiated but it can also be inhibited. In this way, muscular responses that might otherwise have been initiated by local excitation arising from local sensory stimulation can be inhibited.

● What do we call the muscular response initiated by local excitation?

○ Such a response is a reflex.

As shown in Figure 1.26, there are two routes: one from the cortex and one from subcortical structures, which influence 'local levels'. These will now be described.

The corticospinal pathway

CORTICOSPINAL PATHWAY:

* MOTOR CORTEX
    or → local interneurons
↓
MOTOR NEURONS
• Myelinated ⎫ speed!
• large diameter ⎭
• Fine movements
    ↳ acting in isolation

The term **corticospinal pathway** refers to the path of neurons that start in the motor cortex and run to a specific location in the spinal cord, either to motor neurons themselves or to local interneurons that then make contact with the motor neurons (see Figure 1.27). The advantage that such a direct link brings is one of speed. The axons of cells in the corticospinal pathway are myelinated and a percentage of them have large diameters.

● What is the significance of this?

○ Both myelination and a large diameter contribute to a high speed of transmission of action potentials.

Neurons in the corticospinal pathway are mainly involved in the control of fine movements, such as positioning of the fingers. A person is unable to perform such movement if the pathway is damaged. As is shown in Figure 1.27, at the point where the spinal cord meets the brain there is a cross-over in the corticospinal pathway.

INTERACTION
    ↳ smoothness + accuracy

● What is the implication of this?

○ That the motor cortex of one half of the brain is responsible for the control of muscles on the other side of the body.

The non-corticospinal pathway

NON-CORTICOSPINAL PATHWAY
• BRAINSTEM
    ↓
INTERNEURONS (→ SPINAL MOTOR NEURONS)
• whole limb movement
• Branched neurons
    ↳ coordination
        ↳ stability + balance

In addition to the corticospinal pathway, there is another type of control pathway. Neurons of this pathway start in the brainstem and terminate at interneurons associated with the motor neurons in the spinal cord (see Figure 1.26). This so-called **non-corticospinal pathway** is mainly responsible for the control of whole limbs, rather than, for example, the fingers. The non-corticospinal pathway has a particular role in the maintenance of posture and balance as well as in walking. Neurons in this pathway are branched, the branches going to various motor neurons. This means that different parts of the body (e.g. arms and legs) can act in a coordinated way in maintaining stability and in movement. In other words, whereas the corticospinal pathway is involved in individual muscles that exert motor action in isolation (e.g. the fine finger movements of a watchmaker), the non-corticospinal pathway holds more responsibility for coordination of action exerted through larger muscle groups (e.g. in whole-body balance). Smooth and accurate movement is the result of interactions between the two pathways. Loss of one function by damage to one pathway can result in the other pathway taking over some of the responsibility.

Summary of Section 1.10

1 Sensory information arising in dermatomes is conveyed in spinal nerves to the spinal cord. Ascending pathways finally terminate in the somatosensory cortex, where all body parts are mapped (sensory homunculus).

2 Specific identifiable regions of the motor cortex have a responsibility for the motor control of specific parts of the body.

3 Parkinson's disease arises from the degeneration of dopaminergic neurons in the substantia nigra.

4 Information is conveyed from the brain down the spinal cord in two pathways: the corticospinal pathway and the non-corticospinal pathway.

1.11 When things go wrong

Many different environmental and genetic factors have been found to be responsible for causing disease or injury to the nervous system. Epilepsy, traumatic head injury and stroke are three of the most devastating and prevalent conditions that affect us in this modern age – we shall limit our discussion here to the two former conditions and return to the latter in the next book (Book 3, Chapter 2).

1.11.1 Epilepsy

The word epilepsy derives from the Greek *epilambanein* which means to seize or to attack. There are 20–70 new cases per 100 000 people each year (around 30 000 people develop the condition in the UK each year, and 40 million people worldwide). The incidence is higher during the first two decades of life and in older people. In epilepsy, recurrent seizures develop due to sudden, excessive and disorganized activity of neurons. The majority of cases (more than 70%) are **idiopathic** (i.e. no known cause can be found), and most of these patients develop epilepsy before the age of 20. Epileptic seizures are classified as *generalized seizures* (which arise due to excessive electrical activity over a wide area of the brain, often involving both cerebral hemispheres) and *partial* (or focal) *seizures* (which arise due to excessive electrical activity confined to a limited area of the brain – usually the temporal or frontal lobe). Partial seizures (previously known as *petit mal*) are further subdivided according to the level of consciousness, which is either retained (simple partial seizure) or impaired (complex partial seizure). Generalized seizures (previously known as *grand mal*) result in loss of consciousness, convulsions, behavioural changes and changes in muscle tone. The seizure usually only lasts a few minutes and is followed by a drowsy, confused phase and then sleep (see Case Report 1.1). However, a prolonged seizure without recovery of consciousness can occur in some instances, and this may be life-threatening. It may cause permanent brain damage due to lack of oxygen and send the patient into a coma.

Case Report 1.1   Epilepsy

Jack is 21 years old and is a successful hair stylist. He lives with two friends in a flat, and his mother lives in the same town. At the age of 15 years he developed idiopathic epilepsy and takes anti-epileptic medication (carbamazepine) which controls it most of the time. Here is his story of how he developed epilepsy and how it affects his day-to-day life.

'I had my first fit when I was 15 years old. I was at school in class, and I was taken to hospital by ambulance. I can't remember much about it except coming round in casualty. I'd hit my head on the desk as I fell so they had to check me out for that too. We hoped it might be a 'one-off' but it happened again a few weeks later and I was started on tablets. I have had tests, but they can't find a cause. I wanted to do hairdressing and so I got an apprenticeship and went to college. We've always been very open in my family and my mum always said it was important for me to make sure people knew that I have fits, and to explain to them what to do. So I made sure I told people at the salon and at college and they've always been cool about it. I do wear a silver chain which says I have epilepsy. My worst fear is it'll happen when I'm not with people who know me and an ambulance gets called. When I've had a fit I just want to go home and sleep it off – I usually feel a bit off for a day or two. I don't want to go to hospital!

I'm one of the senior stylists at the salon now, and what I've told the staff is, if I have a fit, just to try to make sure I don't hit myself on anything, and when my arms and legs stop shaking, to turn me on my side. I tell them to call my mum, and she'll collect me and take me home. They also know that if the fit should go on a long time or I don't start to wake up after about ten minutes, that's when they should call an ambulance. Fortunately that's not happened yet. They also know that I could wet myself during a fit. I think it's better to tell people what to expect. We're all good mates in the salon – the deputy manager has diabetes and we know how to recognize if she's going hypo too.

The main problem my epilepsy causes me is I haven't been able to learn to drive yet, as you have to be completely free of fits for a year before applying for a licence. The longest I've been without one was 11 months, and I was really hopeful but then I had a fit so I was back at square one. The other thing that's annoying is drinking. Drinking's a big part of going out and although I could get away with having one drink – maybe two – it hardly seems worth it. I can't drink more than that as it would stop my drugs working properly and the alcohol makes it more likely I'll have a fit. I do also avoid strobe lights when I'm out. I make sure I take my tablets and go for my check-ups, but other than that I try to just get on with things. I love my work and I have great friends.'

Treatments prescribed are designed to help control seizures (through anti-convulsant drug therapy) and are effective in at least 80% of cases, allowing the patient to live a normal life. The drugs used act in various ways to prevent the neurons from firing continuously and include:

- *sodium valproate* – inhibits enzymes which degrade the inhibitory neurotransmitter GABA, stimulates enzymes that break down the excitatory neurotransmitter, and limits repetitive neuronal firing by blocking sodium channels on neurons;

- *carbamazepine* – thought to prevent repetitive firing of action potentials in depolarized neurons by blocking sodium channels;

- *phenytoin* – acts on voltage-dependent sodium channels on neurons to prolong the 'inactive' state, reduces calcium entering neurons, blocks the release of neurotransmitters, and increases the action of GABA;

- *diazepam* – a class of benzodiazepine, which enhances the effects of GABA in slowing down neuronal activity.

In many instances, epilepsy can be controlled through treatment with a single drug which lessens the frequency of seizures, but sometimes a combination of drugs is necessary. Success largely depends on the patient following the course of treatment, because often, seizures may return when the medication is stopped. Careful consultation and routine follow-ups are recommended to avoid choosing activities that may involve a risk for triggering epileptic seizures or be deemed dangerous in the event of developing a seizure (for example, certain sports, operating machinery or driving). Some people with epilepsy may also develop depression. With careful monitoring and controlled medication, however, most people who have epilepsy do lead relatively normal and productive lives. After all, some great historical figures, Alexander the Great and Julius Caesar for example, had epilepsy.

1.11.2 Traumatic head injury

An estimated one million people attend hospital as a result of head injury each year in the UK. Minor head injuries are the most common, accounting for three-quarters of all head injuries. These can result from such common incidences as walking into the top of a low door, or knocking the head whilst getting into a car. They can result (but not necessarily) in unconsciousness for up to a quarter of an hour. A moderate head injury causes a longer period of unconsciousness – up to six hours, and patients may still have physical and psychological problems after five years. Severe head injuries cause loss of consciousness for a period that is longer than six hours, and few people are expected back at work within five years after such an incident. Head injury is the most common cause of death and disability amongst young people. Mortality as a result of severe head injury affects one person in every ten thousand in the UK each year. **Traumatic brain injury (TBI)** results from damage to the brain that is caused by an external force to the head, and includes complications that follow as a consequence (e.g. rising pressure inside the skull, bruising and swelling of the brain).

Leading causes of TBI include road traffic accidents, acts of violence (assault), sports and recreational injuries, a blow to the head or a fall. TBI can also occur in the absence of an outward physical evidence of injury (e.g. in the case of 'whiplash' injury).

Closed head injuries (where there are no visible skin or open wounds) are the most common type. What is particularly dangerous is that they may not be detected immediately because the injured person may not have lost consciousness, or may be unaware that they did. Particularly in an accident involving many people, these patients may receive minimal attention until they pass out. **Open head injury** or penetrating wounds (including bullet-wounds where part of the skull is open and the brain exposed) are less common. Crushing injuries are the least common, and often cause damage to the base of the skull and nerves of the brainstem rather than the brain itself. Loss of consciousness may or may not occur in such injuries. In closed head injury, TBI may result from rapid acceleration and deceleration or rotation of the brain, causing stretching and shearing (tearing) of nerve fibres, contusion (bruising) of the brain tissue against the skull, brainstem injuries, and associated oedema (swelling as a result of accumulation of fluid within tissues). The result is a diffuse brain injury. *Diffuse axonal injury* (generalized damage to axons in the central white matter), can result from acceleration/deceleration of the brain alone, but is enhanced with direct impact on the head. This type of injury is most likely to occur in response to strain placed on axons, and within 72 hours or more, leads to a cascade of events that cause death or damage to these axons, and their neural connections.

Secondary injuries such as serious blood loss or lack of oxygen can add further to brain damage. Intracerebral haemorrhage, bruising or swelling in the brain or development of blood clots (**haematoma**) are further consequences of different types of head injury. In particular, **extradural haemorrhage** (bleeding into the space between the dura and the skull), *subdural haemorrhage* (accumulation of blood in the space beneath the dura), or *subarachnoid haemorrhage* (bleeding into the space between the arachnoid and pia mater), often associated with an **aneurysm** (weakening of the wall of the artery which may balloon out into a sac and burst, causing haemorrhage), are all particularly serious complications which rapidly raise the pressure within the skull, and prompt identification (on CT scan) and subsequent treatment is essential. Oedema associated with the brain is another serious problem which has to be resolved with immediate treatment, since the confines of the skull are fixed, and will not expand, so a raised **intracranial** (inside the skull) **pressure (ICP)** can further damage the brain tissue. Oedema can also place pressure on blood vessels within the brain, limiting its blood supply, which can be fatal. One of the earliest and most sensitive indications of a raised ICP is a worsening in the level of consciousness (a decrease in arousal and awareness). Other signs include enlargement of pupils and slowing of pulse rate and abnormal or irregular respiration. ICP is therefore monitored carefully when the patient is admitted to hospital and measures taken to reduce the risk of raised pressure (the patient may be placed on a ventilator ensuring adequate oxygen delivery, and the amount of water and salts in the body controlled to limit the fluid flowing to the brain).

Diagnosis and treatment

Disturbances affecting memory, intellect, mood and general fatigue (tiredness) are frequent complaints of patients with TBI. Personality changes and rapid 'mood swings' are also frequently observed. A mild to moderate head injury can cause **concussion** (for a brief period of time the brain injury may be sufficient to make a person lose consciousness) followed by an alteration in a person's state of consciousness, or impairment in mental functions. Initial symptoms associated with concussion include drowsiness, headache, dizziness or vertigo, nausea and vomiting, confusion, disorientation, poor concentration and attention, and lack of awareness of one's surroundings. However, in some circumstances the effects of minor to moderate brain injuries are not immediately apparent, and may take many months to manifest with symptoms including a variety of mood and cognitive changes including memory dysfunction, difficulty with simple arithmetic or finding words, irritability, anxiety, depression, loss of appetite and sex drive, and sleep disturbances amongst others. Severe head injuries (a crushing blow or penetrating wound to the head) are more life-threatening, and cause more extensive problems including paralysis and severely limited mental abilities.

Severe damage to the nerve fibres in the central parts of the brain and to the brainstem (which normally keeps an individual alert and awake) results in coma where the patient is unresponsive to the outside world. Irrespective of whether the patient has been unconscious, they can suffer from **post-traumatic amnesia (PTA)**, where they are aware of things around them, but are often confused, disorientated, cannot remember everyday matters or conversations and often say or do bizarre things. The duration of PTA, when combined with the length of time in a coma usually gives a better measure of the eventual outcome of TBI. (PTA associated with moderate head injury usually lasts up to 24 hours, and will last longer than this following severe head injury.) Rehabilitation is essential after the acute phase has passed.

Assessing a patient's level of consciousness, motor and reflex responses (using the Glasgow Coma Scale developed by Teasdale and Jennet in 1974) amongst other neurological observations to determine TBI, can be complicated if the individual is intoxicated with alcohol or taking sedatives. (See Case Report 1.2.)

If ICP is raised, the patient may need to spend some time on a neurosurgical intensive care unit in order for this to be managed. A diuretic drug such as *mannitol* administered intravenously (via the vein) is effective in the short term. Ventilation is another means of reducing ICP. By *reducing* levels of circulating carbon dioxide (this normally dilates cerebral arteries and increases the volume of blood flowing to the brain) blood vessels are constricted and the cerebral blood volume reduced. Apart from the rapid haemorrhaging mentioned above, a **chronic subdural haematoma** may occasionally present as a delayed complication several days to weeks after a minor–moderate head injury. Pressure exerted on the brain manifests as headache, drowsiness, and confusion, amongst other signs. The haematoma can be identified on a CT scan and surgically 'drained'. Recent studies have identified an **endogenous** (naturally occurring) cannabinoid compound (arachidonoyl glycerol – a substance chemically related to cannabis) that may protect the brain after head injury (Panikashvili et al., 2001). Rehabilitation at a specialist centre, however, will continue to play an important part on the road to recovery after a severe head injury.

Case Report 1.2 Head injury

William was an 18-year-old youth who had suffered a head injury as a result of a road traffic accident. He had been driving in the early hours of Sunday morning, on his way to drop his friend home after a late-night party. He had failed to stop at a red light, going straight over the crossroads where the accident happened. He was admitted to the Accident and Emergency (A&E) department where a nurse assessed him and found him to have paralysis down his left side, and he was having difficulty focusing and finding words. He had quite severe bruising to his scalp, on the right side, but otherwise no external bleeding or obvious external injuries. His friend John, who had been sitting in the passenger seat at the time, said it had all happened rather quickly. John was miraculously unharmed, but when the car struck their vehicle from the right, William's head had first struck the window to his right and then whiplashed sharply to the left, and he lost consciousness for about ten minutes. A passer-by had called for an ambulance on his mobile phone, and they had arrived at the hospital within half an hour of the accident. He said it had all happened so suddenly and yet at the time he could see every minute detail as if time had slowed down or something. His friend was clearly coherent although still in a state of shock after the incident – the nurse referred him to the A&E doctor who decided it would be vital to have an X-ray. Neither youth seemed to be intoxicated with alcohol. William was referred to the neurosurgical specialist and transferred to the ward where his intracranial pressure was monitored and found to be raised, and he was placed on mechanical ventilation and given mannitol. A CT scan did not show any signs of intracranial, extradural or subdural haemorrhage.

William continued to improve during his two-week stay on the ward and he gradually became more alert and able to follow verbal commands, although occasionally showing signs of disorientation. Movement to his left arm also returned progressively with physical therapy, but he had considerable difficulty with fine motor and rapid alternating activities in his left hand. During his stay, he also showed symptoms of mild hearing loss, which cleared towards the end of the stay. He had excellent support from his parents and two older brothers and his friends, which clearly helped him to improve and interact better. He was referred to a rehabilitation centre where his rehabilitation programme involved a team of specialists including rehabilitation nurses, an occupational therapist, a speech therapist, a physiotherapist and a psychologist. Over a period of three months his coordination problems began to improve through the therapeutic programme of strengthening and other exercises to improve his fine motor skills, and he regained his former level of alertness and mental abilities prior to the accident. He improved from requiring considerable assistance (on admission) with personal hygiene and mobility, to being quite independent. At discharge he had regained almost all of his receptive and expressive language skills, was safety conscious, oriented and adjusted appropriately. He had showed sufficiently good improvement in skills to return home to his family and to the important decision of whether to continue his education at university now that he had completed all his A-levels. The psychologist had particularly impressed him. He thought the subject of neuropsychology would be quite interesting to follow up.

We have journeyed far through the nervous system and have finally come to the end of this chapter. In the next chapter, we will continue our journey with a look at our special senses and how we perceive the world around us through them.

Questions for Chapter 1

Question 1.1 (LOs 1.1 and 1.3)

Supply the missing terms in the following statement:

In the spinal cord, cell bodies are found predominantly in the (a) *Gray matter* whereas the white matter is composed largely of (b) *axons* ; the whitish appearance is due to (c) *Myelin* .

Question 1.2 (LOs 1.1 and 1.3)

Which of the following nerves contain only afferent fibres?

cranial nerves

motor nerves

sensory nerves ✓

spinal nerves

Question 1.3 (LO 1.2)

The brain and spinal cord are organs of which of the following? PNS, (CNS), ANS, CSF.

Peripheral Nervous System
central Nervous system
Autonomic Nervous system
Cerebrospinal fluid

Question 1.4 (LOs 1.1 and 1.5)

Suppose that a peripheral nerve on one side of the body (associated with the spinal cord) is severely damaged (crushed or severed) as a result of an accident. More specifically, let us presume that the damage is done to (a) a dorsal root nerve, (b) a ventral root nerve, or (c) a spinal nerve. What loss of function would be expected in each case?

(a) ventral root nerve = motor neurons
↳ loss of movement on 1 side
↳ specific dermatome.
↳ internal ?
(b) dorsal root nerve = sensory
↳ loss of feeling on 1 side
↳ specific dermatome.
(c) spinal nerve = motor + sensory
↳ loss of movement + feeling

Question 1.5 (LOs 1.2, 1.4 and 1.5)

A new drug is being tested which, when injected, has the effect of (amongst other things) slowing the heart rate and also reducing the strength of heart contractions. What could be its possible mode of action? (*Hint*: look back at Section 1.8.2.)

Heartrate ⇒
↳ smooth muscle
↳ neurotransmitters
↳ noradrenaline
↳ acetylcholine.
↳ slow HR.
↳ ANS
↳ sympathetic
↳ parasympathetic
↳ inhibitory

Heart beats are modulated by ANS, Sympathetic NS is excitory so incr HR + strength, whereas Parasympathetic NS is inhibitory, slowing HR + reducing strength.

In order to reduce pumping activity sympathetic neurons will have be inhibited, releasing less noradrenaline at neuromuscular junctions, and and parasympathetic neurons will be excited, releasing more acetylcholine at neuromuscular junctions.

∴ drug might act as antagonist to noradrenaline by blocking receptor sites, or inhibiting diffusion across cleft, or act as an agonist to acetylcholine, by binding to receptor sites or by blocking reuptake.

References and Further Reading

References

Anderson, B. and Harvey, T. (1996) Alterations in cortical thickness and neuronal density in the frontal cortex of Albert Einstein, *Neuroscience Letters*, **210**, 162–164.

Fried, I., Wilson, C. L., Macdonald, K. A. and Behnke, E. J. (1998) Electric current stimulates laughter, *Nature*, **391**, 650.

Harlow, J. M. (1868) Recovery from the passage of an iron bar through the head, *Publication of the Massachusetts Medical Society*, **2**, 327–347.

Lorber, J. (1981) Is your brain really necessary? *Nursing Mirror*, **152**, 29–30.

Panikashvili, D., Simeonidou, C., Ben-Shabat, S., Hanus, L., Breuer, A., Mechoulam, R. and Shohami, E. (2001) An endogenous cannabinoid (2-AG) is neuroprotective after brain injury, *Nature*, **413**, 527–531.

Shammi, P. and Stuss, D. T. (1999) Humour appreciation: a role of the right frontal lobe, *Brain*, **122**, 657–666.

Teasdale, G. and Jennett, B. (1974) Assessment of coma and impaired consciousness. A practical scale, *Lancet*, **2**, 81–84.

Further Reading

Barker, R., Barasi, S. and Neal, M. J. (2003) *Neuroscience at a Glance*. Oxford: Blackwell Scientific Publishing.

Bayerstein, B. L. (1999) Whence cometh the myth that we only use ten percent of our brains? in Della Sala, S. (ed.), *Mind-Myths: exploring everyday mysteries of the mind and brain*, pp. 3–24. New York: John Wiley and Sons.

Brain Facts: A Primer on the Brain and Nervous System (1997). Washington, DC: Society for Neuroscience.

Carter, R. and Frith, C. D. (1998) *Mapping the Mind*. London, Wiedenfeld & Nicolson.

Neuroscience-Science of the Brain: An Introduction for Young Students (2003). British Neuroscience Association.

Siegel, G. J., Agranoff, B. W., Albers, R. W., Fisher, S. K., Uhler, M. D. (1998) *Basic Neurochemistry: Molecular, Cellular and Medical Aspects*. Lippincott: Williams and Wilkins.

CHAPTER 2

THE SPECIAL SENSES

Learning Outcomes

After completing this chapter, you should be able to:

2.1 Describe the basic structural components of the five sensory systems: the olfactory system, the gustatory system, the skin, the eye and the ear.

2.2 Distinguish between the senses of touch and of pain and their associated pathways within the nervous system, and between referred pain and phantom limb pain.

2.3 Describe the basic anatomy and physiology of the retina.

2.4 Explain how refractive errors can be corrected, discuss the purpose of the light reflex and explain how we see colours.

2.5 Describe the basic anatomy and physiology of the middle and inner ear structures involved in the processes of hearing and balance.

2.6 Outline the central pathways involved in vision and hearing and language.

2.7 Describe some of the main causes of visual and auditory impairment.

2.1 Overview and introduction to the special senses

As you are reading this introduction, you will be focusing your gaze on the words across the page. At the same time you will be aware of sounds in your immediate environment. Perhaps there is also a distinct ambient odour that you can faintly smell. You may be holding a pen, rubbing your chin in deep thought, or savouring the flavours of a mint, a soft drink or a sugary sweet. Indeed, you are probably using two or more of your five senses – vision, hearing, smell, touch and taste – right now. What is so special about our senses? Well, in the previous chapter we learnt that our brain receives information from our senses and makes meaning of this based on our previous experiences. The way we perceive the world around us is unique to each of us. What we can sense physically influences how the brain can conceptualize, interpret and ultimately interact and respond with the outside world– that includes everyday communication with people too!

Our senses develop at different rates as we grow up. Visual input, in particular during the early months has a profound effect on a baby's developing nervous system – we literally learn to see. Infants starting out in life are far-sighted with poor **visual acuity** (i.e. they lack the ability to discriminate fine detail).They also lack colour vision and depth perception at birth. A new-born baby can see light and patterns (such as those associated with an overhead mobile over the cot), but objects beyond about 20 cm appear quite blurred. Research has shown that high contrast images (such as black and white stripes or light and dark contrasting colours) are most easily registered by an infant's brain particularly in the first two months after birth (whereas the pastel colours so often used in toys and nursery

VISUAL ACUITY

decoration, which are aesthetically pleasing to parents, in fact do little to stimulate the infant's nervous system during the early months). Hand–eye coordination begins to develop as the infant starts to track moving objects, and by the end of the second month the baby can focus better on objects, and detect shades of red and blue. Colour vision is almost fully developed by the fourth month. Visual ability continues to mature and develop well into the primary school years.

Although a new-born can hear sounds, the initial responses are reflexive, but as the child develops into a toddler, they begin to listen attentively and initiate sounds with the development of language. By comparison with vision and hearing, our sense of taste and that of smell are most defined at birth. They begin to deteriorate after we reach mid-life and by the age of 80, we lose the ability to discriminate between smells and tastes (this loss can also be seen at earlier stages in patients with neurodegenerative conditions such as Alzheimer's disease, which you can think of as part of a 'rapidly ageing' phenomenon). This gradual decline in sensory ability with age also affects our vision and hearing. We begin the study of the physical senses with smell, taste, touch and pain and concentrate on vision and hearing later in this chapter.

2.1.1 The senses of smell and of taste

Smell

Did you know that we can distinguish between 3000 and 4000 different smells? Smell (**olfaction**) and taste (**gustation**) are often inseparable in our daily lives. For example, the taste and appreciation of food is influenced by our sense of smell, as well as its temperature and texture. Essentially, both depend on the detection of chemicals via specific receptors that are designed to identify them. Have you ever noticed how you suddenly yearn for a curry when you encounter the aroma of Indian spices (or pass by the takeaway around the corner), or how you conjure up pleasant memories of people, places or events when you smell the scent of a particular flower or the waft of a perfume? Odours can help us to recall memories, since **olfactory** (smell-associated) **pathways** are closely linked to the limbic system (which governs memory and emotion, as you may recall from Section 1.4.1). If we smell or taste something prior to or during a negative experience, then that smell and taste are directly associated with that experience, and can be the basis of avoidance behaviour towards certain foods. It can of course work the other way, however, with a positive association linking memory and emotion with certain pleasant odours or tastes.

● Can you think of any immediate difference between smell and taste?

○ Smell, unlike taste, can signal over long distances, and may help to serve in evolutionary terms as an early recognition or warning device, for example in detecting a fire!

Emotions can also be communicated by smell – dogs and horses in particular are sensitive to the 'smell of fear' or rather the diffusion of chemicals in human sweat. For example, chemicals released when the unfortunate postal worker becomes aware of the old snarling dog positioned behind the fence, alert the said

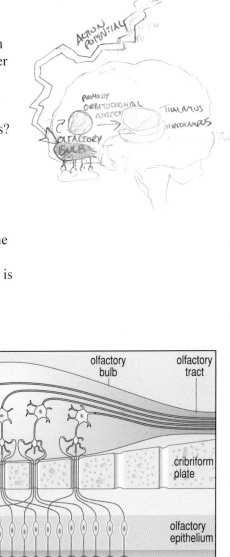

dog long before the ill-fated postal worker arrives to deliver the mail. For a more pleasant illustration, think of the way we can usually alter the ambience of a room by using aromatherapy oil burners or special fragrances. Our likes and dislikes of people and choices of partner can be greatly influenced by the way they smell – a characteristic that has been vastly exploited by companies advertising the sales of perfumes and deodorants. There is evidence women can detect even small differences in the male immune makeup which are unique to an individual (Jacob et al., 2002). Babies as young as a few days old can likewise recognize the distinct smell of their own mothers. So how does the mechanism of olfaction actually work?

Odorous chemicals first have to reach the nasal cavity (sniffing speeds up this process) and bind to receptor proteins in *olfactory receptor neurons* (of which there are around 10 million) (Figure 2.1). These neurons are located in the upper part of the nasal cavity, in the *olfactory epithelium* which is covered by a film of mucus.

● In relation to smell what would you suppose to be the function of the mucus?

● Odorous molecules must dissolve in the mucous film before binding to the receptor proteins.

In humans there are around 350 different types of olfactory receptor proteins associated with olfactory neurons. An olfactory neuron has many receptor proteins but they are all the same, i.e. each neuron only expresses one out of the 350 possible types. Each type of receptor will only bind to one type of odorant molecule, but imagine the possible permutations! No wonder our sense of smell is so rich and subtle!

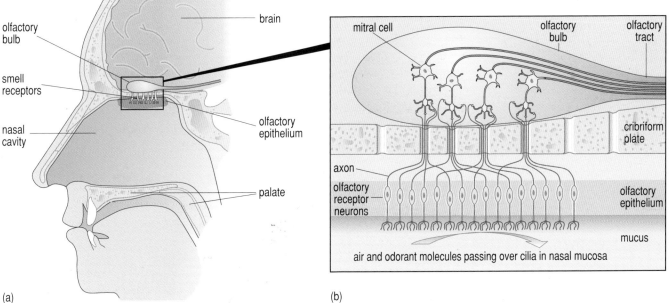

(a)

(b)

Figure 2.1   The anatomy of the olfactory system.

[Handwritten margin notes:]

OLFACTORY NERVE
└→ 2ndary messenger

↓

PRIMARY OLFACTORY CORTEX

↓

THALAMUS

↓

LIMBIC SYSTEM

PRIMARY OLFACTORY CORTEX
(ORBITO FRONTAL CORTEX)
• Olfactory region
• ANOSMIA – TBI
        – Alzheimers

THALAMUS:
• Router for sensory info
        └→ Cerebral cortex

LIMBIC SYSTEM
(AMYGDALA)
(HIPPOCAMPUS)
• Emotions
• memory
        └→ short term → long term

Limbic system? –emotional?

[Printed text:]

Once the odorant has bound to the protein receptor a change occurs on the other side of the cell membrane (inside the neuron). This leads to the synthesis of a molecule, known for obvious reasons as a **second messenger**, which binds to membrane proteins that open ion channels and allow Na^+ and Ca^{2+} to cross the membrane.

● In which direction will these positive ions move?

○ They will be drawn into the neuron by concentration and electrical gradients.

● What will be the consequence of this movement of positive ions?

○ The cell membrane will move from the negative resting potential, become more positive and, once past the threshold value an action potential will be initiated.

In this way information about smells passes along the olfactory receptor cells' axons (which collectively are known as the **olfactory nerve**) through the cribriform plate to a part of the brain called the olfactory bulb (Figure 2.1). Within the olfactory bulb, signals from the olfactory nerve are passed on to mitral cells and forwarded to the **primary olfactory cortex,** then to the thalamus and limbic system as shown in Figure 2.2.

Because olfactory receptor cells are so close to the 'outside world' they are easily damaged by airborne particles. Fortunately they are renewable, although we do not know how long each neuron lives. Presumably this ability for regeneration declines with age hence the decline in the acuity of smell with age, mentioned at the start of the chapter.

Anosmia is the term used to describe the loss of the sense of smell. This can be brought about by traumatic head injury or as a consequence of disease (for example, Alzheimer's disease), or it may be congenital (i.e. some people are born without the capacity for olfaction).

Taste

Our appetites and cravings for certain foods are driven by their taste. Most of us like sweet flavours, and we crave salt in food when our internal levels are low. We can also avoid certain foods and poisons because of their unpleasant taste – most poisons have a bitter taste and when food goes 'off' it turns acidic and becomes 'sour' to the taste. We even have a taste for proteins ('umami'). **Taste cells** (receptors) are located in **taste buds** (oval sensory structures) found on the tongue. Different receptors in distinct areas on the tongue relay information about whether something is sweet, salty, sour, savoury (the taste of certain amino acids – for example, glutamate) or bitter (refer also to Book 1, Section 4.3.2). Some areas of the tongue are more responsive to certain tastes than others. Taste buds (of which there are around 5000 on your tongue, each containing around 50 taste cells) are embedded in specialized epithelium that forms structures called **papillae** – these can be detected on the tongue as little red bumps (Figure 2.3, overleaf). There are four types of papillae – three types are taste sensitive: *fungiform* (innervated by a branch of the facial nerve; Table 1.1) are sweet and salt/sour sensitive and *foliate* and *circumvallate* (both innervated by the glossopharyngeal nerve) detect bitter tastes; the fourth is mechanical non-gustatory *filiform*. Cells that are found within the taste bud include *supporting cells*, *taste cells* which are

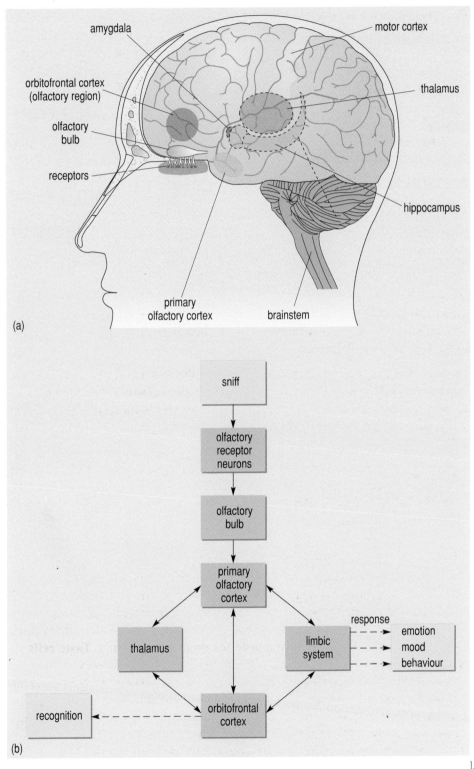

Figure 2.2 Olfactory pathways to the brain. (a) The diagram illustrates the relative positions in the brain of the structures in the olfactory pathway. (b) The processing of information is indicated in the flow diagram. From the receptors the information flows to the olfactory bulb and then to the primary olfactory cortex. From here it has two major routes: one to the limbic system (including the amygdala and hippocampus), and the other to the orbitofrontal cortex via the thalamus. It is the limbic system that is responsible for the 'affective' component of smell (memory, emotional responses). Recognition is thought to occur in the right orbitofrontal region of the brain.

basal cells = proto-taste cells → differentiate

the *sensory receptor cells* and *basal cells* (which differentiate into new taste cells and are replaced roughly once every 10 days). A sour taste is the result of taste receptors on the taste cells detecting hydrogen ions (acidity), salty taste is the detection of metal ions (e.g. sodium and potassium), and a sweet taste comes from the ability to detect sugars (both naturally occurring and synthetic, for example, the artificial sweeteners saccharin and aspartame).

MEDULLA:
- swallowing centre
- vomiting centre
- Basic, necessary activities
  - e.g. breathing + circulation
- Part of BRAINSTEM

PRIMARY GUSTATORY CORTEX:
- Taste perception (+ recognition?)

Figure 2.3 Basic surface anatomy of the tongue showing the regional distribution of taste buds and their cellular composition. Serous glands secrete a fluid that removes taste particles, clearing the taste buds ready for the next stimulus.

● Can you recall the names of the natural sugars?

○ Glucose, fructose, galactose and sucrose.

Once a taste cell (see Figure 2.3) has been activated by the appropriate chemical, synaptic vesicles release **neurotransmitter** into the synaptic cleft between the taste cell and the cell shown in Figure 2.3 as the primary afferent neuron.

● For taste cells in the fungiform papillae which nerve is the primary afferent?

○ The facial nerve (see above).

All of the nerves from the tongue synapse in the *medulla* and relay information to the gustatory centres of the brain, including the **primary gustatory cortex** (which deals with the perception of taste), and to the **limbic system** (which determines the behavioural responses to taste) (Figure 2.4).

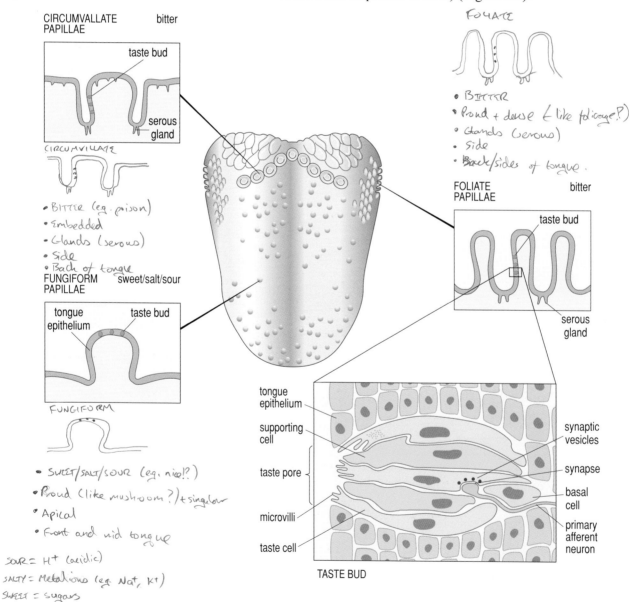

CIRCUMVALLATE PAPILLAE — bitter

taste bud

serous gland

CIRCUMVALLATE
- BITTER (eg. poison)
- Embedded
- Glands (serous)
- Side
- Back of tongue

FUNGIFORM PAPILLAE — sweet/salt/sour

tongue epithelium

taste bud

FUNGIFORM
- SWEET/SALT/SOUR (eg. nice!?)
- Proud (like mushroom?) + singular
- Apical
- Front and mid tongue

SOUR = H+ (acidic)
SALTY = Metal ions (eg. Na+, K+)
SWEET = sugars

FOLIATE

- BITTER
- Proud + dense (like foliage?)
- Glands (serous)
- Side
- Back/sides of tongue.

FOLIATE PAPILLAE — bitter

taste bud

serous gland

tongue epithelium

supporting cell

taste pore

microvilli

taste cell

synaptic vesicles

synapse

basal cell

primary afferent neuron

TASTE BUD

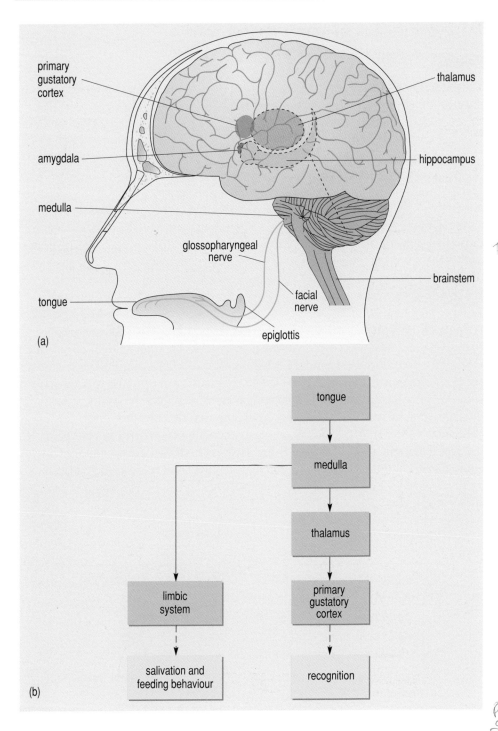

Figure 2.4 Gustatory pathways to the brain. (a) The diagram shows the relative positions of the structures in the gustatory pathway. (b) Flow diagram showing the neural pathway for taste. Nerves from the tongue and inside the mouth relay information to the medulla. From here neurons project to the limbic system or via the thalamus to the primary gustatory cortex.

What we often refer to as 'flavour' is in fact a combination of smell, taste, texture and other sensory components, including vision.

Hold your nose (or use a clothes peg) and close your eyes. See whether you can tell the difference between tea, coffee and water. You may be surprised to find that it is very difficult to distinguish between tastes if smell and vision is eliminated.

MEISSNER'S CORPUSCLES
  ↳ *low freq vibrations*
  ↳ *rapidly adapting*

PACINIAN CORPUSCLES
  ↳ *high freq vibrations*
  ↳ *rapidly adapting*

MERKEL'S DISCS
  ↳ *pressure*
  ↳ *slowly adapting*

RUFFINI ENDINGS
  ↳ *stretch*
  ↳ *slowly adapting.*

2.1.2 The senses of touch and of pain

Touch

Touch (tactile sensation) allows us to detect the size, shape and texture of objects through our skin. There are two main layers to the skin.

● What are these two skin layers called (see Figure 2.20 in Book 1 if you cannot remember).

● There is an outer epidermis and an inner dermis.

A variety of specialized receptor cells can detect and discriminate between certain stimuli. For example, there are receptors that are sensitive to light touch, those that detect a stronger pressure or vibration (both are **mechanoreceptors**) and temperature-sensitive receptors (**thermoreceptors**). Some of these types of receptor are shown in Figure 2.5, and their functions are summarized in Table 2.1. **Discriminative touch** is based on the perception of pressure, vibration and texture. This relies on four different receptors located in the skin: **Meissner's corpuscles**, **Pacinian corpuscles**, **Merkel's discs** and **Ruffini endings**. Meissner's and Pacinian corpuscles are rapidly adapting (they quickly stop firing in response to a constant stimulus), whereas Merkel's discs and Ruffini endings are slowly adapting (that is, they do not stop signalling in response to a constant stimulus). For this to make sense, imagine placing an object, let us say a pencil, in the palm of your hand. As it touches down, the first two receptor types (Meissner's and Pacinian) inform you that something has settled in your palm. If the pencil lies still, they will cease firing. However, Merkel's discs and Ruffini endings will continue to fire and signal that an object still remains in your palm.

Table 2.1 Sensory receptors associated with the skin.

Number on Figure 2.5	Receptor	Function	Location
1	hair follicle ending	respond to displacement of hair	wraps around hair follicle
2	Meissner's corpuscle	respond to vibration (low frequency)	dermis of the skin
3	Merkel's disc	respond to pressure	dermis of the skin
4	Ruffini ending	respond to skin stretch	dermis of the skin
5	Pacinian corpuscle	respond to vibration (high frequency)	dermis of the skin
6	free nerve ending	different responses to mechanical, thermal or noxious stimuli	various types found throughout the skin

There are also receptor cells in muscles and joints that are triggered in response to movement of these tissues, so giving us the sense of 'body awareness' (**proprioception**).

Try this activity. Sit down comfortably, and close your eyes. Touch your nose, elbow or any other body part.

You should find that you can accurately touch any of your own body parts because you are using proprioception independent of visual signals to inform your movements.

Figure 2.5 Schematic representation of the dermis and epidermis showing some of the receptor types.

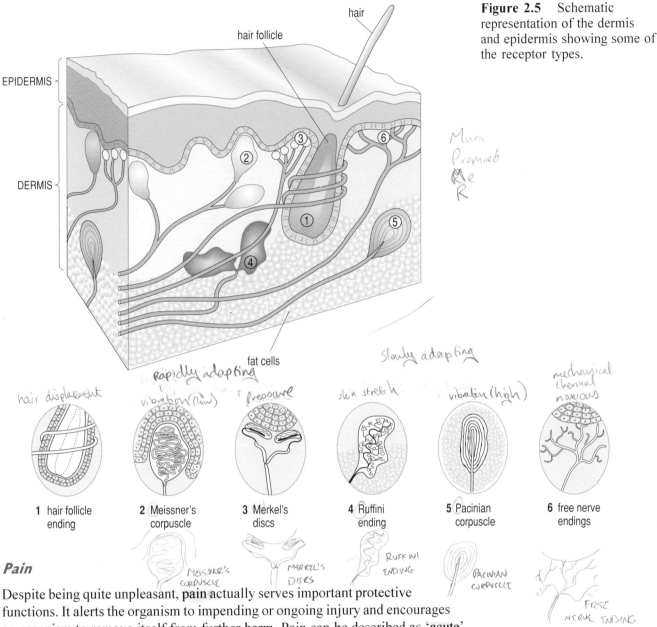

Handwritten notes: Mum Promised Me R; My Mushrooms R Pointy; rapidly adapting; Slowly adapting

1 hair follicle ending
2 Meissner's corpuscle
3 Merkel's discs
4 Ruffini ending
5 Pacinian corpuscle
6 free nerve endings

Handwritten: hair displacement; vibration (low); pressure; skin stretch; vibration (high); mechanical thermal noxious

Pain

Despite being quite unpleasant, **pain** actually serves important protective functions. It alerts the organism to impending or ongoing injury and encourages an organism to remove itself from further harm. Pain can be described as 'acute' or 'chronic'. Put simply, acute pain is short-term pain that usually has an identifiable cause, warning of disease or current damage to tissue. There are a variety of medical interventions that can be effective in blocking acute pain. Chronic pain on the other hand, is long-term pain that is not necessarily associated with any form of injury or disease, though typically it is, and in many instances it is not relieved by medication.

Tissue damage is detected by free nerve endings that are called nociceptors. Nociceptors are found in all parts of the body except for the brain (Section 1.8.2). They can detect different types of pain – **superficial** (i.e. caused by injury to the skin), deep somatic pain (originating from muscles, joints, tendons and blood vessels), and visceral pain (that originates from body organs). Another type of pain, **neuropathic pain** (or 'neuralgia'), occurs as a result of injury or disease to nerve tissue itself, which can disrupt the correct transmission of information.

PHANTOM LIMB PAIN
↳ not psychological
↳ muscle cramping
   ↳ residual limb.
      ↳ damaged nociceptor
        neurons
      ↳ hyperexcitable pathways
      ↳ reduced blood flow
↳ Tingling
   ↳ background cortical activity
   ↳ reorganisation of ..
     somatosensory cortex

REFERRED PAIN
↳ eg heart attack

SPINOTHALMIC TRACT:
• Heat
• Pain
COLUMN-MEDIAL LEMNISCUS TRACT:
• Tactile
• Proprioception
• Vibration
• MEDIAL LEMNISCUS

MEDULLA

THALAMUS

SOMATO SENSORY CORTEX ⟶ CORTICOSPINAL PATHWAY

The concept of **phantom limb pain** is very curious, and quite different. This is the sensation reported by 50–80% of patients who have undergone amputation surgery to remove part or all of a limb. Sensations related by the patients as emanating from their amputated limbs, range from the ability to 'feel' an arm resting on a table, or the fingers to 'detect' the texture of an object, or even the movement of the absent limb, through to sensations of tingling, prickling or shooting pains originating from the missing members of a hand for example, long after the surgery had taken place. There is little evidence that psychological factors cause phantom pain. Instead recent studies indicate that the major muscles in the residual limb 'tense up' several seconds before a cramping phantom limb pain manifests, and these muscles remain tense for most of the duration of this episode. Irritation of damaged nociceptive neurons or hyperexcitability of certain pathways are thought to be responsible for the sensation. Other studies have shown that the burning sensation of phantom limb pain is associated with a reduced flow of blood to the residual limb. Both of these respond to appropriate treatments. As for the non-pain-associated sensations such as tingling, one explanation considers that there is a background level of cortical (brain) activity in the absence of any somatosensory (body) input and it is this activity that the brain perceives as tingling. It is further suggested that a gradual process of reorganization within the somatosensory cortex, reduces both the size and the activity of the brain region devoted to the missing limb, and so these experiences lessen over time.

Referred pain is defined as pain from one region of the body that is perceived in another area, distant from the source. A well known example of this type of pain can be seen in a patient experiencing a heart attack – they often feel pain down the inside of the left arm and the forearm. Other examples of such associations include the gall bladder referring pain to the top of the right shoulder, stomach problems referring to the spine between the shoulder blades, kidney pain felt in the groin area, intestinal dysfunction felt in the middle or lower back, and a problem in the diaphragm felt in the shoulder and neck. The precise mechanisms underlying referred pain are poorly understood, and referred pain does not always give accurate information about the source of the pain.

Once a stimulus has been detected by nociceptors, the neural signal is transmitted towards the spinal cord and the signal crosses over almost immediately within the spinal cord to fibres located on the other side. The pathways for detecting heat follow a similar course as those for detecting pain and are known as the **spinothalamic tract** (shown in Figure 2.6). These ascending fibres relay sensory information up to the brain, and descending pathways relay motor information to control the response within muscle. By contrast, signals from other sensations (such as tactile sensation, joint position and vibration) travel along the **dorsal column–medial lemniscal tract** (Figure 2.6), and up to the brainstem (medulla) before crossing over. The information is relayed via the thalamus to the somatosensory cortex (which localizes the origin of the stimulus). The message received by the brain is processed and an appropriate response sent back down the spinal cord and towards a muscle group to elicit the necessary set of actions – this is the corticospinal pathway (Figure 1.27).

SPINO THALMIC TRACT
↳ heat/pain
DORSAL COLUMN - MEDIAL LEMNISCAL TRACT

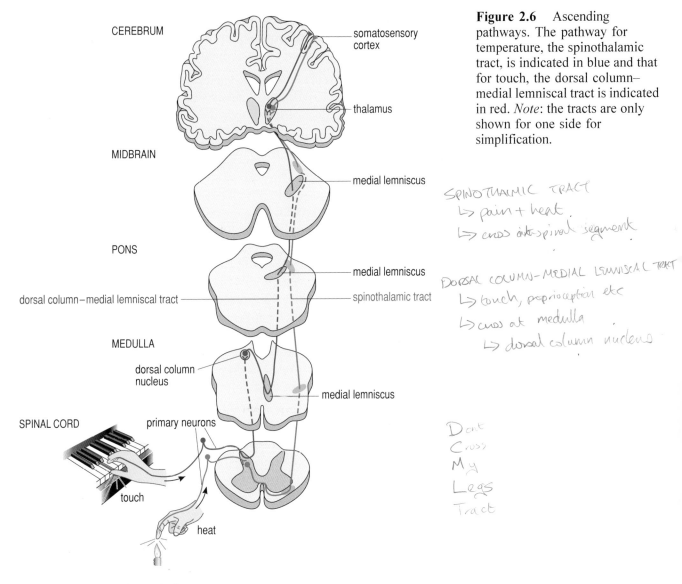

CEREBRUM

somatosensory cortex

thalamus

MIDBRAIN

medial lemniscus

PONS

medial lemniscus

dorsal column–medial lemniscal tract

spinothalamic tract

MEDULLA

dorsal column nucleus

medial lemniscus

SPINAL CORD

primary neurons

touch

heat

Handwritten notes:

SPINOTHALMIC TRACT
↳ pain + heat.
↳ cross onto spinal segment

DORSAL COLUMN-MEDIAL LEMNISCAL TRACT
↳ touch, proprioception etc
↳ cross at medulla
↳ dorsal column nucleus

Dont
Cross
My
Legs
Tract

Figure 2.6 Ascending pathways. The pathway for temperature, the spinothalamic tract, is indicated in blue and that for touch, the dorsal column–medial lemniscal tract is indicated in red. *Note*: the tracts are only shown for one side for simplification.

Summary of Section 2.1

1 We can interpret and interact with the external world through the use of our physical senses – smell, taste, touch, vision and hearing.

2 Our perception of smell is very closely associated with our perception of taste: both depend on the detection of chemicals at specialized receptors and both influence activity within the limbic brain centres, which govern memory and emotion.

3 Specialized receptors within the skin are differentially sensitive to touch, pressure, vibration, tissue damage and temperature.

4 Pain has an important protective function, alerting the person to injury or disease. Acute pain is short-term and usually has an identifiable cause. Chronic pain is long-term and not necessarily associated with any identifiable form of injury or disease.

5　Phantom limb pain refers to the sensation reported by many patients who have undergone an amputation, within the absent limb. Referred pain is pain perceived to be in one area of the body that has originated in another.

6　Sensory signals associated with heat and pain are transmitted along the spinothalamic tract to the brain. Sensory signals associated with touch, joint position and vibration are transmitted via the dorsal column–medial lemniscal tract to the brain. The message(s) are received and processed by the brain and a response is sent back down the spinal cord towards the appropriate group of muscles to elicit an action, via the corticospinal pathway.

2.2 The visual system

2.2.1 Basic anatomy and physiology of the eye and the retina

The human eye weighs about 7.5 g, and the eyeball is about 2.5 cm long. Light is actually a form of energy which has been described both as *waves* and as packets of energy called *photons*. What we see as light is particular wavelengths within the electromagnetic spectrum (Figure 2.7). There is nothing special about these wavelengths, it is just that to us they are visible, whereas bees and butterflies, for example, can see ultraviolet light!

Figure 2.7　Visible light and the electromagnetic spectrum

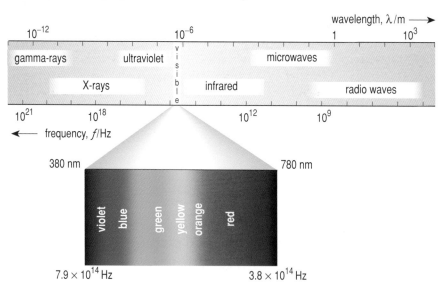

● Look at Figure 2.7. What wavelengths can we see as light?

○ We see wavelengths between 380 nm and 780 nm as light, because we have specialized receptors that are excited by this form of energy.

So how do we actually see? Light reflecting off the surface of objects (or emitted by an object) is detected by the eye (Figure 2.8). This light first encounters the **cornea**, where it is focused, then the **lens**, which varies the focus according to the distance of the object from the eye (the shape of the lens can be altered by the *ciliary smooth muscle* fibres). This focal adjustment by the lens is

smooth muscle - ANS

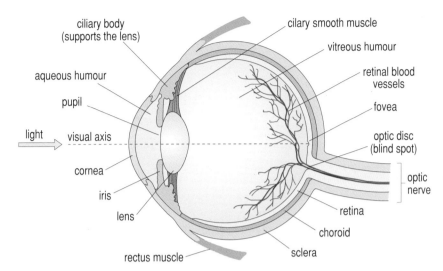

Figure 2.8 Diagram of the human eye.

CORNEA — FOCUS
↓
AQUEOUS HUMOUR —
↓
PUPIL — aperture size — IRIS
↓
LENS — Accommodation (distance)
↓
VITREOUS HUMOUR
↓
RETINA — receptor array

also called **accommodation** (the lens is pulled taut and is elongated and flat for distant vision, and released, adopting its natural rounded shape for near vision). Light rays first pass through the fluid-filled space between the cornea and the lens (the fluid is called **aqueous humour**) and then through the circular aperture of the **pupil** which is surrounded by the **iris** diaphragm muscles, before passing through the lens. The diameter of the pupil determines the amount of light entering the eye, and this in turn is regulated by the **circular** and **radial** smooth muscle fibres of the iris under the control of the autonomic nervous system. When the circular muscles contract the diameter of the aperture decreases (i.e. the pupil becomes smaller). When the radial muscle contracts the aperture enlarges (i.e. the pupil dilates). The image of the object in the visual world is projected onto the **retina**, located at the back of the eye. The receptors are located in the retina. The lens of the eye is transparent and functions much like that of a camera, and consequently, an image falls on the retina upside down and reversed from left to right (Figure 2.9).

LENS — controlled by CILIARY SMOOTH MUSCLE fibres.
↳ PRESBYOPIA

IRIS = altered by CIRCULAR + RADIAL SMOOTH MUSCLE FIBRES.
↳ PHOTOPUPILLARY REFLEX
↳ or LIGHT REFLEX

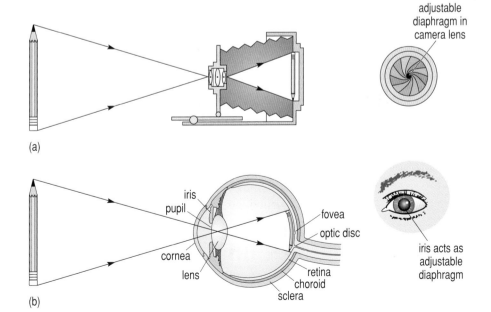

Figure 2.9 Diagram comparing the eye and a camera.

RODS:-
• Sensitive to low light levels
  └> info combined
      └> stronger signal
      └> night-vision.
• Lacks fine detail
• Throughout retina (-fovea)

CONES:
• Colour vision
• Visual acuity
• Info kept separate
  └> fine discrimination
  └> Day-time vision
• Densely packed within FoveA.

PHOTOPIGMENT:
• absorbs light energy
• OPSIN - protein
• RETINIENE - derived from vit A
  └> vit A deficiency
    └> Night 'blindness'.

The main layers of the retina are shown in Figure 2.10. Visible light that reaches the retina must travel through several layers of cells before being detected by specialized **photoreceptors** (Book 1, Section 2.3.2) that lie on the innermost retinal layer. There are two types of photoreceptors, termed **rods** and **cones** (Figure 2.10). Rods are located throughout the retina (except the *fovea* where acute focusing occurs) and are sensitive to low levels of light. The information from many rods is combined to give a stronger signal. This is useful, for example, in night-time vision. Whilst this system is sensitive to very low levels of illumination, it cannot discriminate fine visual detail. For this reason, even though we can detect objects at night, we cannot make out detail. Cones, on the other hand, are responsible for daytime vision, and are essential for visual acuity and colour vision. They are packed densely in the fovea region (where there are no rods) and the signal from each cone is kept separate so that the ability to make fine discriminations is retained. It is the **photopigment** contained within rods and cones that absorbs light energy. The photopigments all have a similar chemical composition and consist of a protein, called **opsin** and a chemical called **retinene** (also called 'retinal') which is related to vitamin A.

● Can you recall from Book 1, Chapter 3, a symptom of vitamin A deficiency?

○ Night 'blindness'.

There are around 125 million photoreceptors which are able to transform the energy received from light into biochemical signals. In turn these generate

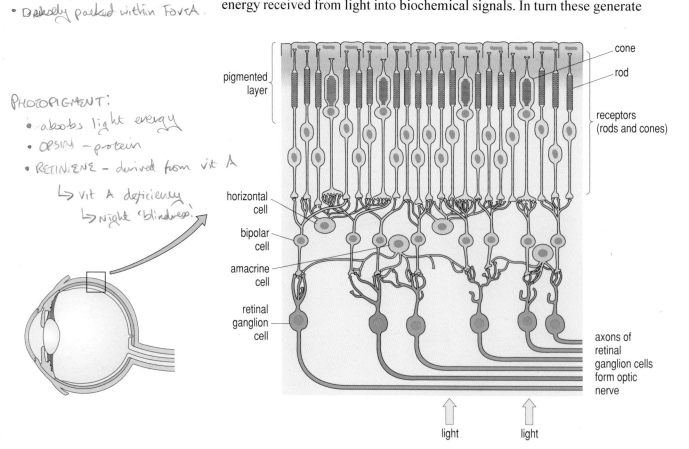

Figure 2.10 Schematic cross-section of the retina showing rod and cones and other cell layers.

electrical signals and there is an initial processing in the retina via synapses on bipolar, amacrine and horizontal cells. Finally **retinal ganglion cells** carry the processed information to the brain, their long axons forming the optic nerve.

In Figure 2.8 you can see the **blind spot** (optic disc) where the optic nerve leaves the back of the eye. This is devoid of any light-sensitive photoreceptor cells.

You can demonstrate your own blind spot by carrying out the following test. Look at the image of a filled circular dot to the left and several centimetres to the right of this, a bold plus sign (shown below). Now close your right eye, focus your left eye on the plus sign while holding the page at arms' length. You should be able to see both symbols. Slowly bring the page closer to your eyes.

●   ✚

At some point the circle vanishes. This demonstrates your blind spot (if you continue moving the page closer to your face, the circle reappears).

2.2.2 Refractive errors and visual acuity

When the functional components of the eye malfunction or do not adjust properly, light is not focused perfectly on the retina and the result is blurred vision, hence the need for corrective glasses and contact lenses. There are three main types of such **refractive error**: nearsightedness (*myopia*) occurs when the focal point falls short of the retina (Figure 2.11a); farsightedness (*hypermetropia*) results when the focal point extends beyond the retina (Figure 2.11b); and *astigmatism* is where an irregular curvature to the cornea and lens gives rise to multiple focal points, none of which gives rise to a perfect image on the retina. *Presbyopia* (or vision in old age) refers to the condition common with ageing, where the lens of the eye becomes hardened and loses its ability to adjust the focal point of the eye – only distant objects can be resolved, making glasses necessary for close activities such as reading. Nearsightedness can be remedied by placing a *concave* lens in front of the eye (Figure 2.11a). Farsightedness is remedied by placing a *convex* lens in front of the eye (Figure 2.11b).

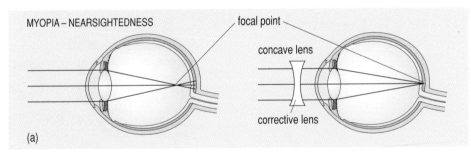

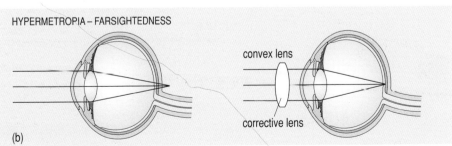

Figure 2.11 Schematic illustrations to show (a) myopia (nearsightedness) and (b) hypermetropia (farsightedness) and their correction.

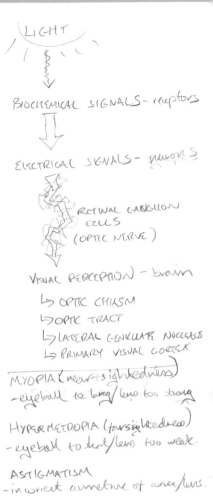

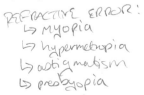

● From Figure 2.11, can you suggest what alterations in the components of the eye can give rise to nearsightedness?

● An excessively long eye. (An overpowerful lens and cornea can also result in nearsightedness.)

Conversely, a short eye and an inadequate cornea and lens can result in far-sightedness.

Visual acuity, or the ability to discriminate fine detail, is defined in clinical terms as the minimum distance that two lines (or points) must be separated in order to appear distinct. The optometrist usually tests this by referring to a **Snellen letter chart** (Figure 2.12). An individual with 'normal' eyesight should be able to read the smallest row of letters at a distance of 6 metres (20 feet). Visual acuity according to this description is referred to as '6/6' or '20/20' vision.

Figure 2.12 A version of the Snellen letter chart from the USA. This version is available online (Division of Driver Licensing, 2004).

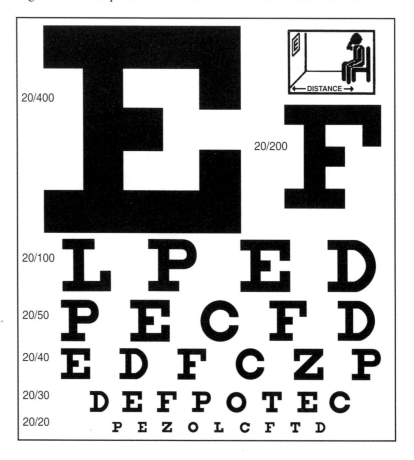

2.2.3 The light reflex and the truth about tears

When a bright light is shone into the eye the pupil constricts. This is the **light reflex** (also referred to as the **photopupillary reflex**).

● Which muscle contracts to cause this constriction?

● The circular muscle of the iris contracts (Figure 2.8).

PHOTOPUPILLARY REFLEX
⤷ (LIGHT REFLEX)
⤷ Parasympathetic NS
⤷ morphine/alcohol
⤷ constriction of pupil
⤷ circular muscle.
contracts
⤷ iris

This reflex is governed by the **parasympathetic nervous system**. Light shone into one eye causes pupillary adjustments in *both* eyes, and is very important in preventing damage to the photoreceptors of the retina.

ANS:
Parasympathetic
opposing sympathetic

● What additional measures should we take to shield our eyes from bright sunlight?

◐ We should wear a peaked hat, a visor or sunglasses to reduce glare. More specifically, we would select sunglasses that offer us uv (ultraviolet) protection.

● Why is this important?

◐ Ultraviolet radiation can be damaging to the retina. It may lead to 'snow blindness' (when reflected off a white surface for excessive periods) and in the longer term, may lead to cataracts (see Section 2.5.2) and premature ageing of the eyes.

By comparison, in dim light the radial muscle of the iris contracts.

● Which branch of the autonomic nervous system will control this muscle contraction and what will be the effect on the pupil?

◐ This contraction will be under the influence of the **sympathetic nervous system**, dilating the pupil.

Drugs can affect the photopupillary reflex through their action on these specific neural pathways. Alcohol or morphine cause the pupil to constrict, whereas cocaine and atropine, for example, cause the pupil to dilate. Pupils that are unequal in diameter or fail to adjust in response to a flash of bright light in a neurological examination, may indicate conditions such as cerebral haemorrhage (bleeding within the brain) that places pressure on the optic nerve. The accommodation of the lens is also a reflex response that is under the control of the parasympathetic nervous system.

ACCOMODATION
↳ parasympathetic NS
↳ beer goggles!

● Will the sympathetic nervous system affect lens shape too?

◐ No, because the lens is pulled taut by the ciliary muscles (under parasympathetic control) but when released it adopts its natural rounded shape (it is not pulled back to that shape by muscles).

Have you also noticed that bright lights often make your eyes water? This is also a reflex response under sympathetic and parasympathetic control. For a long time tears were thought of as no more than a vestigial secretion, or an outlet for human emotions. Research has found that such secretions from the lacrimal (tear) glands, not only lubricate the eyeball and eyelid and prevent dehydration of the cornea, but also help to wash away dust and debris and to supply nutrients to these sites. Tears contain a mixture of water, lipids, salts, antibodies, antibacterial proteins and growth factors. They are distributed when we blink, and are drained through the tear ducts. If you are wondering why onions make us shed involuntary tears, it is because the chemical released by a peeled onion is turned to acid upon contact with the eye and this stimulates release of tears. If not for the tear reflex, it would be quite damaging to the eyes. Furthermore, tears produced under stressful or emotional circumstances have been found to contain many toxic biological

RETINAL GANGLION CELLS
    (OPTIC NERVE)
    ↓
OPTIC CHIASM
    ↓ ↳ Split L/R
    ↓ ↳ crossover
OPTIC TRACT
    ↓ ↳ L/R seperate
THALAMUS – LATERAL GENICULATE NUCLEUS
    ↓ ↳ processed sensory info.
PRIMARY VISUAL CORTEX

substances and the stress hormone adrenocorticotropic hormone (ACTH, see Chapter 3). So, tears have been proposed as a means of removing these chemicals from the body during times of emotional stress! A deficiency in the production of tears (that occurs naturally or as a side-effect of drug treatments or a disease such as diabetes), or rapid dehydration, actually has serious consequences. It leads to a condition called *dry eye syndrome*, where the eye is aggravated by dry air, wind, dust and smoke, and this can lead to an aversion to light and damage to corneal epithelium; it also increases the likelihood of an eye infection.

2.3 Central visual pathways and visual areas

Axons of the retinal ganglion cells form the optic nerve and project to the *optic chiasm*, where there is partial cross-over of fibres (axons). These fibres, now called the *optic tract*, terminate in a region of the thalamus called the *lateral geniculate nucleus (LGN)* (Figure 2.13).

● What does the term *lateral geniculate nucleus* tell you about the anatomy of this structure?

◑ In this context 'nucleus' tells you that the structure contains densely packed neuronal cell bodies. ('Lateral' means side and 'geniculate' refers to the sharp angle – it means 'small knee' in Latin.)

From the LGN the signals are relayed to the **primary visual cortex** (Brodmann area 17) and to secondary visual areas located at the back of the brain (for example, Brodmann areas 18 and 19; see Figure 1.7).

Physiological studies of the visual system suggest that visual information is processed in three ways: (i) according to shape, (ii) according to colour, (iii) according to movement, location and spatial organization. Psychological testing in humans has shown that the perception of movement, depth perspective, relative object size and movement as well as shading and graded textures all depend on our ability to detect contrasts in light intensity rather than colour. The perception of depth is brought about by cortical processing of a 'fusion' of two images (from inputs of the visual fields of each eye).

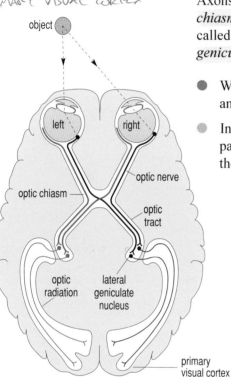

Figure 2.13 The main pathway from the retina to the visual cortex.

Neurons within the retina also project to other brain regions including a specialized area of the hypothalamus called the suprachiasmatic nuclei (SCN), which controls body rhythms. We will learn more about body rhythms in Book 4, particularly in relation to the sleep–wake cycle.

2.4 Colour vision and colour blindness

Seeing the world in colour is central to our lives, and yet at the same time it is one factor that we frequently take for granted in everyday living. Colours shape the way we behave, interact with and respond to social and environmental stimuli, and they invariably affect our mood, perception and how we interpret cues, whether we are consciously aware, or through subliminal awareness of our external world. You may be surprised to learn that 1 in every 12 men and 1 in every 200 women

VISUAL INFO PROCESSED
(1) shape (2D?)
(2) colour
(3) location/movement + spatial org.

suprachiasmatic nuclei (SCN)

are actually affected by some form of 'colour deficiency', more commonly referred to as 'colour blindness'. True colour blindness, however, is quite rare (about 30 in a million people do not see any colours, and the world appears as if in black and white). Colour blindness is hereditary and sex-linked, i.e. associated with the X-chromosome.

2.4.1 How do we see colours?

The wavelength of light determines the colour that we see (Figure 2.7). As you now know, we detect colour using our cones. These are found in the highest densities within the fovea and are principally located in the centre of the retina, the macula. This area provides the clearest, most distinct vision. The cones contain one of three photopigments (you may recollect that these are composed of the proteins opsin and retinene). **L-cones** detect long wavelengths associated with red colours, **M-cones** detect medium wavelengths (green) and **S-cones** detect short (blue) wavelengths. This property is referred to as the **spectral sensitivity** of photoreceptors. It is alterations in photopigments contained within these receptors that lead to colour blindness.

Colour vision, however, is also an active process that depends as much on the function of the brain (based on prior stored experience), as upon the external physical environment. The brain determines which colour we see by comparing the combination of inputs received from the three types of cones.

2.4.2 The different forms of colour blindness

In colour blindness, either one photopigment is missing or it responds maximally to a different wavelength (this is described as a shift in spectral sensitivity). Complete loss of one type of cone is known as **dichromacy**. A shift in the spectral sensitivity of one type of cone is a common form of colour blindness referred to as **anomalous trichromacy**. It typically manifests as a confusion between red and green (i.e. affecting L-cones and M-cones) and occurs due to variation in the cone pigment caused by a difference in amino acid sequences (human red and green pigments differ only at 15 out of 364 amino acid residues).

2.4.3 Some practical considerations

Common forms of colour blindness are not in themselves serious conditions, and people with red–green colour deficiency generally can see most colours. They mostly have trouble distinguishing between some shades of red and green. From a practical point of view, they live their lives coping well with tasks that require normal colour vision. They may not even be aware that their colour vision differs from normal, unless they are the subjects of a colour vision test. In contrast, *dichromats* (who lack one of the three cone types entirely), are usually aware of their colour visual problem, which may affect their lives on a daily basis. Colour acuity is important in some situations and professions, for example the motorist's ability to discriminate between red and green traffic lights, for careers in the armed forces, in aviation and maritime occupations. There is some evidence that red–green colour-deficient individuals are actually better than average at certain jobs, for example at finding green targets against a green background. This tendency to be less confused by camouflage meant that during wartime, armies relied on their colour-blind spotters and snipers to identify camouflaged targets. Colour acuity is also very important for transmitting visual information electronically, for example via the World Wide Web. So much so in fact, that specialized colour charts have been set up for web designers, which take colour deficient vision into consideration.

2.4.4 Is there a cure for colour blindness?

There is, at present, no effective method to recover full tricolour vision for red–green colour blindness. Coloured contact lenses or spectacles are claimed to show some improvements in people with colour deficiencies, but with mixed results. There are, however, alternative methods available for making information in colour pictures detectable by colour-deficient individuals. The easiest method is to increase the red–green contrast, since many colour blind people have some residual capacity to discriminate red from green colours.

2.5 Causes of impaired vision

A loss of vision can be partial or progress through to total loss of sight. Visual disturbances increase with age, and up to one in six adults over the age of 45 report some type of impairment. This figure rises to over one in four of those who are 75 and older.

2.5.1 Diabetic eye disease

Diabetes is the most common cause of visual disturbance and blindness in the modern world. Diabetes causes damage to the capillaries that provide oxygen and nutrients to the retina and this allows blood to escape into the area. Newly formed blood vessels are fragile and frequently also bleed into the **vitreous humour** (the fluid inside the eyeball; Figure 2.8). Symptoms include blurred, distorted or double vision, although many patients may have no outward symptoms. Laser treatment can reduce the risk of developing more severe loss of vision. People with diabetes are also prone to suffer from glaucoma and cataracts and are therefore advised to have retinal screening annually. (See Case Report 2.1.)

2.5.2 Cataracts

A cataract forms as a progressive clouding and swelling of the lens of one or both eyes and occurs predominantly in older individuals (those over 60 years of age). If left untreated, it will ultimately result in blindness. A variety of factors other than ageing are associated with developing a cataract. These include smoking, poor nutrition, eye injuries and long-term exposure to sunlight. Surgical treatment is used to remove the cataract. Following removal of the lens, a small plastic lens is permanently affixed in its place inside the eye.

2.5.3 Macular degeneration

Age-related macular degeneration is also a leading cause of irreversible blindness in older individuals. This may occur as a result of thinning of the layers of the macula (Section 2.4.1), which is a gradual process, or as a consequence of haemorrhage of an associated blood vessel that destroys the macular tissue, which is rapid and devastating. The early symptoms include blurred vision, distortion of objects, and development of a dark spot in the centre of the field of vision.

2.5.4 Glaucoma

Glaucoma is the term used to describe a group of conditions associated with progressive damage to the optic nerve, and is the third most common cause of blindness in western society. A rise in pressure within the eye (intraocular pressure) can come about as a result of inadequate drainage of aqueous humour (the watery fluid produced by ciliary epithelial glands; see Figure 2.8) which bathes internal structures in the eye and may be one indication of a patient who is at risk of developing glaucoma. Patients are usually unaware that they have raised intraocular pressure (see Case Report 2.1). The condition may also develop secondary to other eye diseases, and in patients with a family history of glaucoma. The common effective treatment for glaucoma is a reduction in intraocular pressure, and early identification and diagnosis of those patients at risk.

[Handwritten margin notes: GLAUCOMA: → damage to OPTIC NERVE → INTRAOCULAR PRESSURE → inadequate drainage → aqueous humour → family history → secondary symptom → other eye diseases → early diagnosis if high risk → e.g. diabetes; e.g. diabetes]

Case Report 2.1 Glaucoma

Jeremy is 50 years old. He had been diagnosed with diabetes in his mid-forties. Recently, he had been experiencing a gradual loss of peripheral vision in both eyes. He had gone to his opticians for an eye check and mentioned that he was frequently seeing dark 'blind' spots in his vision and that these were increasing in size. His visual acuity was lessened and he was also beginning to see 'halos' around lights. The optometrist looked at the back of his eye using an ophthalmoscope and could detect some damage to the optic nerve. She tested his field of vision by showing Jeremy a sequence of lightspots and asking him to respond to those he could see. She said that they would also have to carry out a test to check whether the pressure in his eyeballs had risen significantly. This was done with a device that blew a small puff of air directly onto his eyeball. The test found his intraocular pressure to be more than twice normal levels. The optometrist explained that Jeremy had a condition known as 'open-angle' glaucoma. This was the most common form of glaucoma, also known as 'chronic simple glaucoma', and it affects around two out of a hundred people over the age of 40. She asked him if he knew of any close relatives who had had glaucoma. Jeremy mentioned that his grandmother on his mother's side was said to have had glaucoma, but he was not so sure since she passed away before he was born. The optometrist explained that open-angle glaucoma was around six times more likely to develop in someone with a close relative having the condition. Of course, she added,

his diabetes was also a risk factor for developing glaucoma – when was the last time he had his eyes checked? Jeremy replied that he had felt no pain and had experienced no visual problems in his eyes over the past few years, so he had not followed up regular screening checks. The optometrist said that she would have to refer Jeremy to his GP who would locate a consultant ophthalmologist to follow up further assessment and to administer treatment. Hopefully, they could attempt to halt the damage done to his optic nerve before it got worse. She said that it was important for him to receive treatment, as the build-up of pressure inside his eye would be painless but slow and progressive. If it was left untreated, his field of vision would continue to reduce, so that eventually only a small central area would remain (tunnel vision), before his sight was completely lost. She said that options for treatment would be medicine such as a beta-blocker (Book 3, Chapter 3), given as eye drops (these would help to lower the internal pressure of the eye by increasing fluid drainage, but may have some side effects such as causing irritation to the eyes), or laser treatment and surgery, as advised by the ophthalmologist. She added that treatment would not reverse any existing loss of vision, but it would halt any further deterioration. Jeremy thanked her for all her help and advice. He assured the optometrist that he would visit his GP for the follow-up assessments as she had suggested and would make sure that his two children went for regular screening at their local opticians.

Summary of Sections 2.2 to 2.5

1　Light is focused through the cornea, and this focus is varied by the lens according to the distance of the object from the eye (a process called 'accommodation'). The image of an object falls on the retina located at the back of the eye, upside down and reversed from left to right.

2　Visible light that reaches the retina is detected by specialized light receptors (photoreceptors) termed rod and cones. Rods are located throughout the retina and are sensitive to low levels of light (for example, in night vision), but cannot discriminate fine detail, whereas cones are particularly localized to the fovea, are responsible for daytime vision and essential for discriminating fine detail and colour vision.

3　Photoreceptors transform light energy into biochemical signals (through activation of photopigments) and subsequent electrical signals which are passed on to the brain via the optic nerve. The location at the back of the eye where the optic nerve leaves the eye is devoid of photoreceptors and is called the blind spot.

4　Nearsightedness (myopia), farsightedness (hypermetropia) and the inability to adjust the focal point of the eye, common in old age (presbyopia), are all types of refractive error. The first two conditions can be corrected by placing an appropriate lens in front of the eye.

5　The light or 'photopupillary' reflex helps to adjust the level of light reaching the retina, to prevent damage to the photoreceptors. This involuntary reflex action is controlled by the autonomic nervous system.

6　The production of tears is also under the control of the autonomic nervous system. Tears help to lubricate the eye, prevent dehydration of the cornea and wash away dust and debris. They also contain growth and antibacterial factors, and are a means of removing toxic substances that accumulate under stressful conditions.

7　The main visual pathway from the retina to the cerebral cortex crosses over at the optic chiasm, projects to the thalamus (lateral geniculate nucleus), and on to the visual cortex at the back of the brain.

8　The wavelength of light determines the colour we see, and colour is detected by three types of cone photoreceptors with differing photopigments (L-cones for red, M-cones for green, and S-cones for blue). This is referred to as spectral sensitivity. Alterations in, or loss of any of the photopigments within these receptors leads to colour blindness.

9　There are several causes of impaired vision, the more common ones being diabetic eye disease, cataracts, macular degeneration and glaucoma.

2.6 The auditory system

2.6.1 Basic anatomy and physiology of the ears: the process of hearing

Our hearing not only enables us to communicate, but also gives us important information for survival. We can use our hearing independently from our sight, for example, to warn us of an approaching vehicle which may be obscured behind parked cars when stepping out into the road from the pavement.

Sound is transmitted through space as vibrations which cause changes in pressure. The pitch or frequency of sound is measured in units called Hertz (Hz). Humans can hear sounds with frequencies between 20 and 25 000 Hz. In the ear the energy from the vibrations is converted into neural signals (see below). There are three main parts to the human ear – the external, middle and inner compartments (Figure 2.14). Sound is first guided through the *external ear* (pinna) and the *auditory canal* to the *eardrum* (tympanic membrane) which vibrates in response to sound. The human eardrum is only 500 μm thick, so is a very delicate structure. These vibrations are transferred to bones within the middle ear called **ossicles** (the smallest bones in the body) – the **hammer** (**malleus**), attached to the eardrum, the **anvil** (**incus**) and the **stirrup** (**stapes**) which in turn convey the vibrations through the **oval window**, via the **cochlea** to the **inner ear**. The middle ear ossicles increase (amplify) the sound energy that reaches the cochlea more than 20 times. This is brought about because the area of the oval window is much smaller (about 22 times) than that of the eardrum, and the ossicles act as a mechanical lever, increasing the force applied at the interface between the stapes and the oval window. There are also two very small muscles called the *tensor tympani* and *stapedius* attached to the ossicles that contract reflexively in response to very loud sounds.

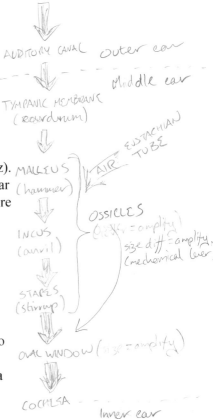

Figure 2.14 Anatomy of the human ear showing the outer, middle and inner compartments.

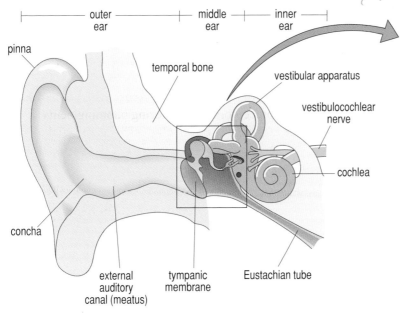

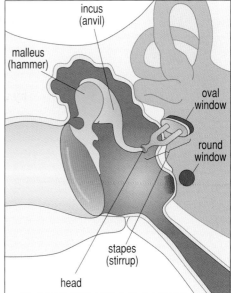

EUSTACHIAN TUBE - equalizes pressure
↳ air IN

OVAL WINDOW - dissipates pressure
↳ from sound waves.

PERILYMPH
↳ scalae vestibuli + tympani
↳ transmission of sound
↳ stapes
ENDOLYMPH
↳ scala media

ORGAN OF CORTI
↳ In scala media
↳ hair cells
↳ mechanoreceptors

PERILYMPH:
• (extracellular fluid)
• outer layers
• SCALA VESTIBULI
  +
  SCALA TYMPANI
• transfer sound waves

ENDOLYMPH:
• (intracellular fluid)
• inner layer
• SCALA MEDIA

- What purpose do you suppose these muscles serve?

- Their function is to dampen the movement of the ossicles and reduce the amplification of sound, therefore helping to preserve the inner ear structures from overload and subsequent damage.

The middle ear contains air that is replenished through the **Eustachian tube** (Figure 2.14) (this exits in the pharynx at the back of the throat) each time that we swallow. Yawning or chewing gum forces air into the Eustachian tube and balance is maintained between the pressure in the outer and middle ear (you have probably heard your ear 'click' or 'pop' when travelling on an aircraft as the cabin pressure changes – this is a change in pressure detected by your eardrums).

The inner ear contains the cochlea, **vestibule** and **semicircular canals** (Figure 2.15). The cochlea is a spiral (coiled) fluid-filled structure that contains around 20 000–30 000 **hair cells** (so termed due to their microscopic hair-like projections – cilia), which respond to the vibrations produced by sound.

- How would you classify these hair cells?

- Receptor cells that respond to pressure or vibration are mechanoreceptors.

There are three channels or *scalae* within the cochlea – the *scala vestibuli, scala media* and *scala tympani* (Figure 2.16). The scala vestibuli and tympani both contain a fluid called **perilymph** (similar to extracellular fluid), the scala media contains **endolymph** (similar to intracellular fluid). Sound pressure transferred via the stapes to the membrane of the oval window, is conducted in the fluid perilymph within the scala vestibuli and scala tympani to the **round window**, where it dissipates (think of this as a pressure release valve) (Figure 2.16). It takes around 5 milliseconds for the vibration from a sound wave to travel the length of the cochlea!

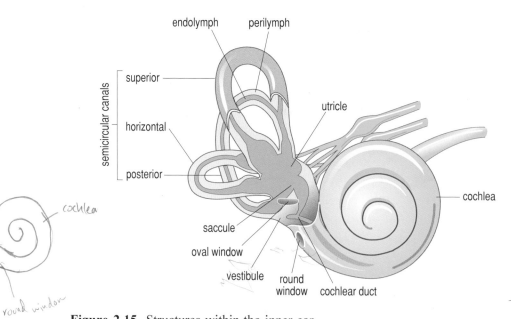

Figure 2.15 Structures within the inner ear.

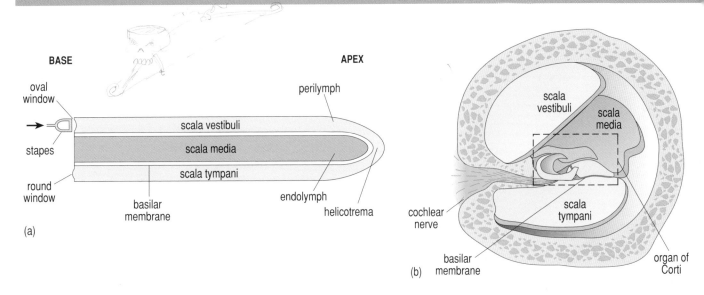

BASE

oval window

stapes

round window

basilar membrane

scala vestibuli

scala media

scala tympani

APEX

perilymph

endolymph

helicotrema

(a)

scala vestibuli

scala media

cochlear nerve

scala tympani

basilar membrane

organ of Corti

(b)

Figure 2.16 (a) Diagrammatic representation of the three channels (scalae) within the cochlea. (b) Cross-section through the cochlea to show the scalae and the organ of Corti.

Hair cells located on the basilar membrane of the **organ of Corti**, which lies within the scala media (see Figure 2.16b and Figure 2.17a, overleaf) translate vibrations into electrical neural signals. At the larger end of the cochlea they respond to very high-pitched sounds, while those at the smaller end and most of the rest of the cochlea respond to low-pitched sounds. A sound of the appropriate pitch causes the cilia on the hair cell to bend (Figure 2.17b, c). Bending of the cilia triggers an electrical current within the hair cell and causes the release of glutamate near the base of the cell, and this neurotransmitter subsequently activates the dendrites of a neuron that is part of the **auditory nerve**. The louder the sound, the greater is the displacement of the cilia and in proportion, the release of glutamate from the hair cell.

Signals from the hair cells are transmitted via the auditory nerve to the medulla in the brainstem where initial processing takes place, then to the *medial geniculate nucleus (MGN)* of the thalamus for further processing and subsequently to the primary auditory cortex (Brodmann areas 41 and 42) and secondary auditory cortex in the temporal lobe – the final areas of the brain involved in processing sound (Figure 2.18, overleaf). Sounds associated with speech, however, are additionally processed within specialized speech and language centres, which were introduced in the preceding chapter (Broca's and Wernicke's areas; Figure 1.7). Due to the structural layout of the hair cells on the basilar membrane (progressing across the range from low-pitched sounds to high-pitched sounds – think of this as representing the keys on a piano – an oversimplified illustration of course!), information regarding the vibration at different locations on the membrane are relayed through to specific regions of the auditory cortex where they are mapped point for point, creating a *tonotopic map* on the auditory cortex (Figure 2.18b).

75

Medial geniculate nucleus (MGN)
↳ Thalamus↲
↓
PRIMARY AUDITORY CORTEX
↳ Tonotopic map

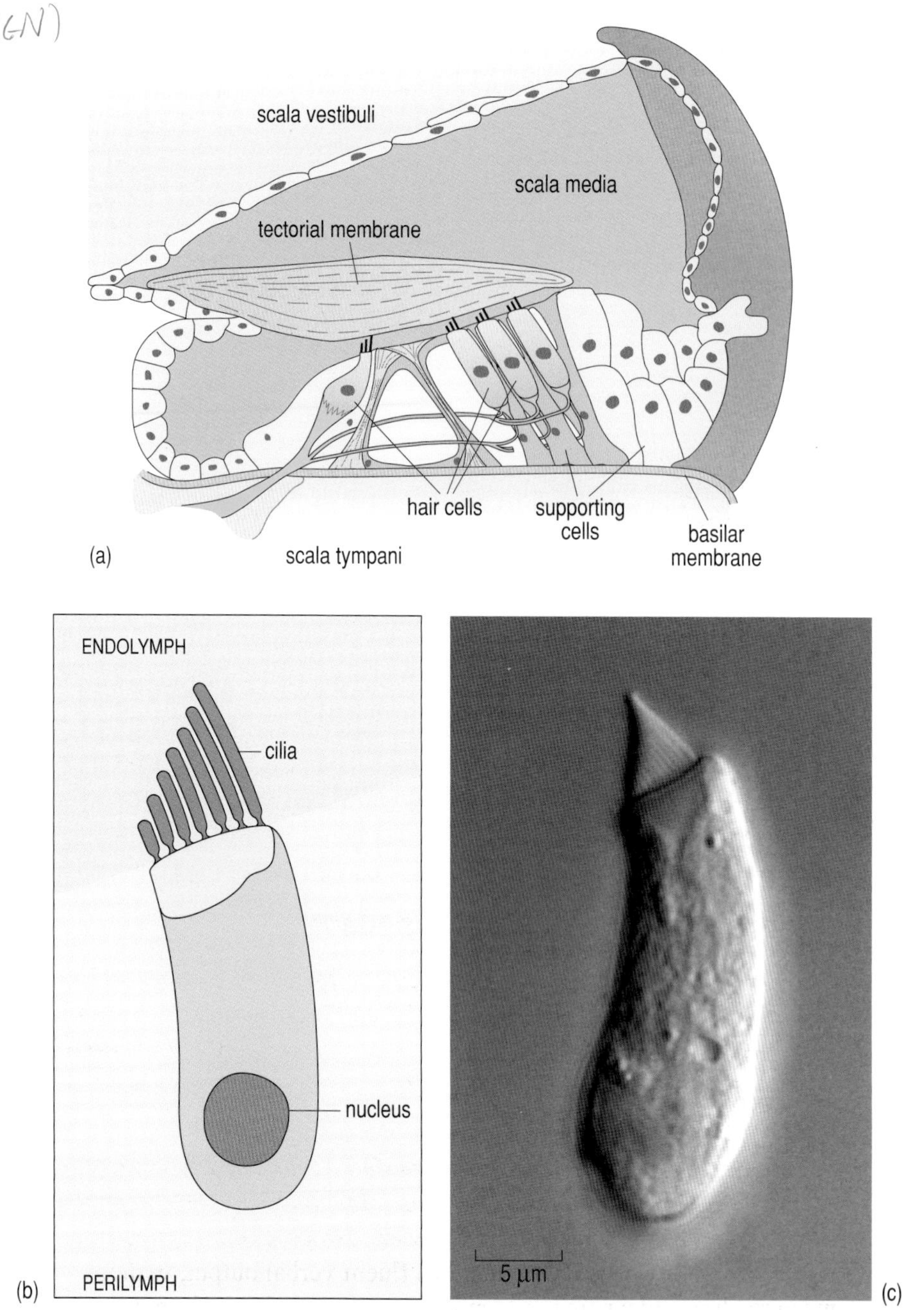

(a)

scala vestibuli

scala media

tectorial membrane

hair cells

supporting cells

basilar membrane

scala tympani

(b)

ENDOLYMPH

cilia

nucleus

PERILYMPH

(c)

5 μm

Figure 2.17 (a) Diagrammatic representation of the organ of Corti showing the basilar membrane, hair cells and overlying tectorial membrane which runs parallel to the basilar membrane. When the basilar membrane vibrates up and down in response to motion at the stapes, so does the tectorial membrane and the hair cells are stimulated. (b) Schematic structure of a hair cell. (c) High power photograph showing a typical hair cell.

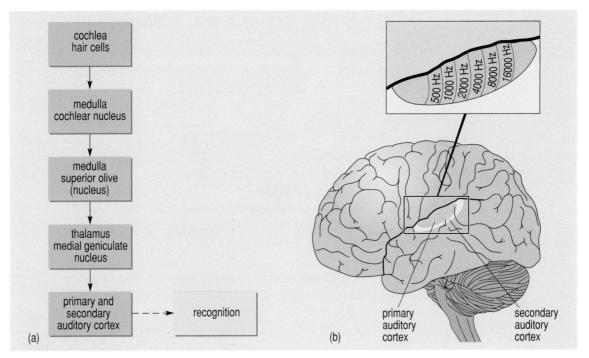

Figure 2.18 (a) The processing of auditory information is indicated in the flow diagram. (b) The primary and secondary auditory cortex in the temporal lobe of the human brain. The inset shows a schema of the tonotopic map in the primary auditory cortex.

THALAMUS :
• Relay centre for sensory info
• Gateway to CEREBRAL CORTEX

2.6.2 Auditory pathways and language

The cortical representation of hearing is very complex. We are only now beginning to understand the various pathways and brain areas (more than 15, of which just a few were mentioned in the previous section) that are involved in processing sound. Outputs are also sent to the **auditory motor cortex** which controls the body's response to sounds.

Disruption to any of these pathways can manifest in several subtle ways. For example, a disruption in the pathways between the **thalamus** and the **primary auditory cortex** in each hemisphere of the brain can give rise to **pure word deafness**, a condition where the patient has fluent verbal output, without problems in reading and writing or identifying non-verbal sounds, but shows severe difficulties in spoken language comprehension and repetition. **Auditory agnosia** is another form of 'central' deafness, where the individual is unable to interpret (recognize) non-verbal sounds (such as a telephone ringing), but is able to interpret speech. Where pure word deafness and auditory agnosia are combined (as a result of severe damage to the auditory cortex), the result is **cortical deafness.** Patients with cortical deafness are unable to interpret either verbal or non-verbal sounds, although they are aware of the occurrence of sound (for example, in producing a startle reaction to a loud noise).

PURE WORD DEAFNESS :
• Thalamus → prim auditory cortex
• Reading/writing/speaking ok
• language comprehension/repetition affected

AUDITORY AGNOSIA
• Interpreting speech ok
• recognising (non-verbal) sounds affected
• Form of CENTRAL DEAFNESS

CORTICAL DEAFNESS :
• Pure word deafness + auditory agnosia

Handwritten margin notes:

VESTIBULAR SYSTEM:
- Balance/posture
- Movements (of head)
- Inner ear.
- OTOLITH ORGANS:
  - (SACCULE + UTRICLE)
  - Linear acceleration
  - MACULAE (receptors)
    - Respond to gravity
    - Static equilibrium
    - position of head
- SEMICIRCULAR CANALS (x3)
  - In 3 planes
  - Angular acceleration
  - CRISTAE (receptors)
    - respond to rotation
- endolymph (scala media)

2.7 The vestibular system and equilibrium

The **vestibular system** is positioned close to the cochlea (Figure 2.15), and responds to movements of the head in relation to position in space, and to the pull of gravity. It is important for balance and posture (for example, as we sit or stand). There are two types of sensors in the vestibular system – the *otolith organs* (**saccule** and **utricle**), which sense changes in the rate of linear movements, and a set of three **semicircular canals** arranged at right angles to each other, which sense changes in the rate of rotational movement in three planes. The vestibular system, like the scala media of the cochlea, is filled with fluid endolymph. Receptors (*cristae*) in the semicircular canals are able to respond continually to angular and rotational movements of the body. They maintain *dynamic equilibrium*. Receptors (*maculae*) within the vestibule are static by comparison and respond to the pull of gravity, giving information regarding the position of the head at any given time – they maintain *static equilibrium*. These, together with other sensory input, are necessary for balance, and send information to the brain via the **vestibular nerve**. Disturbances in the vestibular system lead to symptoms such as vertigo, nausea (as in motion sickness), inability to stand upright and involuntary rolling of the eyes.

Try a little test for yourself – or get a willing friend to take part. Spin around in circles for about 5–10 seconds and then stop suddenly. OK, so you felt dizzy, but why?

Your visual input was telling you that you had stopped moving, but the fluids within your vestibular apparatus were still moving for a short time afterwards.

2.8 Causes of impaired hearing

Impaired hearing is common in old age, and can be partly compensated for, through the use of a hearing aid to amplify sounds. In the case of more severe hearing loss, however, the individual may be unable to distinguish any sounds at all (for instance this may be temporary as a result of an inner ear infection, or more permanent in the case of a ruptured ear drum). One of the most common causes of impaired hearing is an accumulation of earwax within the ear canal, blocking the ear drum. Under normal healthy conditions, wax produced by special glands in the outer part of the ear canal, serves to coat and clean the skin of the canal, collecting dust and germs. It usually accumulates, dries out and is discarded externally. The absence of ear wax can cause dry, itchy ears. However, in cases where wax builds up this can be removed by very gently syringing the ear canal with warm water (a procedure often carried out by the nurse at a local GP surgery). The doctor may alternatively prescribe a drug to soften the wax. You may be familiar with the admonition: 'Never insert a cotton applicator into your ear'. Well, not only is earwax actually there to protect your ears, it is often this very kind of probing that helps to push the wax deeper against the ear drum, which, because of its very thin and delicate structure, is itself prone to being damaged! There are other, more serious types of hearing impairment which we shall now discuss.

2.8.1 Types of hearing impairment and their treatment

Loss of hearing may be conductive, sensorineural or central. **Conductive loss of hearing** affects all frequencies of hearing and is caused by some kind of an impediment to the passage of sound vibrations. This might be the build-up of ear wax already mentioned, fusion of the ossicles, or by disease, such as an ear infection affecting the outer or middle ear. **Sensorineural loss of hearing** results from damage to the inner ear sensory or neural part of the system, for example, to the hair cells in the cochlea or to parts of the vestibulocochlear nerve. Damage may be to part of, rather than to the whole of the sensorineural system and hence may affect specific frequencies more than others, distorting sound. A mixture of these two conditions (i.e. affecting both the inner and the outer ear) can occur. **Central loss of hearing** results from damage to the auditory pathways linking the cochlea and the nervous system or damage to areas of the brain that are associated with processing of auditory information.

Repeated infections of the middle ear are a common cause of conductive hearing loss during childhood. These can cause the Eustachian tube to swell up (it can be filled with fluid instead of air after a severe upper respiratory tract infection), and increased air pressure can cause a hole (or perforation) in the eardrum. This usually heals naturally, but in severe cases, a permanent perforated eardrum may result. A very common cause of sensorineural loss is repeated exposure to very loud noises (for example, in factory environments, at rock concerts or when using a Walkman with the volume turned up high). Central hearing loss is much more rarely encountered by comparison with the other forms described but can result from brain lesions. There are also some genetic causes for hearing loss, and certain types of tumours – *acoustic tumours* – that can interfere with the auditory nerves and their signalling. A hearing aid placed behind the ear or within the ear itself can help to amplify vibrations of sounds, and emphasize voices, but background noise is also enhanced so many people find these of limited use. In more profound cases of hearing loss, an electronic device called a **cochlear implant** (Figure 2.19) placed within the cochlea can stimulate the auditory nerve directly by generating electrical signals in response to vibrations (in this way, it substitutes for the damaged cochlear hair cells).

Figure 2.19 (a) Examples of cochlear implant equipment, and (b) a diagram showing insertion of a cochlear implant electrode.

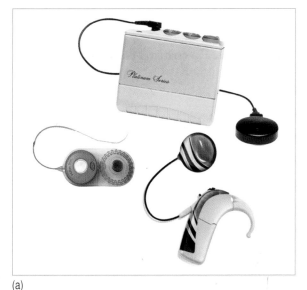
(a)

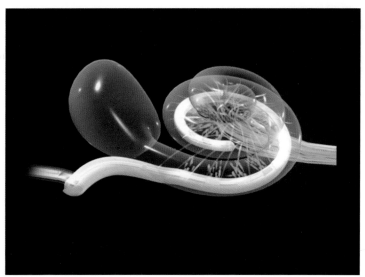
(b)

2.8.2 Infections of the middle ear and Ménière's disease

Middle ear infections (otitis media) will often resolve without any specific course of treatment. Antibiotics can be prescribed for middle ear infections, but are only effective in 15–20% of cases. If fluid persists for more than a couple of months and causes significant loss of hearing, this can be surgically drained. However, prolonged build up of pressure in the inner ear (usually as a result of disturbance between the drainage and production of endolymph and perilymph within the inner ear) can affect both the vestibular apparatus (semicircular canals) and the cochlea, which may subsequently lead to the sensations of dizziness, vertigo (spinning), disorientation, fluctuating loss of hearing and a ringing in the ears (called **tinnitus**) that are symptoms characteristic of Ménière's disease (see Case Report 2.2). Changes in blood supply to the inner ear may result in similar symptoms. Background noise inside a person's head (also referred to as tinnitus), however, can occur in many forms and is not necessarily associated with hearing impairment as such. It may be intermittent, or range in frequency and loudness. If the auditory nerve is irritated in any way, the brain can interpret the impulse it receives as background noise. The main treatment for Ménière's disease is prescription of a diuretic and a diet that is low in sodium. Other drugs are used to stop dizziness (e.g. meclizine and diazepam) or those that may improve blood circulation to the inner ear.

● What is the function of a diuretic?

● A diuretic helps the body to get rid of excess fluid.

Summary of Sections 2.6 to 2.8

1 Sound is transmitted through space as vibrations which cause a change in pressure.

2 There are three main parts to the human ear – the outer, middle and inner ear. Sound travels through the outer canal to the eardrum causing it to vibrate. These vibrations are passed on to the ossicles within the middle ear which in turn amplify and convey the vibrations to the cochlea within the inner ear.

3 The cochlea is a coiled, fluid-filled structure that contains hair cells which respond to the vibrations produced by sound. These are located on the basilar membrane of the organ of Corti. Sound pressure is conducted through fluid-filled channels in the cochlea and dissipated at the round window.

4 Hair cells translate vibrations into electrical neural signals which are passed along the auditory nerve via the brainstem, medulla and thalamus, to the primary and secondary auditory cortex.

5 The vestibular system is positioned close to the cochlea within the inner ear compartment. It responds to movements of the head in relation to position in space and the pull of gravity and is necessary for maintaining balance. There are two types of sensors – otoliths sense linear movements and semicircular canals sense rotational movement in three planes. Information is relayed from the vestibular system to the brain via the vestibular nerve. Disturbances in any of these components can lead to symptoms such as vertigo, nausea, inability to stand upright and involuntary rolling of the eyes.

Case Report 2.2   Ménière's disease

Nicola is a 30-year-old office clerk. For the past several months she had experienced intermittent dizzy spells, where the room spun round anticlockwise and at high speed, making her lose her balance and evoking nausea and vomiting. These symptoms occurred on average three to four times a week, lasting up to one hour on each occasion. She thought it was definitely stress-related and could hardly move at such times. She also experienced a high-pitched whirring and ringing (tinnitus) in her left ear each week. She had felt a pressure or 'heaviness' in this ear. The attacks had progressively worsened recently, and Nicola was now also experiencing some loss of hearing in her left ear, which was worse on some days than on others. Her doctor believed the symptoms were associated with a condition known as Ménière's disease. He explained that although the underlying causes for this condition had not been made clear as yet, it could be associated with fluid build-up in her inner ear, which distorts the delicate membranes of the cochlea and vestibular system, thereby affecting both hearing and balance. Repetitive damage to hair cells would cause them to die and, as they are not replaced, this could lead to more permanent hearing loss.

Her doctor noted from her medical records that she had a particularly intense bout of flu in the last year, accompanied by an inner ear infection, which had preceded the onset of her present symptoms. The viral infection could have been a trigger, although other causes (including an autoimmune component, or a tumour associated with the vestibular nerve supplying the inner ear) could not be ruled out altogether at this stage. Acute labyrinthitis (viral inflammation of the inner ear) is also known to commonly give rise to vertigo syndromes. He would refer her to an ear specialist who would carry out several tests including electronystagmography (to test balance), electrocochleography (which measures the excessive fluid accumulation in the inner ear), brainstem-evoked response audiometry (which measures the function of the cochlea and the acoustic nerve), magnetic resonance brain imaging (to rule out an acoustic or related tumour) and lab tests to detect any inner ear-related immune infections.

[MRI
polarizes
H]

The doctor further explained that in some patients the unilateral (one-sided) disease appears to 'burn-out' with deafness remaining but with the vertigo and tinnitus declining. Others could go on to develop a severe bilateral disorder where the vertigo remains and where surgical intervention becomes necessary. This intervention, however, would probably not be considered unless the attacks of vertigo were extremely severe and did not respond to treatment. In the first instance, treatment would be aimed at preventing the symptoms of vertigo: medication such as valium (diazepam) or other benzodiazepines have a direct effect on the nerves controlling balance and when administered at the onset of a vertigo attack, could help to prevent it from continuing. Another recent drug, betahistine, appears to promote better circulation of the blood supply to the inner ear, reducing the fluid retention. A diuretic drug taken daily (such as hydrochlothiazide) would help the body to reduce fluid retention further. A dietary restriction on salt intake would be essential to reduce fluid accumulating in the inner ear over time. The doctor knew that Nicola smoked. She would be advised to give this up, since smoking is known to constrict and reduce the blood flow through the tiny blood vessels that nourish the inner ear nerve endings. He strongly recommended a change in diet and lifestyle, as cutting down on salt, caffeine, giving up smoking and having a regular exercise programme would be very beneficial.

6   Disruption to auditory pathways and associated brain structures can give rise to pure word deafness (severe difficulties in spoken language comprehension and repetition), or to auditory agnosia (an inability to interpret non-verbal sounds whilst retaining ability to interpret speech). Where these are combined, the result is cortical deafness.

7   There are several causes of hearing impairment. Conductive hearing loss is common during childhood and usually reversible. Sensorineural and central hearing loss are more serious.

2.9 Conclusion

You should now be able to see more clearly how each of our senses functions as a whole and interacts with others and how ultimately our nervous system guides and interprets these sensory perceptions. There now remains one final phenomenon to beguile you with, and this would be the curious condition called synesthesia. In reality, this is a very rare neurological condition where the individual perceives an involuntary blending of two or more senses, resulting in quite unique perspectives. Patients with this condition have described perceiving 'certain colours or sounds as numbers or letters', 'hearing sounds as colours', and 'shapes that evoked distinct tastes' as examples. These observations further emphasize how unique our senses and their interpretation are to each of us, in forming our understanding of the external world. For further reading on this most interesting subject, refer to Ramachandran and Hubbard (2003) and Cytowic (1993).

Questions for Chapter 2

Question 2.1 (LO 2.1)

'Taste buds' are also referred to as 'papillae'. Is this statement true or false? Give a brief explanation for your answer. *False, papillae are enfoldings of epithelium, which contain taste buds.*

Question 2.2 (LO 2.2)

For the following statements say whether they are true or false and justify your answer. *False, mind (monism) involves conscious mind-generating activity (mental) cortex, phantom limb pain, whereas ... causes, ... in actual ...*

(a) Phantom limb pain is all in the mind.

(b) If you sustain an injury to the right half of the spinal cord in the region of the thoracic vertebrae you will subsequently feel neither a touch nor pain from the right leg. *False, pain (and heat) travel up contralateral side of spinal column (ie. x-over) to brain so would be felt. Remaining left half of spinal column etc. SPINOTHALAMIC TRACT! Touch does not x-over until brainstem (medulla) so will be impeded by spinal injury.*

Question 2.3 (LOs 2.3 and 2.4)

Describe how the eye focuses an image on the retina. What types of lens are required to correct nearsightedness and farsightedness? Give a brief explanation for your answer. *The cornea focuses light onto the lens; the lens, by altering its thickness and .. its refractive index, projects the (inverted) image onto the retina (accommodation). The iris diaphragm muscles control the amount of light entering eye. Nearsightedness- due to an excessively large eye/strong lens so ...*

Question 2.4 (LO 2.4) *using smooth ciliary muscle fibres.*

(a) How do we see colours? (b) What is meant by colour blindness? (c) Which is the most common form of colour blindness?

Question 2.5 (LOs 2.6 and 2.7)

(a) List four of the main causes of visual impairment. (b) Which of these is specifically associated with progressive damage to the optic nerve? (c) Briefly explain how this condition arises and suggest a form of treatment.

*Diabetic eye disease
Cataracts
Glaucoma
(b) Macular degeneration*

*⁕ intraocular pressure
↳ inadequate drainage of aqueous humour.
↳ other eye diseases eg. diabetic eye disease.
↳ surgery or beta-blocker eye drops.*

*a) 3 types of cones for L/M/S wavelengths.
↳ spectral sensitivity.
Brain interprets inputs using past experiences*

b) Deficiency in one (or more) photopigments, ie 1 cone type does not respond correctly to the expected wavelength.

*c) red-green anomalous trichromacy.
↳ shift in spectral sensitivity*

Question 2.6 (LOs 2.1, 2.5 and 2.6)

Briefly describe, in less than 250 words, the physiological process by which we can hear sounds. Begin your answer from the moment when sound waves reach the eardrum and end with detection of signals in the primary auditory cortex within the brain.

Question 2.7 (LO 2.7)

(a) List the three main types of hearing impairment, and give a brief definition for each. (b) How is otitis media (infection of the middle ear) usually treated?

(a) • conductive loss of hearing: impediment to passage of sound e.g. ear wax or ossicle desensitisation. – ALL FREQS
• Sensorineural loss of hearing: damage to receptors or neural tissue such as the vestibulocochlea nerve. May affect spec freqs
• Central loss of hearing: Damage to auditory pathways or parts of brain associated with auditory processing. May only affect processing of certain sounds (dependent upon brain region)

(b) Antibiotics may be tried but efficacy is low.
~~Ménière's disease treated by use of a diuretic and low sodium diet to reduce fluid build up. other changes in diet + lifestyle may also be recommended e.g. smoking.~~
Usually clear up on own, may be surgically drained

References and Further Reading

References

Division of Driver Licensing (2004) [online] Available from Kentucky Transportation Cabinet: http://transportation.ky.gov/drlic/eye_test.htm (Accessed September 2004).

Jacob, S., McKlintock, M. K., Zelano, B. and Ober, C. (2002) Paternally inherited HLA alleles are associated with women's choice of male odour. *Nature Genetics*, **30**, 175–179.

Vander, A., Sherman, J.and Luciano, D. (2001) *Human Physiology: the mechanisms of body function*. London: McGraw-Hill.

Further Reading

Cytowic, R. E. (1993) *The Man who Tasted Shapes*. New York: Putnam Press.

Doty, R. L. (2003) *Handbook of Olfaction and Gustation*. New York: Marcel Dekker Publishers, 2nd edition.

Moller, A. R. (2000) *Hearing: its physiology and pathophysiology*. San Diego: Academic Press.

Ramachandran, V. S. and Hubbard, E. M. (2003) Hearing colors, tasting shapes. *Scientific American*, April 15.

Roberts, D. (ed.) (2002). *Signals and Perception: the fundamentals of human sensation*. Open University and Palgrave Macmillan.

Sacks, O. (1997) *The Island of the Colourblind*. London: Picador.

Tympanic membrane is part of the ossicles - amplify sound mechanically. Transfer vibrations through oval window into vestibule the (beginning of the) inner ear. Sound waves travel through the perilymph within the cochlea, although (excess?) pressure is released through the round window at the opening of the cochlea. As the sound energy is transmitted along the cochlea it causes the basilar membrane of the organ of Corti to vibrate which mechanically stimulates hair cells contained within. These hair cells are mechanoreceptors which convert their displacement into electrical stimuli. There is a gradient along the cochlea where hair cells at the wider opening respond to higher pitched sounds and as the cochlea narrows (along its length) the hair cells respond to increasingly lower pitches. The hair cells respond to vibrations by releasing the neurotransmitter glutamate which stimulates dendrites in the auditory nerve. The information received by the ear is processed at the medulla, then the medial geniculate nucleus (thalamus) then to the primary auditory cortex, respectively. Different frequencies are mapped point for point here creating a tonotopic map

CHAPTER 3

THE ENDOCRINE SYSTEM

Learning Outcomes

After completing this chapter, you should be able to:

3.1 Understand and explain the principles of physiological regulation and control and maintenance of homeostasis.

3.2 Interpret and design flow diagrams to show the roles of negative and positive feedback loops in physiological regulation and control.

3.3 Outline the gross anatomical organization of the human endocrine system.

3.4 Outline the functional organization of the endocrine system, and its close integration with the nervous system: the hypothalamic-pituitary axis; endocrine glands and tissues not under the direct control of the hypothalamic-pituitary axis.

3.5 Explain how the interaction of hormones with specific receptor molecules in target cells is the molecular mechanism for hormone specificity.

3.6 Interpret data that relate to hormonal action, e.g. blood levels of hormones, effects of factors on the rate of hormone secretion.

3.7 Explain the roles of representative hormones and cytokines as signalling molecules involved in physiological regulation and control.

3.8 Outline the stages of the life of a hormone: synthesis; release; lifespan in the bloodstream; interaction with target cells.

3.9 Apply knowledge and understanding of the principles of endocrine regulation and control to interpreting clinical effects of endocrine malfunction; for example, hyposecretion and hypersecretion of cortisol and thyroid hormones.

3.1 An introduction to the endocrine system

The word 'hormone', once a specialized scientific term used by physiologists, is now well known. For example, you may have a friend or a relative who has diabetes, which results in the loss of regulation of blood glucose levels and an inability of cells in the body to take up glucose. People with type 1 diabetes, which is caused by a lack of insulin, have to inject themselves regularly with insulin in order to maintain stable blood glucose levels (see Book 1, Section 2.3.2). You may have observed the drastic consequences of thyroid malfunction in people diagnosed with **hyperthyroidism** or **hypothyroidism**, respectively excessive and insufficient production of **thyroid hormones**. People with hyperthyroidism have an elevated metabolic rate, increased heart rate, weight loss and intolerance to high environmental temperatures; bulging eyes (exophthalmos) may occur in some forms of hyperthyroidism. Symptoms of hypothyroidism include lethargy (a consequence of low BMR – basal metabolic rate), weight gain and intolerance to low temperatures. Patients with hypothyroidism are prescribed iodine or thyroid hormone tablets; in contrast, hyperthyroidism requires drugs that inhibit the production of thyroid hormones, or surgical removal of the thyroid gland. An enlarged **thyroid gland**, a goitre, may be normal in an individual but can cause breathing difficulties if it presses on the trachea (windpipe). Goitre may be due to a lack of iodine in the diet; iodine is an essential component of thyroid hormones (Sections 3.5.1 and 3.9.1) and if it is lacking in the diet, the thyroid gland compensates by increasing its activity and size. Iodine occurs naturally in sea salt and, in the past, a lack of iodine was a problem in inland areas of Europe, such as Austria and Switzerland, and also in parts of Britain distant from the sea. Goitre was known as 'Derbyshire neck' in Britain because of its prevalence in Derbyshire. The introduction of iodized table salt resulted in the virtual elimination of goitre, apart from cases caused by other factors such as Graves' disease (Section 3.5.1) and benign or malignant tumours.

Treatment of the effects of hormone deficiencies by administration of the missing hormone has proved successful, as demonstrated by the examples of type 1 diabetes and hypothyroidism. Nevertheless, there may be risks associated with hormone treatment. A well-known example is hormone replacement therapy (HRT) for treatment of unpleasant symptoms of the menopause such as hot flushes and sleep disturbance. Such symptoms are relieved by treatment with the ovarian steroid hormones, **oestrogen** and **progestin** (a synthetic form of progesterone), which compensate for the cessation of sex steroid hormone synthesis by the ovaries. However, there is concern about increased incidence of breast cancer associated with the use of HRT. The Cancer Research UK's 'Million Women Study' survey of 1 million women aged 50–64 indicated that women taking combined oestrogen–progestin HRT are almost twice as likely to develop breast cancer than women who do not take HRT (Newcombe, 2003). The five-year survey showed that of 1000 post-menopausal women who do not take HRT, there will be 32 cases of breast cancer from age 50 to 65. Of 1000 post-menopausal women who take combined HRT for 10 years, there will be 19 extra cases of breast cancer from ages 50 to 65. The risk declines as soon as HRT therapy ceases, falling within 5 years to that for women who are not taking HRT.

Hormones are not only administered for treating conditions relating to deficient hormone secretion. Asthma patients inhale doses of **corticosteroid** hormones (see Box 3.1) which reduce the inflammation and mucus production in the lungs' airways that cause asthma. The adrenal glands (Section 3.3.1) secrete corticosteroids, which are not the same as **anabolic steroids**; the latter are synthetic derivatives of sex steroid hormones such as testosterone. Anabolic steroids are taken by some body builders and athletes, who take advantage of their stimulatory effect on muscle growth; however, their use is illegal for individuals competing in events. Anabolic steroids became notorious following the revelation that they were given to young athletes in Communist East Germany during the 1970s and 1980s. The steroids that were given to young female swimmers, some only 14 years old, were particularly effective in enhancing their swimming performance. The swimming team was known as the 'wonder girls' because of their consistent high performance levels that won them many medals.

The steroid pills given to the girls, who were told that they were vitamins, contained oral-turinabol, a derivative of testosterone. Oral-turinabol increased muscle growth in the girls, speeded up recovery time after injury, and accelerated the rate of formation of red blood cells. Yet side-effects observed in the girls included irreversible masculinization, involving reduction in body fat and breast size, pattern baldness and excessive body hair; long-term effects include a high incidence of liver cancer and miscarriage. Nevertheless, when used appropriately, anabolic steroids have proved useful too, for example, in treating muscle wasting in patients with AIDS (acquired immunodeficiency syndrome).

So we can see that hormones are powerful substances, with far-reaching effects, both when administered inappropriately and as treatment for serious or life-threatening conditions. The power of hormones derives from their role as specific signalling molecules that control the function of cells, tissues and organs in the body.

The term 'hormone' (derived from the Greek for 'I excite'), was proposed originally by Ernest Starling in 1905. Starling and his colleague, William Bayliss, working at University College London, discovered the first substance to be recognized as a hormone, **secretin**, which is released into the bloodstream by cells lining the duodenum, in response to the entry of acidified food from the stomach. Secretin is carried in the bloodstream to the pancreas where it stimulates pancreatic cells to secrete water and bicarbonate ions. The release and action of secretin is an example of classic hormone function, whereby in response to a physiological signal, a hormone is released from an **endocrine gland** into the bloodstream, within which it is transported to its target tissue (Figure 3.1).

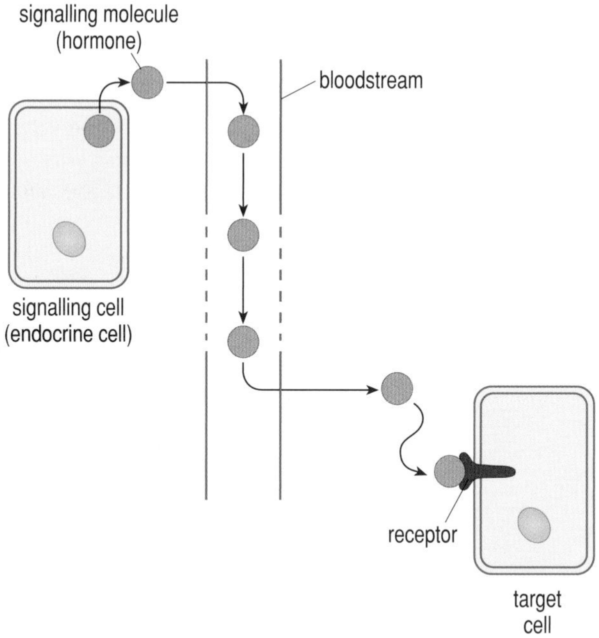

Figure 3.1 Endocrine cells are specialized cells that secrete signalling molecules known as hormones into the bloodstream, where they are carried to all parts of the body. Hormone molecules act on specific target cells at some distance from their site of release. Hormone molecules attach to specific receptor protein molecules in the target cell membrane, or inside the target cell and this attachment initiates the response of the cell to the hormone signal (Section 3.3.2).

Although hormones have access via the bloodstream to cells in all tissues and organs of the body, only specific target cells can respond to a particular hormone. The hormone signal initiates the response in the target tissue via interaction between the hormone molecule and a specific receptor protein molecule (Section 3.3.2) in the target cell.

● What are the target cells for secretin, and what is their response to the hormone?

● Pancreatic cells are the target cells for secretin and they respond by secreting water and bicarbonate ions.

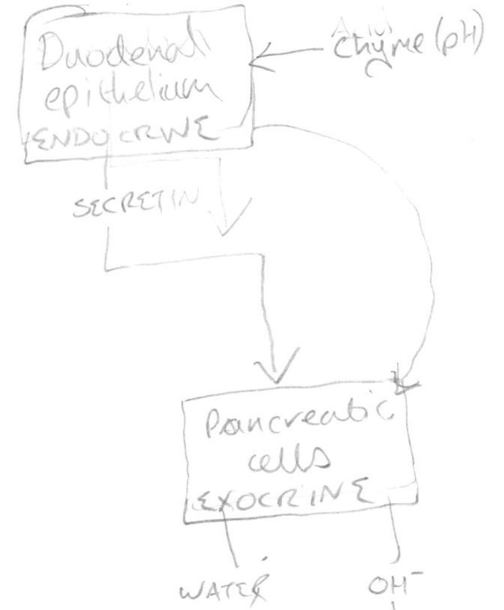

The secretions from the pancreatic cells are collected in the pancreatic duct, which transports the fluids directly into the duodenum contents. Glands such as the pancreas that secrete their products into a duct, are known as **exocrine glands**. The salivary glands, which secrete saliva via a duct into the mouth, are another example.

GLUCOCORTICOIDS:
↳ Metabolism

MINERALOCORTICOIDS
↳ Homeostasis

CORTISOL
• Glucocorticoid
• Anti-inflammatory
• Hydrocortisone

ALDOSTERONE:
• Mineralocorticoid
• Kidney → K⁺   } From urine.
  ↖ Na⁺ + H₂O

Box 3.1   The steroids

The steroids are a group of lipids that all have the particular ring structure that is shown in Figure 3.27. These chemicals include the naturally occurring sex hormones, bile acids, toad poisons and corticosteroids. All steroid molecules that are found in humans are derived from cholesterol which is itself a steroid. Chemists are able to synthesize many of these chemicals as well as steroids that are not found naturally, such as the anabolic steroids descibed in Section 3.1.

The corticosteroids are synthesized by the adrenal *cortex*. (Recall from Section 1.1 that *cortex* means bark or outer layer so the adrenal cortex is the outer layer of the adrenal gland just as the cerebral cortex is the outer layer of the brain.) The corticosteroids all have 21 carbon atoms and are divided into two groups based on their functions. The glucocorticoids influence carbohydrate, lipid and protein metabolism whilst the mineralocorticoids regulate ion and water balance. To complicate matters some of these chemicals do both but the classification is based on their most important role in the body. The major naturally occurring glucocorticoid in humans is **cortisol**. This has the additional role of acting as an anti-inflammatory agent and you might have come across it being used this way medicinally. When cortisol is used pharmacologically it is called hydrocortisone. Corticosterone is another glucocorticoid found naturally and it behaves very like cortisol except that it is not anti-inflammatory. An example of a mineralocorticoid is **aldosterone**. It stimulates the kidney to excrete potassium ions whilst absorbing sodium ions and water from the urine as will be described in Book 3, Chapter 1.

Other steroids that are hormones and will be mentioned in this chapter are the sex hormones testosterone, oestrogen and progesterone. However, a fuller discussion of their roles must wait until Book 4.

In the following sections we begin by examining the anatomical and functional organization of the endocrine system and where appropriate, demonstrate the integration between the nervous and endocrine systems. Our study of the life of a hormone includes the chemical nature of hormones, their secretion by cells and their duration in the bloodstream.

Summary of Section 3.1

1   Endocrine tissues and glands secrete hormones into the bloodstream, within which they are transported to target cells.

2   Hormones are powerful signalling molecules that regulate and control the function of tissues and organ systems.

3   Each individual hormone affects a specific type of target cell, or two or more specific target cells.

4   Hypersecretion and hyposecretion of hormones have serious effects on physiology, as demonstrated by the signs and symptoms of hyperthyroidism and hypothyroidism.

5   Hormones are used to treat hormone deficiency disorders and also as therapy for conditions such as muscle wasting in people with AIDS, and asthma.

6   Abuse of hormones can have devastating effects; female athletes who took doses of anabolic steroids show signs of masculinization and long-term effects include increased incidence of miscarriage and liver tumours.

3.2 The role of the endocrine system

The endocrine system plays a key role in regulating a stable internal environment inside the body even when it is exposed to an extreme external environment, or to changes in intake of nutrients, water and mineral salts. The maintenance of a stable internal environment is known as **homeostasis** (see Book 1, Section 2.4), and includes the maintenance of certain physiological variables, such as body-water volume and mineral salt concentrations in body fluids, at constant levels. At this point, it is useful to remind yourself about the distinction between physiological variables that are regulated and those that are controlled.

●   What is the difference between regulated physiological variables and controlled physiological variables?

○   A **regulated** physiological variable is one that is maintained at near constant levels, sometimes described as a 'set point', and includes blood glucose level, body temperature, and usually, levels of thyroid hormones in the blood. **Controlled** physiological variables need to vary considerably, according to circumstances, to help maintain the regulated variables at the optimum value (e.g. shivering is a controlled variable that assists the regulation of body temperature). (See Book 1, Section 2.4.)

Human body temperature is regulated at 37 °C; blood glucose levels are regulated at around 4–6 millimoles per litre (where 1 millimole of glucose = 180 mg glucose). Prolonged variations in levels of regulated variables have undesirable or lethal physiological consequences. Detectors, e.g. special neurons in the hypothalamus, function by signalling information about the levels of regulated variables. The responses of controlled physiological variables to signals from detectors maintain constancy of regulated variables. For example, the rates of uptake of glucose from the blood by liver, muscle and adipose tissues, are controlled variables, and vary in response to levels of blood glucose. As with blood glucose levels, blood thyroid hormone levels are held relatively constant. So this is a regulated variable, controlled by varying the rate of secretion of thyroid hormone in response to the detected blood levels. However, thyroid hormone secretion can also vary in response to ambient temperature, e.g. thyroid hormone levels rise in a person exposed to freezing temperatures.

● Why might it be helpful to have raised levels of thyroid hormone in freezing conditions?

○ An increase in this hormone would stimulate an increase in BMR and hence increase heat generated by the body.

● Classify the following as either regulated or controlled variables. (a) Rate of drinking, (b) body-water volume, and (c) rate of formation of urine in the kidney.

○ (a) The rate of drinking is a controlled variable (subject to being over-ridden by social factors, e.g. consuming alcoholic drinks at a party). (b) Body-water volume is a regulated variable as it is essential that this should be maintained at a near constant level. (c) The rate of urine formation is a controlled variable.

The processes that contribute to the regulation of body fluid are under coordinated neural and hormonal control. Motivation for drinking is under the control of the nervous system. The rate of urine formation is controlled by hormones; the major hormone involved is **antidiuretic hormone**, **ADH**.

● What does the term diuretic mean? (Check Book 1, Section 3.8 if uncertain.)

○ A diuretic is a substance that increases the rate of elimination of water from the body (in urine).

● What effect will ADH have?

○ ADH will help to conserve body fluids by reducing the amount of water eliminated in the urine.

ADH is a peptide that is secreted by the **hypothalamus** and released by the **posterior pituitary gland**. (The term **secretion** encompasses both synthesis and release of a hormone.) ADH has its effect by promoting the uptake of water from urine in the kidney, thereby conserving body water (Book 3, Chapter 1). If body-water volume increases above the optimum value, release of ADH is suppressed and the rate of urine production increases until excess water has been excreted.

3.2.1 Feedback in physiological regulation and control

The role of ADH illustrates the point that **negative feedback** (introduced in Book 1, Section 2.4) plays a dominant role in physiological regulation and control. The process of negative feedback has two components. When levels of a physiological variable are too high or too low, and require hormone action, detection of the abnormal levels initiates secretion of that hormone. The effects or products of the action of the hormone suppress the further release of that hormone, forming a negative feedback loop. To illustrate the feedback pathways

Handwritten margin notes:

ANTIDIURETIC HORMONE (ADH):
• Rate of urine formation (kidneys)
  ↳ controlled variable
• Hormone
  ↳ Peptide.

Regulation of body fluid

NEURAL   HORMONAL
↓   ↓
Thirst   Urine formation
↓   ↓
Drinking   ADH

SECRETION = synthesis + release

ie. feedback mech

−ve FEEDBACK
• Receptors stimulated
  ↓
  → secretion of hormone
     ↓
     transport to receptors (2ndary)
        ↓
        Effects/products
           ↓
        inhibits [2ry receptors?]
• e.g. SECRETIN
  ↳ Duodenum → pancreas
     ↳ H₂O + OH⁻

90

involved in hormonal regulation and control, a simple way of visualizing all of the components of the system is required. Flow diagrams are popular with physiologists as they can be designed quite quickly and are suitable for both simple and complex endocrine control systems, and it is possible to include neural components too. Figure 3.2 is a simplified flow diagram that illustrates the negative feedback control of the pH (i.e. acidity) of the contents of the duodenum by secretin.

There are six stages highlighted in Figure 3.2. In stage (1), acidic chyme from the stomach enters the duodenum (the small intestine). The high acidity (i.e low pH) of the duodenum contents is detected by specialized endocrine epithelial cells lining the duodenum (2), which respond by releasing secretin into the capillary network that supplies the intestinal wall (3). Secretin is transported in the bloodstream to the pancreas where it stimulates exocrine pancreatic cells to secrete water and bicarbonate ions (4), which are collected into the pancreatic duct. The bicarbonate ions (which are alkaline) are transported via the pancreatic duct (5) into the duodenum, where mixing with the acidic chyme results in neutralization. The resulting neutral pH of the chyme inhibits the release of secretin (6). Figure 3.2 demonstrates that there is one feedback loop in the control system, in which the effect of the action of secretin, i.e. the neutralization of duodenum contents, feeds back to the duodenal epithelial cells and suppresses release of secretin.

It is not surprising that negative feedback is the predominant type of feedback for the maintenance of homeostasis. Negative feedback loops ensure that a deviation from normal, e.g. excessive body-water volume, is eliminated and the normal level is restored. The situation whereby the response to an increase in a physiological variable results in a further increase in that variable is known as **positive feedback**, which has a role in reinforcing physiological processes.

Positive feedback mechanisms are relatively rare in physiology, but one example is the action of the hormone **oxytocin** in controlling uterine muscle contractions during labour. (Note that both the nervous system and the endocrine systems are involved in this process.) Oxytocin is produced in the hypothalamus, a region of the brain (Figure 1.6), and is transported to the posterior pituitary gland (Section 3.4), from where it is released into the bloodstream. Figure 3.3 shows the positive feedback pathway. During labour, oxytocin (1) stimulates contraction of the uterine muscles and therefore enhances labour contractions. As the baby is pushed towards the birth canal (vagina), the cervix dilates and stretch receptors there respond by sending signals (i.e. action potentials, see Chapter 1) via (2), along the spinal cord to the hypothalamus (3), stimulating further release of oxytocin (4). Higher levels of oxytocin in the blood are transported to the uterine muscles, which contract with increasing intensity and frequency. The process continues until the baby is born and the placenta ejected, and then uterine contractions cease as the stretch receptors in the cervix are no longer stimulated.

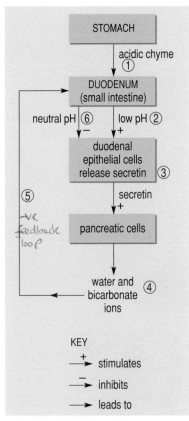

Figure 3.2 A flow diagram showing the negative feedback control of pH of duodenal chyme via secretion of secretin from duodenal epithelial cells. The numbered steps are explained in the text.

Figure 3.3 Positive feedback control of uterine contractions in labour by oxytocin. The + sign indicates a stimulatory effect.

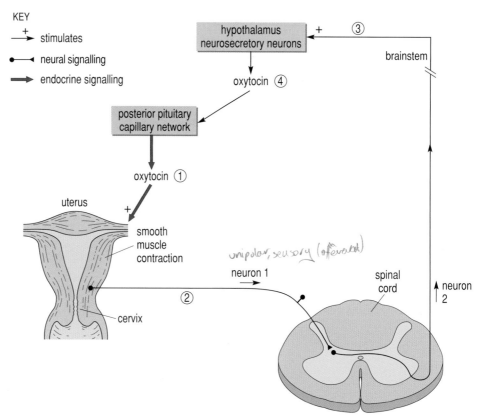

- Why is positive feedback an inappropriate mechanism for controlling secretion of secretin?

- Secretin is released from the intestinal epithelial cells in response to the high acidity (low pH) of chyme in the duodenum. If the effect of secretin, i.e. decreased acidity, promoted release of yet more secretin, and therefore more bicarbonate, then the intestinal contents would become highly alkaline, which would inactivate the enzymes in the small intestine that break down proteins (Book 1, Chapter 4).

As we shall see in Section 3.3, feedback pathways can involve two or more hormones as well as the nervous system. The coordinated action of the nervous system and endocrine system maintain the constancy of regulated variables. The endocrine system also initiates and controls the processes of digestion, reproduction, development, growth, maturation and senescence. We begin our study of the endocrine system in the following section by examining the anatomical organization of the human endocrine system.

Summary of Section 3.2

1 The endocrine system plays a key role in maintaining homeostasis, a stable internal environment, inside the body.

2 Certain physiological variables such as body-water volume, and the concentration of glucose in the blood, are regulated at near constant levels.

3 Appropriate fluctuations of controlled variables such as the rate of uptake of glucose from the blood by liver cells, maintain near constancy of regulated physiological variables.

4   Negative feedback systems, those in which displacements from the norm are corrected, are important in physiological regulation and control.

5   Positive feedback, although rare in physiology, has a role in reinforcing physiological processes.

6   Flow diagrams are used by physiologists for depicting negative and positive feedback systems involved in physiological regulation and control.

3.3 The organization of the endocrine system

It is important to appreciate from the outset that the role of the endocrine system in the control and regulation of the physiological functions of the body is closely integrated with the nervous system. In this section we begin by examining the gross anatomical organization of the endocrine system, a naming of the parts. This provides a reference point for our study of the functional organization of the endocrine system and where relevant, the role of the nervous system in initiating and controlling the secretion of hormones.

3.3.1 Anatomy and functions of the endocrine system

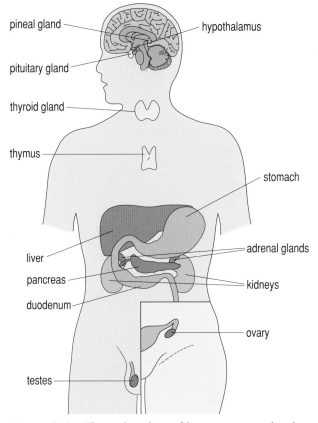

Figure 3.4   The major sites of hormone secretion in humans.

Figure 3.4 shows the major sites of hormone secretion in the human body. Bear in mind that the endocrine glands illustrated each contain a variety of endocrine cell types that secrete a variety of hormones.

A typical example of an endocrine gland is the human **adrenal gland** (Figure 3.5). There are two adrenal glands, each located at the front of the top of a kidney, encased in connective tissue. Each adrenal gland has two distinct hormone-producing regions: an outer cortex packed with cells that secrete corticosteroids, and an inner medulla that secretes adrenalin and noradrenalin.

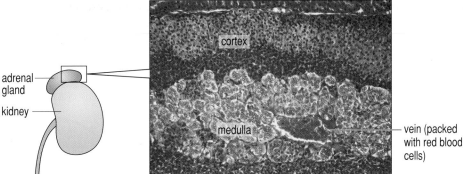

Figure 3.5   Location and microscopic structure of the adrenal gland. The enlargement is a photo of a histological section viewed in a microscope, under low power magnification sufficient to see the layers of tissue.

● Adrenalin and noradrenalin are here being described as hormones. Where else have you come across these two chemicals in this course and how were they described there?

○ In Chapter 1 these two chemicals were described as neurotransmitters of the catecholamine family.

● Catecholamine is a description of their chemical nature, how is it that a chemical can be described in two different ways (i.e. as a neurotransmitter and as a hormone)?

○ The terms 'hormone' and 'neurotransmitter' are descriptors of role not of chemical structure. These chemicals behave differently in different parts of the body (i.e. depending on where they are synthesized and released).

— blood supply or synapse

● The corticosteroids were described in Box 3.1. Name the mineralocorticoid that is secreted by the adrenal cortex.

○ Aldosterone.

● Which is the major glucocorticoid secreted in humans?

○ Cortisol.

Cells in the outer region of the adrenal cortex secrete aldosterone, which stimulates the kidney to excrete potassium ions but absorb sodium ions and water from the urine. Cells in the central area of the cortex produce corticosteroid hormones such as cortisol, which stimulates the production of glucose from glycerol and amino acids (**gluconeogenesis**) in hepatocytes (liver cells) by increasing the levels of enzymes that catalyse the conversion of amino acids into glucose. At the same time cortisol action makes more amino acids available by facilitating the breakdown of proteins (except for liver protein) to amino acids. It also maintains concentrations of those enzymes in adipose tissue that break down fat stores so that fatty acids and glycerol are released during fasting.

● Of what use are fatty acids and glycerol to a body that has had no nutrient intake for some time (i.e. during a fast)?

○ These molecules can be metabolized to provide energy in the form of ATP. (See Book 1, Figure 3.3.)

glycerol → glucose → ATP
fatty acids → Acetyl CoA? → ATP?

Cortisol also facilitates responses to stressful situations by increasing levels of blood glucose via its effects on liver enzymes that break down glycogen stores and release glucose into the blood. Increased lipid breakdown during stress is also enhanced by increased cortisol levels in blood.

● Levels of cortisol can rise as much as twentyfold after stressful incidents, ranging from physical trauma such as accidents to emotional stress. Suggest the advantage of these elevated levels of cortisol.

○ By promoting increased blood glucose levels and breakdown of lipids, cortisol is increasing the availability of energy for cells, facilitating their response to short-term stress, especially in the fight or flight response to danger, but also to repair and renewal of tissue.

[margin notes:]
ALDOSTERONE:
↳ kidney
↳ secrete K+ } from urine
↳ absorb Na+ + H2O }
↳ MINERALOCORTICOID

CORTISOL:
↳ influences metabolism
↳ stims production of glucose.
↳ glycerol } hepatocytes
↳ amino acids } (liver)
↳ enzymatic
↳ GLUCONEOGENESIS
↳ creates more amino acids
↳ breakdown of proteins
↳ (not liver proteins)
↳ adipose tissue
↳ breakdown fat stores
↳ enzymatic
↳ fatty acids + glycerol.
↳ fasting?

The innermost region of the adrenal cortex produces sex steroids. The small amounts of sex steroids secreted by the adrenal cortex are insignificant in comparison to the huge amounts secreted by the **gonads** (ovary and testes). Ovarian output of sex steroids plummets in women who are undergoing the menopause, upsetting the overall balance of sex steroid production. In this case **androgen** (male sex hormones; mostly testosterone) secretion from the adrenal cortex may have masculinizing effects such as hair growth on the face.

Other endocrine glands that contain a variety of endocrine cells include the pituitary, the hypothalamus and the thyroid gland. There are at least eight different types of endocrine cells in the anterior pituitary, each producing a specific hormone. You may be surprised to learn that the hypothalamus, a part of the brain (Figure 3.4), produces at least eight hormones.

The hypothalamus initiates many hormonal and behavioural responses in the body, a function mediated by neural connections with other parts of the nervous system, including the brain. The hypothalamus responds to hormonal signals too. Hypothalamic hormones are known as **neurohormones**, because they are secreted by distinct clusters of nerve cells, known as nuclei. Certain hypothalamic neurotransmitters are known simply as 'peptides' or 'neuropeptides'. The most abundant neuropeptide in the brain, neuropeptide Y, stimulates appetite.

The thyroid gland secretes thyroid hormones, and also **calcitonin**, a hormone that reduces resorption of calcium from bone mineral and from urine in the kidney, thereby reducing blood calcium levels.

- Why does reduced resorption of calcium from bone and urine in kidney reduce blood calcium levels?

- If resorption of calcium from bone is reduced, then calcium remains within bone and does not reach the blood. Reduced resorption of calcium from urine in the kidney means that calcium leaves the body and does not remain in the blood.

Endocrine cells in the islets of Langerhans, in the pancreas secrete the hormones involved in the regulation of blood glucose levels, insulin and glucagon. (This is described in Section 3.7.1.) You will notice in Figure 3.4 that a number of hormone-producing sites are not what would traditionally be regarded as 'endocrine glands' and include the liver, kidney, stomach and duodenum. Liver cells, hepatocytes, respond to growth hormone in the blood by secreting insulin-like growth factors (IGFs), which mediate the growth-promoting effects on the skeleton. Specialized hormone-secreting cells in the inner cortex of the kidney produce **erythropoietin** (Book 3, Chapter 1), which stimulates cell division in **haematopoietic stem cells** in the bone marrow. Haematopoietic stem cells are the source of all blood cells; they divide to form daughter cells, which mature into blood cells and enter the circulation. Different types of haematopoietic stem cells produce particular types of blood cells (Book 3, Chapter 4).

Endocrine glands, and groups of endocrine cells within organs such as the pancreas, are supplied with dense capillary networks.

95

[Handwritten margin notes: ENDOCRINE TISSUE → dense cappillary network → facilitates secretion → fenestrated structure → not continuous lining → rapid transfer of hormones]

● Explain the functional significance of the dense capillary network in an endocrine gland.

● Endocrine glands secrete hormones into the bloodstream and this is facilitated by a dense capillary network that ensures that as many endocrine cells as possible are adjacent to or close to capillaries.

The walls of capillaries in networks that supply endocrine tissue typically have a fenestrated structure. The fenestrations are gaps in the endothelial lining of capillaries where the cytosol of the cells does not provide a continuous lining. Fenestrations permit the rapid transport of hormone molecules, from endocrine cells into the blood. Without these fenestrations, molecules as large as hormones would not be able to cross endothelial cell membranes.

3.3.2 Interaction of hormones with their target cells

As hormones are released into the bloodstream, hormone molecules gain access to every cell in the body, suggesting a lack of functional organization! However, individual hormones can only affect specific target cells, because each target cell has specific receptor protein molecules either in the cell membrane or inside the cell, in the cytosol, nucleus or organelles. It is the structure of the receptor protein molecule that confers the specificity of hormone and target cell interaction.

● Give examples of target cells for (a) oxytocin; (b) growth hormone; (c) cortisol; (d) erythropoietin.

● The target cells are: (a) uterine muscle cells; (b) liver cells; (c) liver cells and fat cells; (d) haematopoietic stem cells.

Although liver cells are targets for both growth hormone and cortisol, each hormone exerts a different effect. One effect of cortisol on hepatocytes is activation of enzymes that break down glycogen; in contrast, growth hormone stimulates release of other signalling molecules, of which IGF-1 is the most important. So hormone specificity allows different hormones to have different effects on the same target cell. The salient point is that only those cells that have the appropriate receptor protein molecules for a particular hormone can respond to that hormone.

Receptor proteins are proteins in cell membranes or inside the cell that provide binding sites for specific signalling molecules, including hormones, or metabolic intermediates, known collectively as **ligands.** A cell can have many thousands of receptor molecules for a ligand and the number can be varied.

● Suggest how the number of receptor protein molecules of a cell can be varied. (*Hint*: recall Book 1, Section 2.3.2.)

● Control of differential gene expression can vary the number of receptor protein molecules expressed by a cell.

An analogy is helpful for understanding how receptor proteins work. A card key for an office provides a useful analogy with a hormonal ligand. The pattern of holes that has been punched in the card is unique for the door of a particular room. The lock of each room, the 'receptor', contains a pattern of studs, which provide a 'binding site' that can only fit the pattern of holes in a particular card. If an incorrect card is inserted into the slit of a lock there is no response and the door remains locked. If the correct card is inserted, the mechanism of the lock responds by initiating a sequence of actions that enable the door to be opened. Receptor protein molecules function in a similar way. An incorrect signalling molecule does not fit the receptor protein and induces no response. The correct signalling molecule fits perfectly into the binding site and triggers a change in shape in the receptor protein. The change in shape then initiates a sequence of events in the target cells that leads to an appropriate response. Binding of a ligand, e.g. a hormone, to its specific receptor (Figure 3.1), triggers a cascade of biochemical responses inside the cell that initiate the appropriate cellular response to the signal. If receptors are absent, or have an abnormal chemical structure they cannot bind to their ligands, just as the wrong lock for a specific card key cannot respond to that card key.

[handwritten margin notes: BIOCHEMICAL RESPONSES — change in shape ↓ ↓ CELLULAR RESPONSE — e.g. differential gene expression]

The crucial role of receptors is illustrated by diseases caused by **autoimmune responses** to protein receptors in which antibodies to receptor proteins are produced. An antibody is a protein produced by the body's defence (immune) system that binds selectively to another protein detected as a 'danger' signal by the immune system (Book 3, Chapter 4). Autoimmune responses involve production of antibodies to the body's own essential proteins. Antibodies to a protein hormone receptor will bind to the receptor and prevent the hormone from doing so, disrupting endocrine control function.

Summary of Section 3.3

1   Hormones are secreted by cells in endocrine glands, such as the thyroid and pituitary, and also from endocrine cells and tissues in organs not regarded as typical endocrine 'glands' such as liver and kidney.

2   Endocrine tissues contain cells that secrete hormones; cells in the adrenal medulla secrete adrenalin and noradrenalin; adrenal cortex cells secrete corticosteroids.

3   Endocrine glands and tissues contain dense capillary networks; fenestrated capillary walls allow hormones to leave the bloodstream and gain access to their target cells.

4   Although hormones are released into the bloodstream, each hormone can affect just one or a specific range of target cells. Receptor protein molecules for specific hormones in target cell membranes, or inside target cells, provide hormone specificity, a crucial aspect of the functional organization of the endocrine system.

5   Individual hormones can only affect those target cells that have the appropriate receptor protein molecules.

[Handwritten margin notes:]
HYPOTHALAMIC-PITUITY AXIS
- 3-tier system
- control of physiological processes
  - POSTERIOR LOBE
  - ANTERIOR LOBE

NEUROSECRETORY NEURONS
- HYPOTHALAMIC NUCLEI → capillaries
- Depolarisation - slower
- Action potentials - last longer
- Axonal endings - more
  - large amounts of NEUROHORMONES
  - terminate into capillaries
    - (not post synaptic membrane)

3.4 The hypothalamic-pituitary axis

So far in our overview of the endocrine system we have mentioned a bewildering variety of endocrine glands and tissues. We now move on to examine the functional organization of the endocrine system so that we can link apparently disparate components and functions, and identify an organizational framework that you can refer to throughout the course.

The term **hypothalamic-pituitary axis** describes the pivotal role of the close interaction between hypothalamus and pituitary gland in the regulation and control of homeostasis and processes such as growth, reproduction, development and senescence. We examined the nervous system in detail in Chapter 1.

● Complete Table 3.1a, a summary of the comparisons of signalling in the nervous system and the endocrine system that can be identified from the information provided in Chapter 1, and Sections 3.1 and 3.2.

Table 3.1a Comparisons of signalling in the nervous and endocrine systems. (To be completed.)

Process	Hormonal signalling	Neural signalling
Release of signalling molecules	Hormones released into bloodstream and reach every organ and tissue	*Neurotransmitters released into synaptic cleft and reach receptors in post synaptic membrane.*
Medium used for long-distance signalling	Hormone molecules	*Action potentials/axons*
Speed of communication	*slower - dependent upon rate of blood flow (+ distance)*	Rapid; speed of saltatory conduction in myelinated axons is up to $100\,\mathrm{m\,s^{-1}}$

● The completed Table 3.1a is provided as Table 3.1b overleaf.

The hypothalamus contains specialized neurosecretory neurons with cell bodies that are clustered into nuclei (Figure 3.6).

Changes in potential of neurosecretory neurons are slower than those in conventional neurons, and the resultant action potentials last longer. Neurosecretory neurons also have more axonal endings (Figure 3.7), which enable them to secrete relatively large amounts of neurohormones. Axons that originate in nerve cell bodies within hypothalamic nuclei end in capillaries, and release their products into the bloodstream.

We can now examine how neurohormones secreted by hypothalamic neurons reach the pituitary gland. The pituitary gland is quite small, only 0.5–0.8 g in mass, and is located in the floor of the skull just above the roof of the mouth, and below the hypothalamus (Figure 3.4). A stalk connects the pituitary gland to the hypothalamus (Figure 3.6).

The pituitary gland consists of an anterior and posterior lobe. Two neurohormones, ADH and oxytocin, are synthesized by hypothalamic nuclei, and released by the posterior pituitary (Figure 3.6).

[Handwritten margin notes:]
POSTERIOR LOBE:
- oxytocin
  - (+ve feedback - labour)
  - regulatory
- ADH (ANTI DIURETIC HORMONE)
  - rate of urine formation
  - controlling physiological variable
- Action potentials
  - from HYPOTHALAMIC NUCLEI

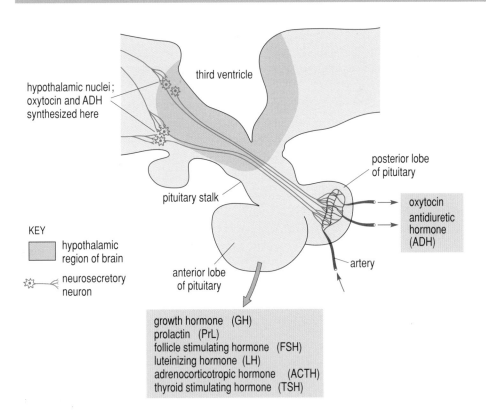

third ventricle

hypothalamic nuclei;
oxytocin and ADH
synthesized here

posterior lobe
of pituitary

pituitary stalk

oxytocin
antidiuretic
hormone
(ADH)

KEY

hypothalamic
region of brain

neurosecretory
neuron

anterior lobe
of pituitary

artery

growth hormone   (GH)
prolactin (PrL)
follicle stimulating hormone   (FSH)
luteinizing hormone (LH)
adrenocorticotropic hormone   (ACTH)
thyroid stimulating hormone (TSH)

Figure 3.6   The location of nuclei involved in the secretion of neurohormones via neurosecretory axons into the capillary network supplying the posterior pituitary is shown. For simplicity, the capillary network supplying the anterior pituitary is omitted. The toned boxes list the hormones released by each of the anterior and posterior pituitary.

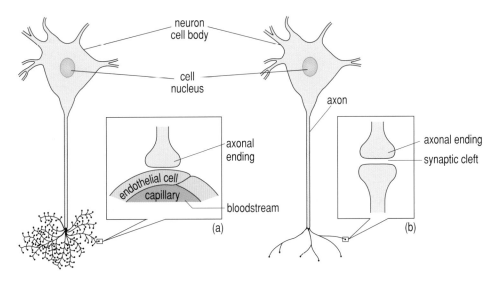

neuron
cell body

cell
nucleus

axon

axonal
ending

endothelial cell

capillary

bloodstream

(a)

axonal ending

synaptic cleft

(b)

Figure 3.7   Comparison of the structure of (a) a neurosecretory neuron and (b) a conventional neuron.

● Examine the blood supply (drawn in red) of the posterior pituitary gland in Figure 3.6, and explain how ADH and oxytocin reach their target cells.

● Neurosecretory axonal endings of axons originating in hypothalamic nuclei, secrete ADH and oxytocin into the capillary network in the posterior pituitary. The capillary network draining the posterior lobe transports the hormones in the bloodstream, thus they reach the target cells in kidney and uterine smooth muscle, respectively.

Table 3.1b Comparisons of signalling in the nervous and endocrine systems. (The completed Table 3.1a.)

Process	Hormonal signalling	Neural signalling
Release of signalling molecules	Hormones released into bloodstream and reach every organ and tissue	Neurotransmitter molecules released into synaptic cleft
Medium used for long-distance signalling	Hormone molecules	Electrical impulses (action potentials), are transmitted along axonal processes
Speed of communication	Depends on rate of blood flow, and distance between endocrine tissue and target cells	Rapid; speed of saltatory conduction in myelinated axons is about $100\,\mathrm{m\,s^{-1}}$

3.4.1 Control of secretion of posterior pituitary hormones

Although ADH and oxytocin are described as 'posterior pituitary hormones', both originate in hypothalamic neurons, so secretion comprises synthesis in hypothalamic nuclei and release from neurosecretory axonal endings in the posterior pituitary. In Section 3.2, we saw how ADH secretion plays a crucial role in the regulation of body-water volume, by controlling the rate of water loss in urine production. This is crucial for maintaining homeostasis. In contrast, oxytocin is involved in controlling a process, the milk ejection reflex, by which milk stored in the breast is made available to a suckling infant (Figure 3.8).

ADH = regulatory ⎫ *physiological*
oxytocin = controlling ⎭ *variable.*

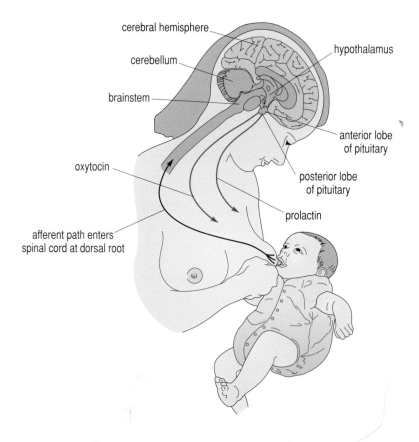

Figure 3.8 The role of oxytocin in milk ejection during breastfeeding. Suckling also stimulates secretion of prolactin which promotes milk synthesis in the breast.

- Summarize the stages in the stimulation of milk ejection in response to suckling by the infant. Figures 3.6 and 3.8 include all the information you need.

- The tactile stimulation of suckling generates action potentials in sensory neurons around the nipple that carry signals via the spinal cord and the brainstem to nuclei in the hypothalamus. Secretion of oxytocin from the posterior lobe of the pituitary and secretion of prolactin from the anterior lobe of the pituitary are stimulated and the hormones are released into the bloodstream. Prolactin stimulates the synthesis of breast milk and oxytocin stimulates milk ejection.

[handwritten note: oxytocin: • labour • lactation → milk ejection ↳ suckling]

Oxytocin stimulates the contraction of specialized muscular cells surrounding milk-secreting glands in the breasts. The milk is squeezed into ducts, which fill up and dilate, causing increased pressure, known as the milk ejection reflex, or 'let-down'. Milk ejection is controlled by coordinated action of the nervous and endocrine systems. In the following section we examine interactions between hypothalamic and anterior pituitary hormones, which also involve neuro-endocrine coordination.

Summary of Section 3.4

1 The hypothalamus contains specialized neurosecretory neurons that secrete neurohormones into the blood supply of the anterior and posterior lobes of the pituitary gland.

2 ADH and oxytocin, neurohormones, are secreted by hypothalamic nuclei, and axonal ending of the axons release these hormones into the capillary network of the posterior pituitary, which functions as a hormone-releasing site.

3 Release of oxytocin during suckling is stimulated via neural pathways beginning with the response of sensory neurons in the nipple to suckling, and transmission of the signal for oxytocin release via the spinal cord and brainstem to the hypothalamus.

3.5 The function of the hypothalamic-anterior pituitary axis

Interaction of hypothalamic hormones with the hormone-secreting cells of the anterior pituitary is complex. The arterial blood supply of the anterior pituitary enters at the base of the pituitary stalk where it branches into a capillary network (Figure 3.9). This capillary network drains the pituitary stalk, and converges to form two **portal veins** that supply the anterior pituitary. Portal veins are defined as blood vessels that connect two capillary networks. (More usually blood from a capillary network is returned to the heart to be pumped to the lungs for reoxygenation.)

[handwritten note: PORTAL VEINS ↳ connects 2 capillary networks]

Figure 3.9   Blood is brought to the pituitary by an artery (1), which in the pituitary stalk (2), branches into a capillary network that receives the hormone secretions from neurosecretory neurons. A portal vein collects the blood from the capillary networks in the pituitary stalk and carries the blood to the anterior lobe of the pituitary, where it branches to form a dense capillary network (3). Blood draining the anterior pituitary is collected into veins that carry the blood away. The posterior lobe of the pituitary has a separate blood supply brought in by a small artery (4).

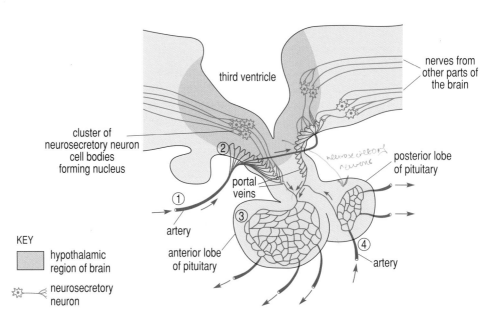

Examine Figure 3.9 and trace the portal veins in the pituitary stalk that carry blood into the capillary network that supplies the anterior lobe. The capillary network is so extensive that no cell in the anterior pituitary is more than a few cells away from a capillary. You can see from Figures 3.6 and 3.9, that the blood supplies for the anterior and posterior pituitary lobes comprise two almost separate capillary networks. The functional significance of the capillary network at the base of the pituitary stalk can be appreciated by examining the anatomical links between the locations of the endings of the neurosecretory neurons, and the blood supply of the pituitary gland.

One of the hypothalamic nuclei secretes six neurohormones, which control the secretion of hormones from the anterior pituitary.

● Examine Figure 3.9 and suggest how neurohormones secreted by the hypothalamus gain access to endocrine cells in the anterior lobe of the pituitary, and control their hormonal secretion.

○ The capillaries that supply the anterior pituitary contain blood that has flowed through the base of the pituitary stalk, where neurons originating in a hypothalamic nucleus secrete neurohormones into the capillary network. The blood flowing out of the pituitary stalk transports neurohormones into the capillary network supplying the anterior pituitary, where endocrine cells are located. Therefore neurohormones in the blood supplying the anterior pituitary can control the secretory activity of hormone-producing cells in the anterior pituitary.

Figure 3.10 summarizes the hormones secreted by the hypothalamus, the pituitary, and those endocrine glands controlled by hormones secreted by the pituitary. This is a complex diagram that you should find useful for reference and you should not attempt to learn it!

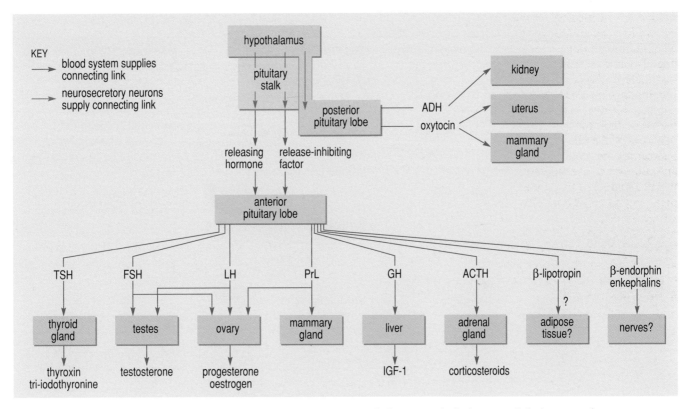

Figure 3.10 A summary of the hormones secreted by the hypothalamus and pituitary, and their target tissues.

It is useful at this point to consider the salient features in Figure 3.10. A hypothalamic nucleus secretes neurohormones into the capillary network supplying the anterior pituitary. The full names and abbreviations for the main neurohormones are provided in Table 3.2. Five of the neurohormones, GnRH, CRH, TRH, GRH and SIF are peptides and polypeptides; four of these are 'releasing hormones' that stimulate release of a hormone from the anterior pituitary lobe; in contrast, somatostatin (SIF), is a release-inhibiting factor. (In some texts releasing hormones are called releasing factors.) The sixth neurohormone, PIF, which blocks prolactin release (and is therefore a release-inhibiting factor), has been isolated and discovered to be a small molecule called dopamine (a catecholamine derived from the amino acid tyrosine – see Figure 3.25 for the structural formula).

- Dopamine is the neurohormone PIF. What other role does dopamine have?

- Dopamine is a neurotransmitter. (See Section 1.9.2.)

- In each case the chemical released is identical. On what is the classification as neurohormone or neurotransmitter based?

- In each case dopamine is synthesized and released from neurons, the difference is in how the target cells are reached – via the bloodstream or across a synapse.

103

Table 3.2 Summary of the main releasing hormones and release-inhibiting factors produced by the hypothalamus.

Neurohormone: hypothalamic releasing hormone or release-inhibiting factor	Chemical nature of neurohormone	Function of neurohormone in controlling secretion of anterior pituitary hormone	Anterior pituitary hormones and their main effects
GnRH (gonadotropin-releasing hormone)	Peptide	Stimulates release of gonadotropins, LH (luteinizing hormone) and FSH (follicle-stimulating hormone)	LH and FSH stimulate secretion of sex steroid hormones by ovary and testis
CRH (adrenocorticotropic hormone-releasing hormone)	Polypeptide	Stimulates release of ACTH (adrenocorticotropic hormone), β-lipotropin and β-endorphin	ACTH stimulates secretion of cortisol by adrenal gland
			Effect of β-lipotropin not known; endorphins have role in pain relief
TRH (thyroid-stimulating hormone-releasing hormone)	Peptide	Stimulates release of TSH (thyroid-stimulating hormone) and PrL (prolactin)*	TSH stimulates secretion of thyroxin by thyroid gland
			PrL stimulates growth of breast and milk production
PIF (prolactin release-inhibiting factor)	Catecholamine (dopamine)	Inhibits release of PrL	
GRH (growth hormone-releasing hormone)	Polypeptide	Stimulates release of GH (growth hormone)	GH stimulates secretion of IGF-1 by liver and kidney
SIF (somatostatin) also known as GIF (growth hormone release-inhibiting factor) DOPAMINE	Polypeptide	Inhibits secretion of GH and TSH	

*TRH can therefore be regarded as a prolactin-releasing hormone (PRH).

The target cells for the hypothalamic neurohormones are specialized endocrine cells in the anterior pituitary; each cell type secretes a specific hormone, or hormones in response to stimulation by a hypothalamic neurohormone (Table 3.2).

● Examine Table 3.2 and identify the response of anterior pituitary target cells to GnRH.

○ GnRH stimulates its anterior pituitary target cells to secrete LH and FSH.

● Examine Table 3.2 and identify the hypothalamic neurohormones that control the release of GH (growth hormone).

○ GRH stimulates release of GH from anterior pituitary cells. SIF inhibits the release of GH.

● How does the hypothalamic control of the release of FSH differ from the control of GH release?

○ Control of release of FSH involves a releasing hormone, GnRH. In contrast control of secretion of GH involves both a hypothalamic releasing hormone, GRH, and a release-inhibiting factor, SIF.

You should find it helpful to refer back to Figures 3.6 and 3.10 and Table 3.2 when reading about specific aspects of hormonal regulation and control in later chapters. The hypothalamic-anterior pituitary axis provides a **three-tier system** of control of physiological processes. Individual hypothalamic neurohormones control release of specific hormones from the anterior pituitary. In turn, specialized endocrine cells in the anterior pituitary secrete hormones that control secretion of hormones from endocrine glands and tissues elsewhere in the body. In the following two sections, our detailed examination of the control of secretion of thyroid hormones and cortisol, respectively, demonstrates the three tiers of hormonal control.

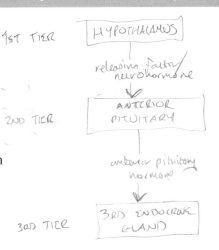

1st TIER
HYPOTHALAMUS
releasing factor/ neurohormone
2ND TIER
ANTERIOR PITUITARY
anterior pituitary hormone
3rd TIER
3RD ENDOCRINE GLAND

3.5.1 Regulation and control of secretion of thyroid hormones

The butterfly-shaped thyroid gland is located in the neck (Figure 3.4), where each 'wing' is wrapped around the front of the trachea (windpipe). Epithelial cells in the thyroid secrete two hormones, thyroxin and tri-iodothyronine. Both hormones are derived from the amino acid tyrosine and their synthesis is explained in Section 3.9.1.

● Which other molecule is derived from tyrosine? *MONOAMINE (NEUROTRANSMITTER)*

○ Dopamine is also derived from tyrosine.

A thyroxin molecule contains four atoms of iodine (and hence is often called T_4); a molecule of **tri-iodothyronine** (T_3), contains three atoms of iodine. The concentrations of thyroid hormones in the blood are regulated at near constant levels. Recall from Section 3.1 that thyroid hormones control the rate of metabolism, and that hyposecretion and hypersecretion of thyroid hormones have serious effects on health. *Thyroid malfunction*

● Referring to Table 3.2 and Figure 3.10, outline the three-tier hormonal control of secretion of thyroid hormone.

○ Regulation of thyroid hormone levels in the blood begins with the hypothalamus, which releases thyroid-stimulating-hormone-releasing hormone, TRH, into the capillary network of the anterior pituitary. TRH stimulates anterior pituitary cells to release thyroid-stimulating hormone, TSH, into the bloodstream. TSH stimulates the **thyroid gland** to release thyroid hormones.

Regulation of levels of thyroid hormones in the blood is a classic example of the three-tier control system that includes the hypothalamus, the anterior pituitary and a third endocrine gland. A flow diagram is a useful way of depicting the hormonal control of thyroid hormone secretion, as we can see from Figure 3.11. Excessive levels of thyroid hormones in the blood are decreased by their negative feedback effects on release of TSH by the anterior pituitary and also on release of TRH by the hypothalamus. Inhibition of release of TRH from the hypothalamus, in turn decreases release of TSH. TSH release is increased when thyroid hormone levels are low, and stimulates the thyroid to release T_3 and T_4. TSH also stimulates development and growth of the hormone-producing thyroid epithelial cells when thyroid hormone levels are persistently low.

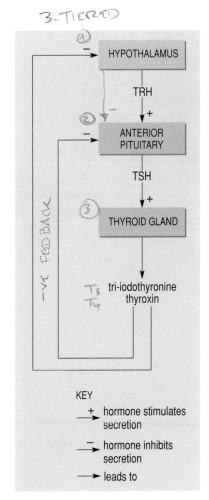

3-TIERED

Figure 3.11 A flow diagram showing the feedback control of the release of thyroid hormones from the thyroid gland.

THYROID GLAND?
↳T3I-IODO.THYRONINE (T3)
↳THYROXINE (T4)
↳ stimulated by TSH*
↳ anterior pituitary lobe
↳ stimulated by TRH*
↳ hypothalamic nuclei
↳ when thyroid hormone
levels ≤ low.
*TSH = Thyroid stim hormone
TRH = Thyroid stim releasing factor

Thyroid epithelial cells need a continual supply of iodine for synthesis of thyroid hormones.

● Suggest the response of the three-tier control system to a prolonged shortage of iodine in the diet.

● Prolonged low iodine levels in the diet would mean a reduction in the secretion of thyroid hormones. Low levels of thyroid hormones in the blood stimulate release of TSH by the anterior pituitary and TRH by the hypothalamus. Prolonged high levels of TSH result in further growth and hence enlargement of the thyroid.

Enlargement of the thyroid is visible as a swelling on the front of the neck, a goitre (Figure 3.12). The enlarged thyroid gland is more likely to capture the low levels of iodine in the blood and may be able to secrete sufficient thyroid hormone for promoting a normal metabolic rate.

GOITRE:
↳ enlarged thyroid
↳ lack of iodine in diet
↳ reduction in thyroid
hormones
↳ stims release of TRH
↳ TSH
↳ thyroid
growth

Figure 3.12 A patient with a goitre formed by enlargement of the thyroid gland in response to inadequate iodine in the diet.

Stimulation of release of thyroid hormones from the thyroid gland by TSH involves the interaction of TSH with target cell receptors. **Graves' disease** is an autoimmune disease in which antibodies against the TSH receptor in thyroid epithelial cell membranes, bind to it permanently and mimic the effects of TSH binding.

GRAVES DISEASE:
↳ autoimmune disease
↳ antibodies bind to
TSH receptors
↳ (in thyroid)
↳ mimic TSH binding
↳ continuous/
unrelenting
↳ excessive thyroid
hormone production
↳ hyperactivity
↳ BMR

● What do we call a chemical when it behaves in this way?

● It is called an agonist. (See Section 1.9.2.)

● Suggest the response of thyroid epithelial cells to binding of the TSH receptor antibody to the TSH receptor. How does this affect the hypothalamic-pituitary axis control of this response?

● Binding of the antibody to the TSH receptor mimics the effect of TSH, so the thyroid epithelial cells secrete T_4 and T_3 excessively and continuously. Hence, the hypothalamic-pituitary axis of control of thyroid function is blocked.

The incidence of Graves' disease (Case Report 3.1) is quite high, affecting up to 5% of women and a much smaller proportion of men.

Case Report 3.1 Graves' disease

Margie, aged 38, moved house to be near her mother, but there were problems, as the two women argued so much. Margie's brother complained that Margie was short-tempered and impatient. Margie was disappointed that her efforts were unappreciated, especially as her responsibilities were wearing her out. She was feeling unwell and anxious and suffering panic attacks. Her appetite was excellent but she was losing weight and she had trouble sleeping. After an argument with a colleague at work she was persuaded by her friends to visit the doctor.

On clinical examination the GP saw that Margie was an anxious, active, talkative person. Her skin was moist and her hair was lank and greasy. Her pulse was rapid and when she held out her hands, the fine tremor characteristic for an overactive thyroid gland (Graves' disease) could be seen. Margie's eyes protruded slightly (see for example, Figure 3.13) and her thyroid gland was enlarged (goitre) but not dramatically so. Her blood pressure and temperature were normal.

Margie attended the medical outpatient department for further investigations. Blood tests revealed raised levels of thyroxin and very low levels of thyroid-stimulating hormone. An electrocardiogram was also performed as untreated Graves' disease can result in cardiac arrhythmias which can be dangerous. Fortunately Margie had no cardiac involvement. Initially she was prescribed carbimazole 15 mg to take three times a day for four weeks, followed by a reduced daily maintenance dose. The practice nurse explained that after Margie had been taking the tablets for a few weeks she should be feeling better and gaining weight. Carbimazole prevents the conversion of iodine to a form that can be incorporated into the hormone but cannot remove thyroxin that is already circulating in the bloodstream, hence it will be a while before the benefit of taking the drug is seen. For 18 months Margie felt well but then developed a recurrence of her symptoms and was admitted to hospital to undergo partial thyroidectomy. The surgeon removed most of her thyroid gland, leaving enough tissue to maintain normal thyroid function and the parathyroid glands, which are important in calcium metabolism (Chapter 4). Margie's recovery was good.

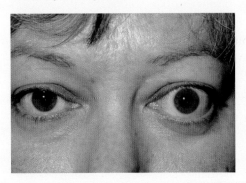

Figure 3.13   A woman's bulging eye due to Graves' disease. The eyeball on the right is bulging, in contrast to the normal eye, giving a staring appearance. Swelling of soft tissue in the eye socket pushes the eye forwards, restricting movement and causing double vision.

AETIOLOGY:
↳ study of causative factors.

The study of the factors that cause Graves' disease (i.e. its **aetiology**) demonstrates the importance of understanding the role of receptors for hormones.

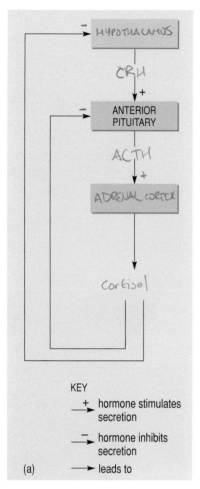

KEY

+   hormone stimulates secretion

  hormone inhibits secretion

(a)   ⟶ leads to

Figure 3.14a A flow diagram showing the feedback control of the secretion of cortisol from the adrenal cortex. (To be completed.)

3.5.2 Regulation and control of cortisol secretion

The family of **steroid hormones** are all derived from cholesterol, and they are not very soluble in water, but are highly soluble in oily solvents. Therefore steroids are very different from the peptide and polypeptide hormones discussed so far. Unlike peptide and polypeptide hormones, steroid hormones can penetrate cell membranes, and interact with receptors located inside target cells (Figure 3.1). Cortisol is the major steroid hormone secreted by the **adrenal cortex**. Normal (basal) levels of cortisol in the blood are regulated by the hypothalamic-pituitary-adrenal gland axis.

● Fill in the boxes provided in the flow diagram in Figure 3.14a with the relevant endocrine glands, showing the relevant hormone secreted by each one, and complete the feedback loops involved in the control of blood cortisol levels in a normal individual. (To complete Figure 3.14a you will need to draw on information in Figure 3.10 and Table 3.2.)

○ The completed Figure 3.14a (given as Figure 3.14b), is shown overleaf. Control of blood cortisol is achieved by negative feedback of cortisol on endocrine cells in the anterior pituitary and hypothalamus.

In humans, levels of corticosteroid, including cortisol, show a distinct pattern over 24 hours (Figure 3.15), i.e. a **diurnal** rhythm.

● Describe the pattern of blood corticosteroid levels in human blood over a 24-hour period (Figure 3.15). Quote representative values for corticosteroid levels from the graph, using the appropriate units of measurement, micrograms of hormone per millilitre, abbreviated as $\mu g\ ml^{-1}$.

○ Blood corticosteroid levels increase from 06.00 to 08.00, reaching $0.35\ \mu g\ ml^{-1}$ at about 08.00. Corticosteroid levels reach a nadir just after midnight, dipping to around $0.05\ \mu g\ ml^{-1}$. There are sharp peaks and deep troughs.

● What do the sharp peaks and deep troughs suggest about the way that the hormone is released?

○ The sharp peaks and deep troughs suggest that secretion is not smoothly continuous but pulsed.

The pulsatile and diurnal patterns of corticosteroid secretion are derived from neural rhythms in the central nervous system that influence secretion of CRH by hypothalamic neurons (Table 3.2).

The housekeeping task of cortisol is to facilitate many essential metabolic processes, including the breakdown of protein, glucose synthesis from proteins, breakdown of lipids, and resorption of calcium in bone. Cortisol also inhibits the kidneys' response to ADH, when there is an excess water load in the body, thereby facilitating excretion of excess water. The role of hormones such as cortisol, which facilitate aspects of metabolism, is described as **permissive**, a term that implies allowing important processes to occur rather than initiating these processes. Cortisol is known as the 'stress hormone', as release of this hormone is increased sharply during stress. Increased levels of cortisol in the blood during

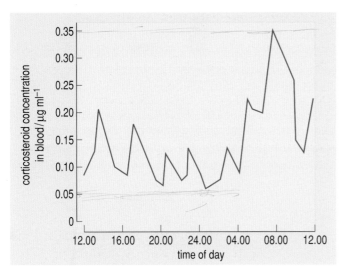

Figure 3.15 Changes in human blood corticosteroid levels over a 24-hour period. Levels are generally lower at night, and higher during the day, especially the morning. Humans are most active during the day.

[Handwritten notes in right margin:]

PERMISIVE:
↳ allow rather than initiate
↳ ie. facilitates

cortisol related diseases/disorders:
↳ ADDISON'S DISEASE
↳ cortisol deficiency.
↳ damaged adrenal glands
↳ tumour
↳ tuberculosis
↳ excessive production
↳ CRH
↳ ACTH
↳ MELANOCYTES
↳ (e.g. Jane Austen)

↳ CUSHING'S SYNDROME:
↳ cortisol excess
↳ cortisol tissue tumour
↳ e.g. adrenal gland
↳ also pituitary tumour
↳ (ACTH)
↳ also prolonged use of corticosteroids medicinally
↳ asthma/arthritis
↳ hydrocortizone?
↳ HBP, muscle wasting, glucose in urine etc

stress promote high rates of lipid and protein breakdown and increased synthesis of glucose from amino acids. Uptake of glucose by muscle and adipose tissue cells is decreased. Overall, levels of amino acids, glucose and free fatty acids in blood are increased.

Deficiency of cortisol, Addison's disease, is therefore life-threatening. This is a rare disease that affects about 1 in 100 000 people. Signs and symptoms include loss of appetite, weight loss, hypoglycaemia, and lack of tolerance to stress.

● Explain the effect of a persistent deficiency in blood cortisol levels on hormone secretion in the hypothalamus and anterior pituitary.

◐ A deficiency in blood cortisol levels stimulates secretion of CRH (adrenocorticotropic hormone-releasing hormone) from the hypothalamus and ACTH (adrenocorticotropic hormone), from the anterior pituitary. Levels of CRH and ACTH in the blood rise sharply.

Abnormally high levels of ACTH in human blood stimulate proliferation of **melanocytes**, pigmented cells in the basal layer of the epidermis of the skin. This causes patchy brown and black pigmentation of the skin. Damage or destruction of the adrenal glands, resulting in lack of cortisol in the blood, may be caused by tuberculosis or an adrenal gland tumour. Jane Austen's journal and letters written during the last year of her life suggest that the cause of her death at the age of just 42, was Addison's disease. In March 1817 she wrote: 'I certainly have not been very well for many weeks, and about a week ago I was very poorly, I have had a good deal of fever at times and indifferent nights, but am considerably better now and recovering my looks a little, which have been bad enough, black and white and every wrong colour. I must not depend upon ever being blooming again.'

Austen's writing suggests that she was affected by one of the signs of Addison's disease, patches of skin pigmentation.

Cushing's syndrome, which is caused by prolonged excessive secretion of cortisol, is also a serious condition, as would be expected for a hormone that facilitates breakdown of protein and lipid. Excess secretion of cortisol may be

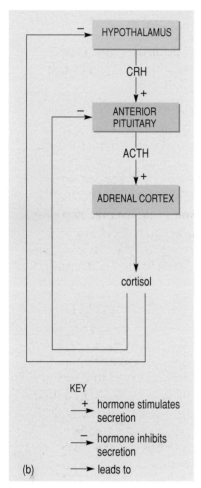

KEY

+ → hormone stimulates secretion

⁻↗ hormone inhibits secretion

→ leads to

(b)

Figure 3.14b A flow diagram showing the feedback control of the secretion of cortisol from the adrenal cortex. (A completed version of Figure 3.14a.)

caused by a pituitary tumour affecting cells that secrete ACTH, an adrenal gland tumour or a tumour elsewhere that secretes cortisol. Cushing's syndrome can also result from prolonged use of **corticosteroids** for treatment of arthritis or asthma. Incidence of all types of Cushing's syndrome is about 2 in 10 000. Patients with Cushing's syndrome show a suite of alarming signs and symptoms as illustrated by Case Report 3.2. *— eg hydrocortisone*

Our final group of endocrine glands and tissues are those that are not under the direct control of the hypothalamic-pituitary axis. Nevertheless most of these tissues have links with either or both of the autonomic nervous system and the hypothalamus.

Summary of Section 3.5

1   The blood supplies of the anterior and posterior pituitary gland are virtually separate.

2   Six neurohormones are known to be secreted from neurosecretory cells originating in hypothalamic nuclei.

3   Five of the hypothalamic neurohormones are peptides or polypeptides; four of these, GnRH, CRH, TRH and GRH, stimulate secretion of a hormone from the anterior pituitary; one, SIF, inhibits secretion. One of the neurohormones, PIF/dopamine, is a catecholamine, and inhibits release of prolactin from the anterior pituitary. Each hypothalamic neurohormone has specific target cells in the anterior pituitary.

4   Specialized endocrine cells in the anterior pituitary secrete hormones that control secretion of hormones from endocrine glands and tissues elsewhere in the body. TSH, for example, stimulates release of thyroid hormones from the thyroid gland.

5   Blood levels of thyroid hormones are regulated. Regulation breaks down in Graves' disease where the thyroid epithelial cells are switched on permanently resulting in excess secretion of hormones.

6   The three-tier system of control of hormone secretion operates by negative feedback loops.

7   The three-tier system of control of thyroid hormone levels can compensate for low dietary iodine by stimulating growth of the thyroid forming a goitre.

8   Both hyposecretion and hypersecretion of cortisol result in serious illness, Addison's disease and Cushing's syndrome respectively.

Case Report 3.2 Cushing's syndrome

Sarah is 41 years old and has always enjoyed good health, despite being a little overweight. Sarah is unmarried and lives alone, but her mother and married sister live locally and Sarah has a busy social life. She commutes every day into the nearest large town where she works in the Human Resources Department of the university. Looking in the mirror, Sarah is critical about what she sees. Her complexion is beginning to look poor and she dreads doing her hair because so much seems to be coming out in her comb. Sarah has always worried about her size, but in the past year she has noticed a distressing tendency towards weight gain, especially around her middle. Her arms and legs are still thin and Sarah persuades herself that she is worrying about nothing. An old friend visiting Sarah's sister remarks that Sarah does not look herself at all. She comments that Sarah seems to have put on a lot of weight and looks flushed, with a very red complexion when previously she had clear, pale skin which was never blemished as it is now. This information was tactfully conveyed to Sarah – her sister had also thought that recently she had not been looking well, although she could not quite have explained how. Sarah did not receive the information well, but she decided to join the health club at the university, hoping that exercise would help her lose a few pounds since dieting alone had failed.

At Sarah's first visit to the health club the fitness instructor undertook an assessment to check that she was fit to perform strenuous exercise. Sarah's blood pressure was found to be elevated (140/100). The instructor showed Sarah some simple stretching exercises and weighed her, confirming that her body mass index was 28 (Book 1, Chapter 3). Once Sarah appeared relaxed and was talking happily about the aims of her intended exercise programme, her blood pressure was recorded a second time, but was still high. The instructor recommended an appointment with the GP before the programme was planned and Sarah, now rather anxious, complied.

On examination Sarah presented as a tall, well-built woman with a plump 'moon' face and adipose trunk showing pronounced striae (stretch marks). In contrast her limbs appeared thin (like sticks) and there was evidence of muscle wasting. Her urine tested positive for glucose and when carefully questioned by the doctor, Sarah could remember that over the past year or so she had not felt well, complaining of tiredness more than usual and with repeated episodes of chest infection. The GP referred Sarah to the Endocrine Clinic in the local hospital.

The consultant suspected that Sarah may have Cushing's syndrome. This condition develops in response to excess levels of cortisol which may either result from medication or from over-secretion from a tumour. Sarah was not taking any medication and as the most common site for such a tumour is the anterior pituitary gland, she had a special X-ray of the skull which revealed a small, localized tumour of the anterior pituitary. Sarah was reassured that such tumours are inevitably benign but she was still very shocked at her diagnosis. She was informed that treatment would involve removal of the tumour. After the operation Sarah would require long-term follow-up in the Endocrine Clinic and might have to take medication for life in order to maintain normal pituitary function (it is not possible to control how much healthy hormone-secreting tissue is removed and this must be assessed after surgery so that replacement is possible as necessary). However, in the long-term Sarah's condition should be controllable. She will be able to return to work and live an independent life. Her appearance should return to normal over time.

3.6 Endocrine tissues that are outside the hypothalamic-pituitary axis

In this section we examine examples of endocrine cells and tissues that are not controlled directly by the hypothalamic-pituitary axis. Given the close interaction between the various components of the endocrine and nervous systems, it is unlikely that any endocrine tissue is completely beyond the control of the hypothalamus or other parts of the nervous system. Even in those endocrine control systems that have no identified link with the hypothalamus, the nervous system may be integrated with hormonal action in some way. Integrated neural and endocrine control is common in physiological regulation.

3.6.1 Digestive hormones

The neural control of digestion of food is mediated by the **enteric nervous system,** and many of the neural reflexes linked to digestive processes take place independently of the central nervous system. The enteric nervous system is part of the autonomic nervous system (ANS) (Section 1.8.2), comprising sympathetic and parasympathetic neurons.

● What functions are controlled by the ANS?

○ The ANS controls all involuntary body functions, including digestion of food.

Certain neurons from the sympathetic and parasympathetic nervous systems synapse with neurons from the enteric nervous system, and provide links to the central nervous system. Hormones involved in control of digestion are secreted into the bloodstream from endocrine cells in the epithelium lining the stomach and small intestine. The apical ('upper') surfaces of the epithelial endocrine cells are in direct contact with the contents of the stomach and intestine and respond to chemical signals in the chyme by secreting molecules of the hormone secretin into the bloodstream from the basal cell membrane. The secretion of hormone molecules from epithelial cells lining the stomach and small intestine may also be mediated by parasympathetic nerves.

The hormone gastrin, a polypeptide, is secreted by the specialized epithelial cells lining the stomach, in response to distension of the stomach by incoming food. Gastrin stimulates epithelial cells lining the stomach to release acid and pepsinogen (Book 1, Section 4.3.4), the precursor molecule from which protein-digesting enzymes are formed. Stimulation of the branch of the vagus nerve that innervates the stomach results in secretion of acid, mucus and pepsinogen into the stomach. The vagus nerve has axonal endings in the stomach which secrete a gastrin-releasing peptide in response to stomach filling. So there appears to be both neural and endocrine control of acid, mucus and pepsinogen release.

The control of appetite also involves the nervous and endocrine systems as we shall see in the following section.

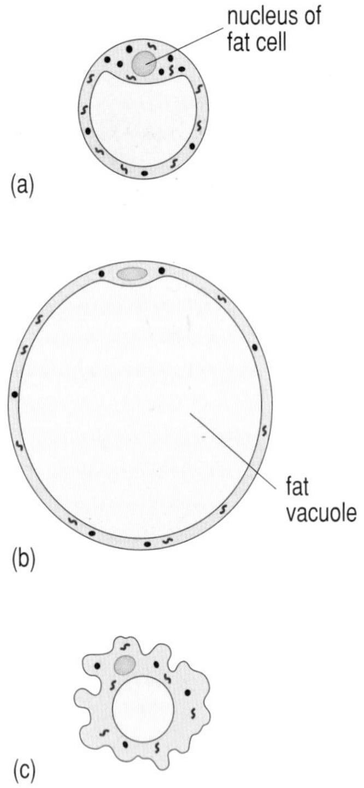

3.6.2 Adipose tissue hormones

Body fat, white adipose tissue (WAT), consists of closely packed fat cells, each loaded with a lipid droplet. In replete fat cells, the lipid droplet takes up most of the cell and the cytosol forms a thin sheath enclosing the fat droplet (Figure 3.16).

(a)

(b)

(c)

Figure 3.16 Fat cells in white adipose tissue. (a) A developing cell. The nucleus is round and the main part of the cell that lies outside the nucleus (the cytosol) contains a single large fat vacuole. (b) A mature cell. The nucleus is compressed against the cell membrane. The large single fat vacuole occupies most of the cell. (c) A fat-depleted cell.

nucleus of fat cell

fat vacuole

In the 1990s, to the surprise of physiologists, it was discovered that fat cells secrete hormones; in 1994 Jeffrey Friedman and his colleagues discovered **leptin**, a polypeptide (Friedman, 2002; Guerre-Millo, 2002; Mantzoros, 1999). The researchers found that the level of leptin in the bloodstream signals the stored lipid content of adipose tissue. When the adipose tissue is replete, leptin release into the bloodstream is maximal. Target cells for leptin are found in many areas of the brain, including the hypothalamus, cortex, cerebellum and brain capillary endothelium. Leptin depresses secretion of **neuropeptide Y**, in the hypothalamus, which suppresses appetite. So leptin exerts a negative feedback effect on hypothalamic secretion of neuropeptide Y, an appetite stimulant, by signalling information about the amount of fat stored in the body, to the brain (Figure 3.17). High levels of leptin increase metabolic rate by activating the thyroid gland via enhanced hypothalamic secretion of TRH.

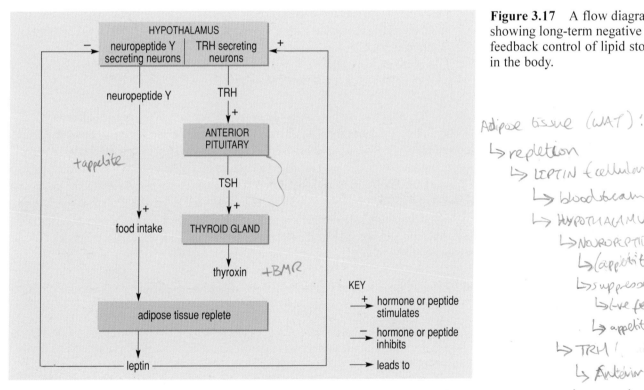

Figure 3.17 A flow diagram showing long-term negative feedback control of lipid stores in the body.

Unfortunately control of food intake in humans is not as simple as suggested in Figure 3.17. Hormonal and neuronal negative feedback pathways that control food intake are affected by motivation, in particular by responses to varied attractive foods. The brain can override the feedback pathway shown in Figure 3.17. The easy availability of low-cost and diverse high-fat attractive foods in the West, coupled with reduced levels of physical activity in western populations, correlate with a sharp increase in the incidence of clinical obesity. Currently (2004) 20% of the adult population of the UK is classified as obese (see Book 1, Section 3.2.2). The number of obese children has doubled since 1982, 10% of six year olds and 17% of fifteen year olds are classified as obese.

- Suggest how leptin might be used to treat clinical obesity; explain your rationale.

- Clinically obese people may have a deficiency of leptin and could be treated by injections of leptin. The rationale would be based on the negative feedback effect of leptin on secretion of neuropeptide Y, an appetite stimulant.

113

Most patients presenting with clinical obesity do not lack leptin; on the contrary, they have high levels of leptin in the blood, as would be expected in individuals with replete fat stores. Nevertheless, clinical trials in which leptin was administered to obese patients were carried out. The results were not promising. The degree of weight loss was no greater than observed with other weight-reducing drugs. After about 6 months of treatment with leptin, body weight reaches a plateau. As very few obese people lack leptin, treatment with leptin may be pointless. Exceptions are a small minority of extremely obese patients who have a mutant (faulty) leptin gene that codes for a leptin with a slightly different amino acid sequence (Friedman, 2002).

● Explain why a person having a mutant leptin gene is clinically obese.

◐ The mutant gene codes for a slightly different amino acid sequence rather than the correct one for normal active leptin. Mutant leptin is likely to be inactive, as the molecule would be unable to bind to specific leptin receptors in target tissues, in particular those in the hypothalamus (Figure 3.17). Therefore neuropeptide Y secretion would not be inhibited, so appetite is undiminished even when WAT is replete.

Interest has also focused on possible deficiencies in receptors for leptin in obese people. Very few patients with clinical obesity have been found to have deficient leptin receptors. The most likely explanation for the lack of sensitivity to leptin in obese patients is nevertheless linked to receptors (Manzoros, 1999). Continued exposure of receptors to a signal often results in reduction of response (known as **downregulation**) of those receptors. The receptors either lose their sensitivity to the signalling molecule or become reduced in number. Clinically obese patients may have developed resistance to leptin, linked to persistent high levels of the hormone in the blood.

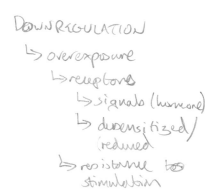

DOWNREGULATION
↳ overexposure
  ↳ receptors
    ↳ signals (hormone)
      ↳ desensitized/
        reduced
        ↳ resistance to
          stimulation

● Predict the effect of leptin injections in an obese patient with mutant receptor protein.

◐ There would be no effects of leptin injection. As the patient's leptin receptors are non-functional, this means that there can be no cellular response to leptin.

Human obesity has many causes and is an intransigent problem with no easy solution.

Summary of Section 3.6

1 The functions of many endocrine tissues that are outside the direct control of the hypothalamic-pituitary axis are integrated with the nervous system.

2 Secretion of gastrin, a digestive hormone, is promoted by peptides released by branches of the vagus nerve, part of the autonomic nervous system.

3 Leptin, a protein hormone secreted by adipose tissue cells, signals a replete state for adipose tissue to the hypothalamus. Low blood leptin levels signal inadequate fat stores.

4 Leptin has a negative feedback effect on secretion of the appetite stimulant, neuropeptide Y, in the brain.

5   Very few obese people have either mutant genes for leptin or its receptors. Loss of sensitivity of the hypothalamus to leptin after prolonged exposure to the hormone, may explain human obesity. The use of leptin for treatment of obesity in people has not been successful.

3.7 Regulation of blood glucose levels

The major fuel for metabolizing cells is glucose, which is broken down to carbon dioxide and water by the process of respiration, providing energy for life processes such as growth, muscular movement and excretion.

● Which macromolecule is digested to glucose and where is most of it absorbed?

● Glucose is a product of carbohydrate digestion, and it enters the bloodstream supplying the small intestine (Book 1, Chapter 4). The bloodstream transports glucose to all cells. The greatest uptake will be in areas where cells have the highest metabolic demands, such as the brain.

● Examine Figure 3.18, which shows blood glucose levels in a volunteer measured over a 24-hour period during which time they ate three meals and slept overnight. Describe the pattern of blood glucose levels quoting values for concentration in the correct units of measurement, millimoles per litre (mmol l^{-1}). Is the level of glucose in the blood a regulated or a controlled variable?

● Blood glucose levels vary between 4 and 6 mmol l^{-1} over the whole period; peaks occur after meals. During sleep blood glucose is maintained at about 4.0–4.5 mmol l^{-1}. The near-constancy of blood glucose levels indicates that blood glucose level is a regulated variable (Section 3.2).

BLOOD GLUCOSE LEVELS
↳ REGULATED VARIABLE

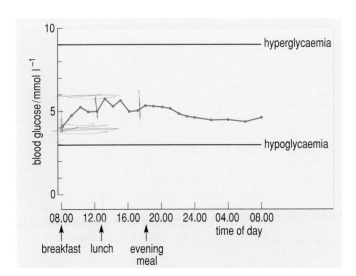

Figure 3.18 The level of glucose in the blood over a period of 24 hours during which three meals were eaten and there was a period of sleep. (Note that mmol l^{-1} means millimoles per litre, where 1 millimole of glucose = 180 mg glucose.) (Hypoglycaemia and hyperglycaemia are discussed in Sections 3.7.1 and 3.7.2.)

Regulation of blood glucose level is an important part of homeostasis, the maintenance of a constant internal environment. The nervous system and the endocrine systems are involved, but not the hypothalamic-pituitary axis. Pancreatic hormones control blood glucose levels.

[Handwritten margin notes, top left:]
Feed forward
↳ Dual control
↳ PARASYMPATHETIC NS
↳ INSULIN
↳ Gastric inhibitory peptide (GIP)
↳ small intestine
↳ fats + glucose
↳ INSULIN

3.7.1 The role of pancreatic hormones

About 98% of the tissue in the pancreas comprises cells that secrete digestive enzymes, bicarbonate ions and water, which are channelled into the pancreatic duct (i.e. the pancreas tissue is 98% exocrine). The remaining 2% of tissue comprises 'islands' of endocrine tissue, the **islets of Langerhans**. Specialized endocrine cells within the islets (known as α and β cells) secrete **glucagon** and **insulin**, respectively (Figure 3.19), polypeptide hormones involved in controlling blood glucose levels. The effects of the two hormones on their target tissues are antagonistic. But, as we shall see, this does not mean that they fight one another; rather, by having opposing actions they work together to achieve a regulated blood glucose level. Control of secretion of hormones from the pancreas involves the autonomic nervous system and feedback from hormones and glucose and other nutrients in the bloodstream.

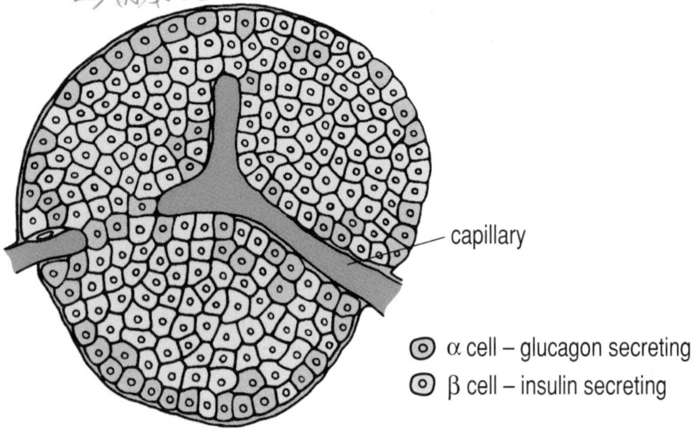

Release of insulin into the bloodstream is stimulated by high blood glucose levels, about 6 mmol l^{-1}, that build up after a person has eaten a meal. After digestion, blood glucose levels are much higher than those in tissue cells. The action of insulin exerts a negative feedback effect on blood glucose levels by promoting uptake of glucose into cells in the target tissues, liver, muscle and adipose tissue (Figure 3.20: for simplicity, muscle is omitted).

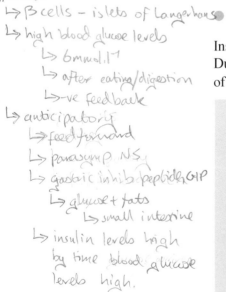

— capillary

⊙ α cell – glucagon secreting
⊙ β cell – insulin secreting

Figure 3.19 Distribution of α and β cells in the islets of Langerhans in a human pancreas. α cells, which secrete glucagon, are situated around the edge of an islet, while insulin-secreting β cells, which comprise 60% of the mass of islet tissue, make up the core. A network of capillaries supplies the islet tissue.

● In what sense are these target tissues?

They are tissues where glucose can be converted into a storage product.

Insulin secretion is also modulated by autonomic neurons that innervate the islets. During eating, parasympathetic neurons are activated and stimulate secretion of insulin.

[Handwritten margin notes, lower left:]
INSULIN
↳ β cells – islets of Langerhans
↳ high blood glucose levels
↳ 6 mmol.l^{-1}
↳ after eating/digestion
↳ -ve feedback
↳ anticipatory
↳ feedforward
↳ parasymp. NS
↳ gastric inhib peptide GIP
↳ glucose + fats
↳ small intestine
↳ insulin levels high by time blood glucose levels high.

Figure 3.20 A flow diagram showing the role of insulin in the regulation of blood glucose. The level of insulin in the blood is controlled by negative feedback of lowered blood glucose on insulin secretion.

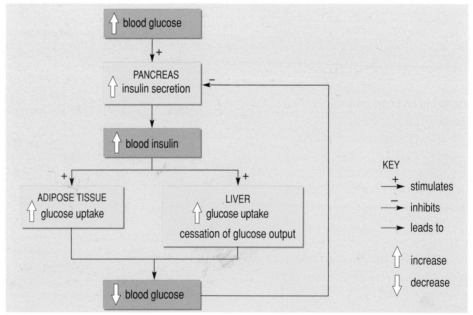

● Suggest the advantage of dual control of insulin secretion mediated by raised blood glucose level, and the response of the autonomic nervous system to eating.

● The parasympathetic nervous system responds quickly to neural signals generated by eating before food is digested, so that by the time blood glucose rises, insulin is already in the blood facilitating transport of glucose into target cells.

The action of the parasympathetic nervous system in stimulating insulin secretion just before blood glucose levels rise, is an example of **feedforward**, a process in which a signalling mechanism pre-empts a response to a physiological change, facilitating a faster response (Book 1, Section 2.4). A hormonal signal is also involved in mediating feedforward. **Gastric inhibitory peptide, GIP**, released by endocrine cells in the small intestine in response to the presence of fats and glucose in the small intestine, stimulates insulin release prior to the arrival of glucose in the circulation.

So during eating and digestion, insulin floods into the bloodstream, and promotes entry of glucose into target cells. After a meal glucose levels are higher in blood than in tissue cells, but glucose can only enter the cells by crossing their membranes via protein membrane transport molecules. Insulin increases the number of glucose transport molecules in **muscle** and **fat cell** membranes (Rea and James, 1997; Watson et al., 2004). When insulin levels are low, glucose transport molecules float around in the cytosol of fat and muscle cells. Interaction of insulin with receptor molecules triggers migration of the transport molecules into the cell membrane, facilitating entry of glucose into the cell.

Entry of glucose into liver cells also depends on insulin, and in order to understand why, we need to look at the biochemistry of liver cell metabolism.

Figure 3.21 summarizes the effects of insulin at the biochemical level. In liver cells, insulin increases glucose uptake by activating glycogen synthase, the enzyme that converts glucose into the carbohydrate glycogen, the form in which glucose is stored in liver and muscle. Insulin deactivates glycogen phosphorylase, the enzyme that promotes the first stage of glycogen breakdown to glucose. Insulin also stimulates fat storage in adipocytes by activating enzymes involved in triacylglycerol (lipid) synthesis from glucose and free fatty acids (Book 1, Section 3.4).

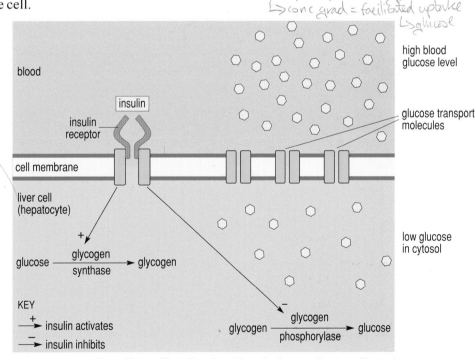

Figure 3.21 The effect of insulin signalling in liver cells. Insulin activates glycogen synthase, the enzyme that promotes conversion of glucose into glycogen thereby removing glucose from the cytosol. The resulting low glucose concentration inside the cell maintains a concentration gradient between high blood glucose and low cell glucose promoting entry of glucose into the cell via glucose membrane transport proteins (facilitated diffusion).

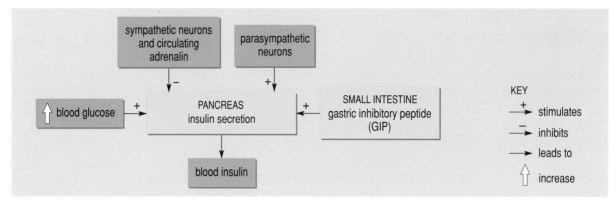

Figure 3.22   A flow diagram summarizing the major factors that control secretion of insulin.

● If insulin is absent, glycogen synthase is not activated. Suggest an explanation for why glucose does not enter liver cells in the absence of insulin.

○ If insulin is absent, there is no glycogen synthesis, so glucose builds up inside liver cells. Hence there will be no concentration gradient between blood and liver cell cytosol and therefore no movement of glucose across the cell membrane by facilitated diffusion.

Insulin secretion is inhibited when blood glucose levels are low, and during times of stress, by the activity of noradrenalin-secreting sympathetic neurons that innervate the islets, and by adrenalin secreted from the adrenal medulla. The complex picture of neural and endocrine control of insulin secretion is summarized in Figure 3.22.

Insulin levels plummet as blood glucose levels decline and both of these factors stimulate secretion of glucagon by the α cells (high levels of insulin inhibit glucagon secretion). The effects of glucagon on target cells are antagonistic to those of insulin, in that they promote increases in the levels of blood glucose. The housekeeping role of glucagon is to maintain levels of blood glucose during the postabsorptive phase, when digestion and transport of blood glucose derived from digestion to target cells are complete.

During prolonged starvation between meals or intensive prolonged exercise, blood glucose levels decline and if this were allowed to continue, the brain would not have access to sufficient glucose for metabolism. Glucose is the only molecule that the brain can use to provide energy in the short term. You may have experienced feelings of dizziness or 'light-headedness' when you are very hungry. These effects are caused by low blood glucose level, less than 3–4 mmol l^{-1}, a condition known as **hypoglycaemia**.

Glucagon raises blood glucose levels by stimulating the breakdown of glycogen stored in the liver. Glycogen phosphorylase, the enzyme that catalyses glycogen breakdown (Figure 3.21), is activated by glucagon, and glycogen synthase is deactivated. (This is the opposite effect to insulin.) During prolonged starvation insulin is virtually absent from the blood and lipid breakdown is enhanced by glucagon. Lipids are broken down to their constituent glycerol and fatty acids. Glucagon also activates the enzymes involved in **gluconeogenesis**.

● Which two building blocks are needed for gluconeogenesis?

○ Amino acids and glycerol.

Note that glucose can be synthesized only from the glycerol portion of fat molecules, not from fatty acids. The fatty acids can, however, be converted into acetyl coenzyme A (acetyl CoA) and be used to produce ATP (see Figure 3.3 of Book 1). Although not shown on Figure 3.3, acetyl CoA must first combine with oxaloacetate which is derived from glucose. Hence once glucose is depleted, excess acetyl CoA enters an alternative pathway in the liver cells and **ketone bodies** are produced. Ketone bodies are released from the liver to the blood circulation. They can be used by other tissues, including the brain, as a fuel source. Unfortunately at high concentrations they are toxic. Ketone bodies have a characteristic alcoholic smell. Because they evaporate at body temperature they can leave the blood as it flows through the lungs and so a starved person's breath smells of alcohol. In the final stages of starvation glucagon also stimulates breakdown of muscle protein into amino acids, which are converted into glucose.

● Which other hormone promotes breakdown of muscle protein to amino acids?

○ Cortisol.

Secretion of glucagon is also controlled by the sympathetic nervous system. A low blood glucose level is detected by glucose receptors in the hypothalamus, which activate the sympathetic neural pathway that innervates the islets.

● Which neurotransmitter is released by the sympathetic nervous system?

○ Noradrenalin is secreted by the sympathetic nervous system.

Stimulation of the sympathetic nervous system pathway causes the release of noradrenalin which in turn promotes glucagon secretion. The physiological significance of the relationship between the sympathetic nervous system and the response to stress and exercise are explored in detail in Book 4.

We have examined the hormonal control of blood glucose levels, a critical aspect of homeostasis. Disturbances of homeostasis of blood glucose have serious consequences as we shall see in the following section.

3.7.2 Diabetes mellitus

In the West, diabetes affects about 2% of the population. About 15% of people who have diabetes have type 1 (insulin-dependent diabetes mellitus), a metabolic disorder caused by a complete or near complete loss of function of the β islet cells with resulting lack of insulin. Patients suffer rapid loss of weight despite increased food intake, and depletion of fat stores and muscle wasting occurs. Blood glucose levels are always abnormally high, greater than 10 mmol l^{-1}, a state known as **hyperglycaemia**.

● Explain the weight loss and hyperglycaemia observed in patients with type 1 diabetes mellitus in terms of the lack of insulin.

- In patients with type 1 diabetes, increased blood glucose cannot initiate release of insulin, so blood glucose cannot be transported across cell membranes into target cells in the liver, muscle and adipose tissue, hence the hyperglycaemia. Therefore, despite hyperglycaemia, cells cannot access blood glucose derived from digested food and the body starves. The physiological response of the body to starvation, mediated by glucagon, is to draw on glycogen reserves, lipid stores, and finally, muscle protein. Without insulin, there is no inhibition of break down of glycogen, fat or protein, so rapid weight loss is observed.

Treatment of type 1 diabetes mellitus involves regular injections of insulin. Patients test their blood at regular intervals to check that their blood glucose levels are within the norm.

People who have type 2 diabetes (non-insulin-dependent diabetes mellitus) have insulin in the bloodstream but blood glucose levels remain high. Patients with type 2 diabetes are mostly middle-aged and older, and often overweight or obese (although recently there has been an increase in the number of cases of children with type 2 diabetes).

- Suggest an explanation for the lack of response of target tissues to insulin.

- Patients who are obese are likely to be eating more food than non-obese people. Continued high levels of blood glucose mean continual high levels of insulin in the blood. Receptors for insulin in the target tissues are likely to be downregulated after prolonged exposure to high blood glucose levels, meaning that glucose is not taken up by target cells.

Type 2 diabetes is treated by exercise, a controlled diet and medication, which ensures that there are prolonged periods during the day when blood glucose levels are close to the regulated norm.

The absence or ineffectiveness of insulin in diabetes mellitus results in elevation of blood glucose levels. Blood glucose levels greater than 10 mmol l^{-1} result in loss of glucose in urine. Prolonged exposure of tissues to high blood glucose levels causes damage. Such damage may be caused by **glycation**, a process whereby glucose molecules bind to protein molecules and cause irreversible structural changes including formation of Amadori product, damaged proteins with abnormally rigid structures. Amadori product is linked to increased incidence of cataracts, peripheral nervous system damage and arteriosclerosis. Another, rather different effect of high glucose levels in blood is that by providing a nutrient-rich environment for pathogens such as bacteria, it contributes to an increased susceptibility to infection.

Our overview of hormone secretion that is not under the direct control of the hypothalamic-pituitary axis is far from complete. New discoveries of sites of hormone secretion are made quite frequently. The picture is also complicated by the existence of cytokines, polypeptide signalling molecules that were not recognized initially as having an endocrine role, the subject of our next section.

Summary of Section 3.7

1   Pancreatic hormones, insulin and glucagon, secreted by type α and β endocrine cells in the islets of Langerhans, control processes that regulate levels of glucose in the blood.

2   Insulin released from β islet cells after a meal, promotes uptake of blood glucose by target cells. In adipose tissue and muscle cells, insulin activates the glucose transporter molecules, thereby preventing prolonged peaks of blood glucose following a meal. In liver cells, insulin activates glycogen synthase, thereby removing glucose from cytosol, and maintaining a glucose concentration gradient between cytosol and blood.

3   Two feedforward mechanisms promote release of insulin into the blood during a meal. Parasympathetic neurons stimulate insulin secretion during eating. Gastric inhibitory peptide, GIP, released by intestinal cells in response to fats and glucose in the intestine also stimulates insulin release.

4   Noradrenalin released by sympathetic neurons in the islets and adrenalin secreted by the adrenal medulla inhibit insulin secretion.

5   Glucagon, secreted when blood glucose and insulin levels are low, promotes breakdown of glycogen by the liver, which provides glucose for secretion into the blood. In long-term starvation, glucagon also promotes gluconeogenesis, synthesis of glucose from amino acids and glycerol, and the breakdown of lipids.

6   Type 1 diabetes is a metabolic disorder caused by a complete or near-complete loss of function of the β cells in pancreatic islets. As insulin activates transport of glucose into target cells, this means that cells do not have access to glucose, even though blood glucose levels are always elevated. Hence people with type 1 diabetes starve to death unless treated with insulin injections.

7   Type 2 diabetes is a metabolic disorder caused by insensitivity of target cells to insulin. Many patients are middle-aged and obese, and have elevated blood glucose levels. (Increasingly, children are also being affected.) Treatment comprises dietary controls, exercise and medication, designed to promote lowering of blood glucose levels and increased sensitivity of target cells to insulin.

3.8 Cytokines and growth factors

Cytokines are signalling molecules that consist of one or two polypeptide chains (Ibelgauft, 2004) (from the Greek, *cytos* a cell, *kineo* to move). So far hundreds of different cytokines have been discovered, and in order to establish molecular relationships between diverse cytokines, physiologists have classified them into families based on similarities of chemical structure. Initially, cytokines were distinguished from conventional protein hormones by a number of criteria. Cytokines are not secreted by defined endocrine glands or tissues, but by a diversity of cell types. Many scientists define cytokines as being signalling molecules secreted by the immune system only, and classify cytokine-like

CYTOKINES
↳ cell movers
↳ AUTOCRINE
↳ affect cells including them
↳ positive feedback?
↳ PARACRINE
↳ local affect
↳ with tissue

CYTOKINES:
↳ structurally classified
   ↳ (with growth factors)
↳ stim' variety of cell types
   ↳ AUTOCRINE
      ↳ affect cells that secrete them
         ↳ amplify signals
      ↳ e.g. INTERLEUKINS
         ↳ immune response
            ↳ cytotoxic T-cells
            ↳ melanoma
            ↳ renal cell carcinoma
↳ PARACRINE
   ↳ affect local cells
      ↳ (secreted within tissues)
      ↳ IGF-1
         ↳ Insulin-like growth factor
         ↳ bone growth plates
            ↳ proliferating cartilage cells
↳ ENDOCRINE
   ↳ can be secreted into blood
      ↳ IGF-1
         ↳ liver
            ↳ response to growth hormone

signalling molecules secreted by other tissues, e.g. insulin-like growth factors, IGFs, as growth factors. A cytokine or growth factor may target a variety of cell types and act to modulate the effects of another cytokine or hormone. The effects of one cytokine or growth factor may overlap with the effects of another. Many cytokines modulate the effects of conventional endocrine hormones. Usually cytokines and growth factors act in an **autocrine** or **paracrine** way. Signalling molecules that act autocrinally affect the cells that secrete them; such a response enables cells to amplify signals. Paracrine signalling molecules secreted by cells within a tissue act locally, exerting effects on cells close by. However, some cytokines and growth factors have been found to operate in an endocrine way, in that they are secreted into the bloodstream. Hence it is difficult to distinguish cytokines and growth factors from hormones.

Interleukins are examples of cytokines secreted by specialized white cells, involved in immune responses to infection and inflammation. We met interleukin-1 in Section 2.12 of Book 1 in connection with wound healing. Interleukin-2 (IL-2) is a glycoprotein secreted by white cells called T lymphocytes. (*T* because these cells mature in the thymus which is an endocrine gland shown in Figure 3.4, *lympho* because the thymus is also part of the lymphatic system shown in Figure 1.10 of Book 1 and *cytos* meaning cell.) IL-2 controls immune responses and anti-inflammatory reactions in the body, by stimulating proliferation and growth of particular types of T cells, each of which have slightly different roles in fighting off infection. (This will be explained in more detail in Book 3, Chapter 4.) One type that is targeted by IL-2 is a cytotoxic T cell (i.e. a cell-killing T cell) that is particularly effective in destroying the tumour cells found in patients with advanced melanoma and renal cell carcinoma. These two conditions are resistant to other treatments and prognosis is poor. Although there are problems with IL-2 because it has (unsurprisingly) toxic side-effects that limit treatment it has been found that treatment with IL-2 can substantially enhance life expectancy for a proportion of this group of patients. Side-effects include diarrhoea and vomiting, low blood pressure, high cardiac output, kidney and liver toxicity, but all these effects are reversible on cessation of treatment. The treatment requires that IL-2 is administered over 15 minutes three times a day; 14 doses are the maximum a patient can tolerate, followed by a rest period of 5–9 days. Of 255 patients with advanced renal cell carcinoma, responses were reported in 15% of patients. The median duration of response was 54 months and for those with complete responses, 80 months, which demonstrates the benefit of IL-2 treatment in a significant proportion of IL-2 treated patients. Median survival for all patients was 16.3 months and 10–20% of patients were thought to be alive 5–10 years following treatment (Fisher et al., 2000). Research continues with the aim of improving survival rates.

As an example of a cytokine secreted by tissues other than those of the immune system we will briefly consider the insulin-like growth factor (IGF) family (Ibelgauft, 2004). These include proteins (polypeptides) that have paracrine and endocrine modes of action. IGF-1 is secreted into the bloodstream by liver cells in response to circulating growth hormone (Section 3.5) and stimulates cartilage cell proliferation in epiphyseal growth plates, and therefore growth of long bones of babies and children (Section 4.4.3).

- Does IGF-1 secreted by the liver function in an endocrine, paracrine or autocrine way in stimulating bone growth?

- Liver-derived IGF-1 functions as a hormone, in an endocrine way, as it is transported in the blood to the target cells in growth plates of bone.

The liver secretes large quantities of IGF-1, around 10 mg day^{-1}. Smaller amounts are secreted by the kidneys, heart, lungs and adipose tissue. IGF-1 is also secreted by proliferating cartilage cells in bone growth plates, where it functions in a paracrine way.

You have no doubt noticed by now that the distinction between the function of cytokines, growth factors and hormones is not so clear-cut after all.

Summary of Section 3.8

1   Cytokines and growth factors are diverse groups of polypeptide signalling molecules, classified by their chemical structure into families. Examples include interleukins (ILs) and insulin-like growth factors (IGFs).

2   T-cells, specialized lymphocytes (white cells) involved in immune responses, secrete interleukins, cytokines that stimulate the T-cells to proliferate, enhancing immune and anti-inflammatory responses.

autocrine

3   Interleukins, e.g. IL-2, are used in treating certain cancers, such as melanoma and renal cell carcinoma.

4   IGF-1 secreted by liver cells functions endocrinally, stimulating proliferation of cartilage cells in growth plates of bones of babies and children. Cartilage cells also secrete IGF-1, which stimulates cartilage cell proliferation paracrinally.

Hormonal release
↳ pulsatile
↳ intermittent
↳ continuous

3.9 The life of a hormone

So far in this chapter we have used the endocrine system itself as a reference point for a classification system that enables us to understand the functional organization of endocrine regulation and control. For a clearer understanding of hormone secretion and hormone specificity we need to consider the chemistry of hormones, their synthesis and how they are released from endocrine cells.

The 'life' of a hormone begins with its synthesis in the endocrine cell. Stored hormones may be bound to a larger polypeptide, or be part of a larger parent polypeptide. Release of hormones may be pulsatile, intermittent or continuous, and takes place in response to nervous or chemical stimuli. Hormones are carried in the blood, where they may be bound to plasma proteins. The **half-life** of a hormone is defined as the time it takes for half the amount of hormone present in blood at any one time to be broken down or removed from the blood. Therefore the half-life of a hormone depends on how quickly it is removed by one or more of three possible processes:

- metabolism in the liver;

- deactivation by enzymes inside target cells;

- excretion by the kidney.

HALF-LIFE
↳ ½ time in blood before hormone
is broken down or removed
↳ metabolism — liver
↳ deactivation — cellular enzymes
↳ excretion — kidney
↳ increased by PLASMA PROTEINS
↳ e.g. globulins
↳ steroids
↳ increase molec size
↳ not filtered out into urine (kidney)
↳ e.g. cortisol
↳ 90% bound
↳ available supplementary reservoir

[handwritten margin notes:]
Plasma proteins
↳ globins
↳ steroid + thyroid
↳ protects against excretion
* ↳ kidney*

Peptide and catecholamine hormones circulate as free molecules in the blood. In contrast circulating steroid and thyroid hormones are bound to large plasma proteins, mostly globulins, which are synthesized in the liver. Binding of steroid hormones to plasma proteins increases their half-life, because the molecular size of the hormone–protein complex is too large to filter into the primary urine in the kidney (Book 3, Chapter 1). For example, about 90% of the cortisol in blood is bound to a globulin protein; the remaining 10% of cortisol in blood is unbound. Thus the bound cortisol probably acts as a readily available reservoir that can smooth out fluctuations in or supplement free cortisol levels. We next examine a number of aspects of the life of a hormone, including hormone synthesis and release, and the persistence of hormones in the bloodstream.

3.9.1 Synthesis and release of hormones

Sections 3.1–3.3 mention a diverse range of hormones, which can be grouped into five categories of molecules according to their chemical nature. Our examination of hormone synthesis must therefore include secretion of peptides and polypeptides, modified amino acids, catecholamines and steroids. Table 3.3 classifies named examples of hormones into categories defined by their chemical nature.

In the following sections we examine secretion of the types of hormones defined in Table 3.3.

Table 3.3   Classification of categories of hormone structure and examples.

Type of hormone molecule	Site of secretion	Secreted hormones and/or cytokines
polypeptides: more than 10 amino acids	hypothalamus	CRH, GRH, SIF
	anterior pituitary	ACTH, GH, FSH, LH, TSH, PrL
	intestine/stomach	secretin, gastrin
	pancreas islets	insulin, glucagon
	adipose tissue	leptin
	kidney	erythropoietin
	liver	IGF-1
(small) peptides: 2–10 amino acids	hypothalamus	GnRH, TRH
	posterior pituitary	ADH, oxytocin
thyroid hormones (derived from two molecules of the amino acid, tyrosine)	thyroid gland	thyroxin, tri-iodothyronine
catecholamines	adrenal medulla	adrenalin, noradrenalin
	hypothalamus	PIF (dopamine)
steroids	adrenal cortex	cortisol, aldosterone
	testis	testosterone
	ovary	oestrogen, testosterone

Secretion of polypeptide and small peptide hormones

Most hormones are polypeptides (or peptides) (Table 3.3). Their synthesis involves transcription of DNA into mRNA, followed by translation, chemical linking of amino acids and protein processing (Book 1, Section 2.7). For many polypeptide hormones, the initial synthesis produces what is known as pre-pro-hormones which enter the cell's secretory pathway, beginning with cleavage into pro-hormones by enzymes, proteases, in the rough endoplasmic reticulum (RER). The pro-hormone is then transferred into the Golgi apparatus where it is cleaved to form the active hormone, and other active peptides. The stages of insulin secretion provide a classic example of the secretory pathway, following synthesis of a polypeptide hormone. Pancreatic islet β cells (Section 3.7.1) synthesize the parent molecule, pre-pro-insulin which is 110 amino acids in length. Subsequently pre-pro-insulin enters the inside of the RER (Figure 3.23), losing part of the amino acid chain and forming pro-insulin.

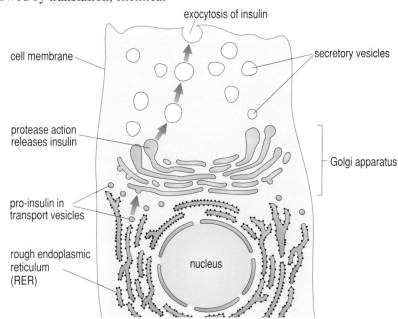

Figure 3.23   Stages in the secretion of insulin in β cells of the islets of Langerhans.

Pro-hormones may be cleaved to form a number of active peptides. In the case of pro-insulin, the molecule is packaged into vesicles in the Golgi apparatus where it is cut into two parts by a protease, forming insulin and a connecting peptide (Figure 3.24).

— cheap to make — ∴ receptors have to be very good at identifying correct hormone!

When stimulated by high concentrations of glucose inside the β cell, the vesicles containing insulin (and the connecting peptide) release their contents by fusing with the cell membrane, the process of exocytosis (Figure 3.23). All small peptide and polypeptide hormones are released from endocrine cells in this way.

TRANSCRIPTION / TRANSLATION → CLEAVAGE → CLEAVAGE → EXOCYTOSIS

Nucleus   PRE-PRO HORMONE   e ∴ Pre-pro-insulin (110 amino acids)
↓ (proteases)   ↓
RER   PRO-HORMONE   Pro-insulin
GOLGI APP/   ↓   ↓
VESICLES   ACTIVE HORMONE   Insulin + connecting peptide
(+ connecting pep)

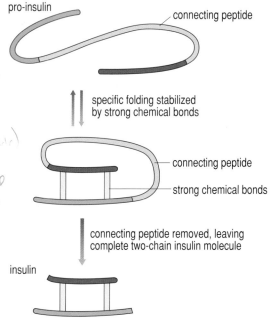

Figure 3.24   Conversion of the inactive precursor protein pro-insulin to the active hormone insulin by removal of the connecting peptide. (a) Insulin is synthesized as a larger polypeptide, pro-insulin; (b) pro-insulin folds to form a stabilized molecule; (c) pro-insulin is cleaved into two parts, a connecting peptide and insulin. Insulin consists of two polypeptide chains held together by two strong chemical (covalent) bonds.

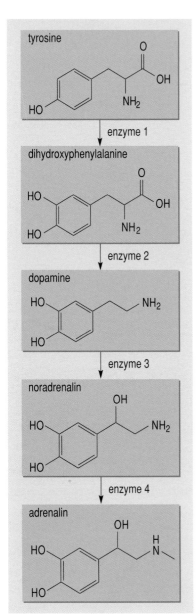

Figure 3.25 Synthetic pathways for catecholamine hormones; each step in the pathway is controlled by a specific enzyme. You are not expected to recall the structures of each of these hormones, but you should be aware how relatively small changes in the tyrosine molecule create a family of catecholamine hormones. *Note:* These are *skeleton* representations – none of the carbon atoms and directly attached hydrogen atoms are shown. Each line denotes a single carbon to carbon bond (C—C bond), with the C atoms at the ends of the lines and H atoms attached to them. Thus a 'free end' represents a CH_3 group, a bend is a CH_2 group and where three lines converge, it means that is a CH group.

Secretion of catecholamine hormones

Adrenalin, noradrenalin and dopamine are all synthesized from the amino acid tyrosine by a series of enzyme-controlled reactions summarized in Figure 3.25. As applies to all sequences of chemical reactions, you should not attempt to learn the molecular structures but appreciate how a family of hormones have the same basic structure. Different hormones in the family each have a slight variation of structure.

Catecholamine hormones are stored in secretory granules and released in a similar way to that for polypeptide hormones. The adrenal medulla is a specialized sympathetic ganglion, a collection of nerve cells, known as **chromaffin cells**, which do not have axons. The cells synthesize adrenalin and noradrenalin by the sequence of reactions summarized in Figure 3.25. The intermediates move backwards and forwards between cytosol and secretory granules. Stimulation of synthesis of noradrenalin and its conversion to adrenalin are activated by sympathetic stimulation in response to stress.

Secretion of thyroid hormones

The main secretory product of the thyroid gland is thyroxin, derived from two molecules of tyrosine linked to four atoms of iodine (Figure 3.26). Thyroxin, T_4, is a pro-hormone for the more active tri-iodothyronine, T_3. Small amounts of T_3 are secreted by the thyroid gland but most T_3 is produced by the removal of iodine from T_4 molecules within target tissues.

The thyroid gland consists of many follicles (each is a tiny ball of the protein thyroglobulin, enclosed in a layer of epithelial cells) which synthesize thyroid hormones. Thyroglobulin is the form in which thyroid hormones are stored inside the follicles of the thyroid gland. Thyroid hormones are synthesized by the attachment of one or two atoms of iodine to individual residues of the amino acid tyrosine within the thyroglobulin molecule. Two iodinated tyrosine molecules then react together, forming mostly T_4 and very little T_3. Iodinated thyroglobulin is stored inside thyroid follicles as thyroid colloid.

The first stage in the release of thyroid hormones into the blood involves entry of thyroglobulin into an epithelial cell by endocytosis. The cell membrane forms a small pocket, which engulfs some of the colloid, and pinches off into the cytosol. Release of thyroid hormones follows the same secretory pathway as that for protein and peptide signalling molecules. Protease enzymes inside lysosomes cleave T_4 and T_3 from the thyroglobulin. Free T_4 and T_3 exit the cell by exocytosis and enter the blood in the thyroid capillary network.

Figure 3.26 Molecular structures of tyrosine, thyroxin (T$_4$) and tri-iodothyronine (T$_3$). The thyroxin molecule has four iodine (I) atoms attached; tri-iodothyronine has three iodine atoms attached. (See the caption for Figure 3.25 for an explanation of these skeleton structures.)

tyrosine

thyroxin (T$_4$)

tri-iodothyronine (T$_3$)

Secretion of steroid hormones

All steroid hormones in humans are derived from the same parent molecule, cholesterol, so they are very different from polypeptide hormones. Steroid hormone molecules all contain four rings of carbon atoms and examples are shown in Figure 3.27, where key differences can be seen between steroid molecules. The molecular structure is complex, but differences between individual steroid hormones are quite small.

● Examine the cholesterol molecule Figure 3.27a and the steroid hormone molecules, Figures 3.27b, c, d and e. What general changes have to be made to the cholesterol molecule in order to transform it into the hormone molecules?

● Synthesis of steroid hormones involves removal or addition of oxygen and/or hydrogen and carbon atoms to/from the basic four ring steroid nucleus of cholesterol.

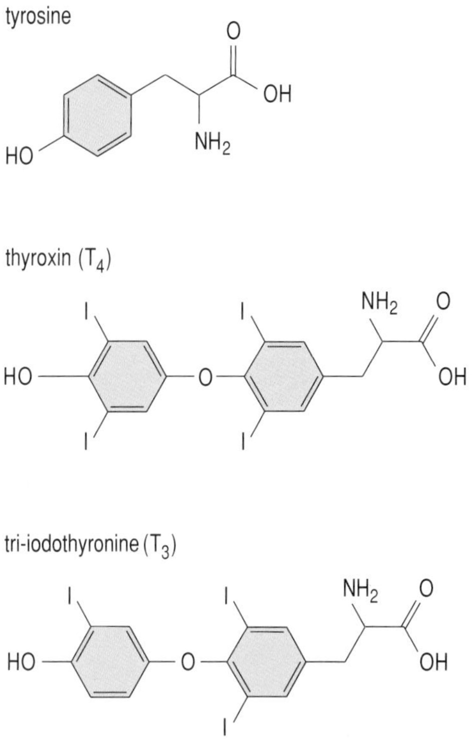

STEROID HORMONES
↳ cholesterol
↳ 4 carbon rings

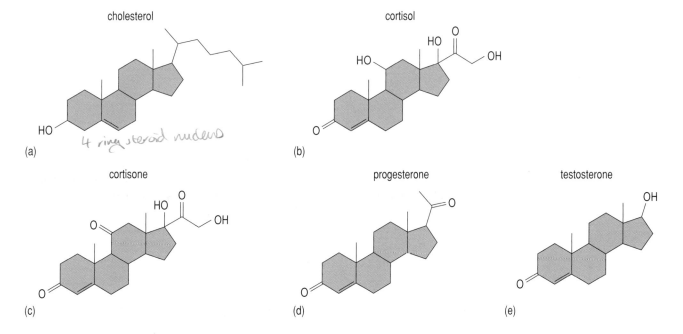

4 ring steroid nucleus

Figure 3.27 The relationship between (a) the parent cholesterol molecule, and four examples of steroid hormones: (b) cortisol; (c) cortisone; (d) progesterone and (e) testosterone. The four rings in cholesterol are coloured purple so that you can trace them in each of the four hormone molecules. (See the caption for Figure 3.25 for an explanation of these skeleton structures.)

Cells that synthesize steroid hormones do not store them. Lipid droplets in cell cytosol contain cholesterol (the hormone precursor molecule), not the hormones themselves. Increases in secretion of steroid hormones are initiated by activation of biosynthesis from cholesterol. There is no apparent special release mechanism for steroid hormones; they pass freely through cell membranes. For example, the response of cells in the adrenal cortex to the hormone ACTH is the initiation of synthesis and rapid release of cortisol.

● Imagine that you spot a bull as you cross a field. You are terrified; your heart beats faster, your mouth feels dry, but you walk slowly. A couple of minutes later the bull moves towards you, and you run to the stile. Your blood cortisol increases to a high level, stimulating increased carbohydrate metabolism. Suggest the mechanisms that increase blood cortisol in response to danger, and initiate the recovery phase when the stress is over.

● Perception of a danger by the brain initiates signals that stimulate the hypothalamus to release CRH into the blood capillary network supplying the anterior pituitary. CRH stimulates the release of ACTH from the anterior pituitary, which in turn stimulates cortisol secretion from the adrenal glands. Once the danger is over, the hypothalamus stops releasing CRH, and blood cortisol levels fall to normal (see Figure 3.10).

The sequence of stages of the acute stress response is rapid and involves other hormones and the neurotransmitter noradrenalin too (Book 4, Chapter 3). A salient point is that cortisol can be synthesized rapidly from cholesterol and released quickly into the bloodstream in response to stress.

3.9.3 Hormone turnover and lifespan

The lifespan of a hormone in the bloodstream is determined by the rate of breakdown and/or excretion via the kidneys of that hormone (Section 3.9). The half-life of growth hormone in the blood is 15–25 minutes; the half-life of plasma oxytocin is just 2–5 minutes. Binding of catecholamines and steroid hormones to plasma proteins increases their half-life, because the molecular size of the hormone–protein complex is too large to filter into the primary urine in the kidney. For example, protein-bound cortisol has a half-life of about 90 minutes; protein-bound thyroxin has a half-life of up to 7 days. A slow-release rate of hormone molecules bound to protein carrier molecules is possible because the amount of hormone bound to plasma proteins is in equilibrium with a small amount of free hormone. Receptors in membranes of target cells have a higher affinity (attraction), for the hormone than do the plasma-binding proteins, so free hormone binds readily to receptors. This loss of free hormone from the blood disturbs the equilibrium between protein-bound hormone, free-hormone and receptor-bound hormone and in response, some of the hormone which was bound to protein, separates and circulates subsequently as free hormone (Figure 3.28).

The low rate of kidney excretion of large protein hormones, such as growth hormone, and hormones that are bound to plasma proteins, explains why such hormones have longer half-lives than small unbound peptide hormones such as oxytocin. The kidney and liver break down hormones, a process which is also slowed down when hormones are bound to large plasma proteins. Hormones may

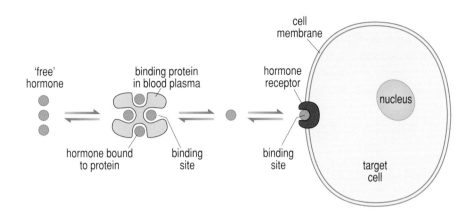

Figure 3.28 Equilibrium between free unbound hormone, protein-bound hormone in blood plasma and receptor-bound hormone. The double-headed arrows indicate that the process whereby the hormone binds to plasma proteins and receptors is reversible.

also be removed from the bloodstream by irreversible uptake into target cells and subsequent destruction by enzymes.

The rate of secretion of a hormone can be determined from measurements of blood and/or urine concentrations of that hormone. Hormone concentrations in blood and urine are usually very low and require special techniques for measurement.

Summary of Section 3.9

1   The first stage of the life of a hormone is its synthesis in an endocrine cell.

2   Protein hormone synthesis begins with transcription of DNA to mRNA, followed by translation, which involves chemical linking of amino acids and processing from pre-pro-hormones into active hormones.

3   Catecholamines and thyroid hormones are synthesized from the amino acid tyrosine. Thyroid hormones consist of two tyrosine molecules linked together.

4   Steroid hormones such as cortisol, are synthesized from cholesterol in specialized cells only when stimulated to do so by hormonal or neural signals. Synthesis is followed by immediate release into the bloodstream.

5   Protein, peptide, thyroid and catecholamine hormones are released into the bloodstream by the protein secretory pathway, involving stages in the rough endoplasmic reticulum, Golgi apparatus and secretory vesicles.

6   The half-life of a hormone in the bloodstream depends on its molecular size and on whether it is bound to a plasma protein.

3.10 Conclusion

There are two over-arching themes in this chapter. The power of hormones as signalling molecules links to their specificity, which is determined by the unique molecular structure of individual hormones, and their interaction with specific receptor protein molecules in target cells. Physiological regulation and control require close integration between the signalling functions of the endocrine and nervous systems.

As you study the remaining chapters of the course, you will come across more examples of hormonal function in regulation and control of physiological processes.

For example, the following chapter includes an examination of the hormonal control of growth, which relies on neuro-endocrine coordination. Therefore you should find it helpful to return to this chapter at various points to remind yourself of the anatomical and functional organization of the endocrine system, in particular the hypothalamic-pituitary axis.

Questions for Chapter 3

Question 3.1 (LOs 3.1 and 3.4)

Classify each of the following statements as true, partly true, or false. Write a brief explanation for your view.

(a) It would be expected that patients with Graves' disease would have high levels of TSH in their blood. *F. Antibodies mimic TSH, so TSH levels would be reduced due to high levels of thyroid hormones produced.*

(b) Growth hormone secretion from the anterior pituitary is inhibited by somatostatin (SIF) and stimulated by growth-hormone releasing hormone (GRH) both of which are secreted by the hypothalamus.

(c) Levels of glucose in the blood are controlled by positive feedback mechanisms involving the hormones insulin and glucagon.

(d) The hypothalamus is a part of the brain that contains neurosecretory neurons, which secrete neurohormones into the bloodstream from their axonal endings.

(e) The hormones FSH, LH and GH are secreted by the posterior pituitary gland.

(f) Cytokines are distinguishable from hormones because they have a local paracrine action and they are never released into the bloodstream.

Question 3.2 (LOs 3.3, 3.4 and 3.7)

Women who are infertile because of hypothalamic malfunction may be treated by administration of GnRH (gonadotropin-releasing hormone).

(a) Explain the rationale for administration of GnRH, by outlining the effects of the neurohormone on the pituitary and ovary.

(b) Why are daily single injections of GnRH ineffective?

Question 3.3 (LO 3.9)

Read through Sarah's case report (Cushing's syndrome), in Section 3.5.2 (Case Report 3.2). Using your knowledge of the hormonal effects of elevated plasma cortisol, explain the signs and symptoms that Sarah was experiencing.

Question 3.4 (LOs 3.5 and 3.7)

Explain how leptin controls: (i) the amount of stored lipid in adipose tissue; (ii) appetite.

Question 3.5 (LO 3.2)

Design and draw a flow chart that summarizes the roles of glucagon in increasing blood glucose and ketone levels during starvation.

Question 3.6 (LOs 3.1, 3.6 and 3.8)

Examine Figure 3.29a and b, which are summaries of measurements made on plasma samples from two volunteers taking a glucose tolerance test. Participant A was a 50-year-old postman of normal weight. Participant B was a 55-year-old office worker, who was obese. For the test, a participant starves for 10 hours and then takes a drink containing 75 g glucose. Samples of blood are taken at regular intervals for 2 hours, and analysed for glucose and insulin. Figure 3.29a and b include plotted values of blood glucose (solid green line) and blood insulin (broken brown line) measured against time.

(a) Describe the pattern of blood glucose, and insulin levels from time zero to 2 hours in participants A and B.

(b) Suggest an interpretation for the pattern of blood glucose and insulin levels in the blood of participants A and B.

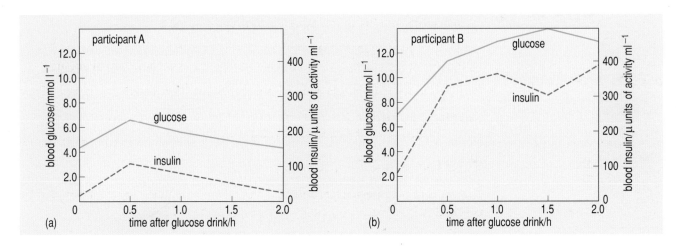

Figure 3.29   Results of glucose tolerance test: (a) Participant A; (b) Participant B. Blood glucose and insulin levels in patients receiving 75 g glucose drink at time zero.

Question 3.7 (LO 3.8)

List four factors that determine which target cells respond to a particular hormone, and the duration of the response.

References and Further Reading

References

Fisher, R. I., Rosenberg, S. A. and Fyfe, G. (2000) Long-term survival update for high-dose recombinant interleukin-2 in patients with renal cell carcinoma. *Cancer Journal from Scientific American*, **6**, Supplement 1, S55–S57.

Friedman, J. M. (2002) The function of leptin in nutrition; weight and physiology, *Nutrition Reviews*, **60**, Part 2, S1–S14.

Guerre-Millo, M. (2002) Adipose tissue hormones, *Journal of Endocrinological Investigation*, **25**, 855–861.

Ibelgauft, H. (2004) [online] Cytokines Online Pathfinder Encyclopaedia. Available from: http://www.copewithcytokines.de/cope.cgi [Accessed July 2004]

Mantzoros, C. S. (1999) The role of leptin in human obesity and disease: A review of current evidence, *Annals of Internal Medicine*, **130**, 671–680.

Newcombe, R. (2003) [online] HRT increases breast Cancer Risk BUPA Investigative News. Available from: http://www.bupa.co.uk/health_information/html/health_news/190803hrt.html [Accessed July 2004]

Rea, S. and James, D. E. (1997) Moving GLUT 4: The biogenesis and trafficking of GLUT 4 storage vesicles, *Diabetes*, **46**, 1667–1677.

Watson, R. T., Kanzaki, M. and Pessin, J. E. (2004) Regulated membrane trafficking of the insulin-responsive glucose transporter 4 in adipocytes, *Endocrine Reviews*, **25**, 177–204.

Further Reading

Berne, R. M. and Levy, M. N. (2000) *Principles of Physiology*. St Louis, MO: Mosby.

Johnson, M. H. and Everitt, B. J. (2000) *Essential Reproduction*, 5th edn. Oxford: Blackwell Science.

Vander, A., Sherman, J. and Luciano, D. (2001) *Human Physiology: The Mechanisms of Body Function*. Boston, MA: McGraw-Hill.

BODY ORGANIZATION AND GROWTH

Learning Outcomes

After completing this chapter, you should be able to:

4.1 List the main functions of the musculo-skeletal system.

4.2 Describe the processes of ossification, bone growth and bone healing.

4.3 Identify the many influences on growth and development and describe and explain the physical changes observed over an individual's lifespan.

4.4 Describe the structure and function of skeletal muscles and synovial joints.

4.5 Explain the role of the musculo-skeletal system and the consequences of bipedalism in the overall health and well-being of humans.

4.1 Introduction

At the end of the previous chapter, you were left racing across a meadow pursued by a bull, an experience that, with luck, few of you have actually experienced! Both nervous and endocrine systems were involved in coordinating your escape and contributed to the emotions you experienced. In describing that experience, the participation of one system was omitted. Being chased implies that you were running away and the activity of the muscles and bones (the **musculo-skeletal system**) in bringing about movement is arguably one of the most important of human activities. Indeed it has been suggested that the nervous system evolved as a consequence of the advantage that movement conferred on animals, i.e. an ability to move away from danger and toward sources of food and drink.

● Can you suggest any evidence to support this idea?

● Plants do not move around nor do they have a nervous system.

There is even a simple animal, known as a sea squirt, that swims around as a juvenile but as an adult attaches to a rock and moves no more. At this point its nervous system degenerates, there being no advantage to an animal in keeping a body system that is using energy but is no longer required.

The example of being chased by a bull may be extreme, but our ancestors, hunting in groups, may well have had similar unpleasant surprises and been glad of the way that their endocrine and nervous systems functioned in concert to prime the body to have the best chance of gaining safety. If you infrequently find yourself running to catch the last train home, your performance may impress you, and whilst recovering from the exertion you might reflect how well adapted we seem to be for making short sprints.

MUSCULO-SKELETAL SYSTEM:
▷ support (frame)
▷ Protection of organs
▷ Mineral storage
▷ Blood cell production
↳ long bones – marrow (red)

Although the function of the musculo-skeletal system is to enable movement via the action of muscles attached to the skeleton, it has four other functions, namely:

- as a supporting framework for the soft tissues and organs of the body;
- protecting delicate internal organs such as the lungs, heart, bladder, brain, etc.;
- storing minerals within bone tissue;
- producing blood cells from tissue (the marrow) found in the cavities of long bones (where lipids are also stored).

Each of these functions will be described.

Perhaps more than any other body system, the musculo-skeletal system is taken for granted until something happens to bring our attention to it. Most of us assume that we will be able to move freely and easily without pain, so that when we do suffer restricted movement it can affect our whole lives and well-being.

The growth of muscles and bones also defines various stages of human development. Parents keenly watch their children's increasing height. The rapid changes at adolescence signal the beginning of adulthood and can cause a great deal of self-consciousness. As the musculo-skeletal system is put under heavy, daily strain, signs of 'wear and tear' ageing are often first noticed in this system.

● Can you think of other instances during our lives when we might become more aware of our musculo-skeletal systems?

◐ Such instances include the following:

- People can suffer fractures (broken bones) and have reduced mobility whilst the bone heals.
- The musculo-skeletal system may be damaged during sporting or other strenuous activities, resulting in sprains, 'pulled' muscles and tendons, cramp, injured joints, etc.
- Many people suffer from back pain throughout their adult lives or at certain times of life, e.g. during pregnancy.

As we grow older, we may experience reduced mobility due to wear and tear at our joints (a type of arthritis) or reduced joint flexibility due to a decrease in the elasticity of certain tissues. Older people, especially women, often suffer from a 'thinning' of their bones, in which there is a decrease in the density of solid bone, which makes the bones prone to fractures. Literally, the bones become more porous, full of pores or spaces, causing a condition called osteoporosis. The condition of **osteoporosis** is said to exist when the level of bone density falls below a critical point (see Section 4.3).

Some working practices can cause or exacerbate musculo-skeletal disorders, e.g. heavy lifting or repetitive movement. In 2002 there were 8206 diagnoses of work-related musculo-skeletal disorders reported in the UK (**Annual Abstract of Statistics**). In 1994 the Clinical Standards Advisory Group on Back Pain reported that back pain alone affected 16.5 million people in the UK and cost the NHS in the order of £480 million. In 1998 40% of the adults that responded to the National Statistics Omnibus Survey said they had suffered back pain that had lasted for more than one day in the previous 12 months, whilst of those over 65 years of age, one in three men and one in four women had suffered persistent pain over the previous 12 months. Currently (2004) the Health and Safety Executive estimate that in 2001/02, 5.7 million working days were lost in the UK due to back pain that was caused by or made worse by work. This does not take into account injuries caused by leisure pursuits, e.g. sports, or by household or caring activities such as the frequent lifting of a house-bound person by their carer. Thus BUPA (a private health insurance organization) estimates that a total of 120 million working days are lost in the UK each year due to back pain. Many incidents of back pain or other injuries may go unreported to the medical profession or employers, as people suffer in silence for fear of losing their jobs, or seek treatment from complementary therapists.

● What is the significance of the under-reporting of musculo-skeletal problems?

● Health problems that go undiagnosed by the medical profession do not appear in official morbidity statistics (Book 1, Chapter 2). These statistics are used to assess and plan health care interventions in the population and as a result, inadequate resources may be allocated. Under-reporting of work-related disorders of the musculo-skeletal system will reduce concern about health and safety issues in certain workplaces.

Human health throughout the lifespan is thus closely related to the health or otherwise of the musculo-skeletal system. So an understanding of the structure and function of this system will be needed as background knowledge for discussions about health in many other parts of this course.

4.2 The pros and cons of standing on our own two feet

Most of the health problems associated with our musculo-skeletal systems, `outlined in the previous section, can be explained by the unique upright posture of humans standing on two legs (**bipedalism**) instead of four. Humans are permanently bipedal.

● Can you think what the advantages might be of an upright posture?

● Only two limbs are involved in standing and walking, leaving the other two free for carrying things, complex manipulations and tool use. The eyes are brought up higher into a highly mobile skull, which improves the ability to spot potential food or enemies from a distance. Some scientists have suggested that standing on two legs minimized the amount of the body exposed to the sun, an advantage on the hot plains of Africa where early humans began walking upright.

Whatever the trigger for bipedalism was, it arose very early on in our ancestry. Skeletons of our bipedal ape-like ancestors dated at about 3–4 million years old have been found in Africa. This indicates that there was a strong evolutionary advantage in this way of standing and moving.

We see, from the high occurrence of musculo-skeletal problems in humans, that standing on two legs has many disadvantages too. They can be summarized by saying that humans have problems with gravity.

BIPEDALISM
● ADVANTAGES
  – Free hands
  – Better visual range
  – less exposure to sun.
● DISADVANTAGES
  – Problems with gravity
    ↳ circulation (brain)
    ↳ uneven strain on spine
    ↳ balance
    ↳ Postural hypotension

Getting blood to the brain against gravity and bringing blood back from the lower body both cause problems. Compensating mechanisms have evolved, but these are not perfect. For example, varicose veins are the result of blood pooling in the superficial veins of the leg. The blood supply to the brain can be temporarily interrupted by standing up too quickly (postural fainting, also known as *postural hypotension*). The steroid hormone aldosterone (see Box 3.1 in the previous chapter) is secreted by the adrenal glands in response to physiological emergencies such as blood loss and acute anxiety. Interestingly, aldosterone is produced when we simply stand up. This is because standing causes blood to fall from the top of the body towards the feet. This sudden change in blood distribution is detected by receptors in the neck that are sensitive to blood pressure changes.

● What kind of change in blood pressure will be recorded, and why would it cause aldosterone to be secreted?

○ As blood falls toward the feet, the neck area will experience a temporary drop in blood pressure. This would be equivalent to losing blood through a severe cut, a physiological emergency which causes aldosterone to be secreted.

Production of aldosterone is then triggered and it causes a momentary rise in blood pressure to compensate. (You will learn more about the action of aldosterone in Book 3, Chapters 1 and 2.)

In animals that walk on four legs, the weight of the internal organs is evenly distributed alone the spine. When we are standing, on our two legs, there is considerable and uneven strain on the spine. The vertebrae become more and more compressed during the course of the day (we are taller in the morning than in the evening, due to the effects of gravity) and we lose height as we (and our spines) age. Sometimes the vertebral discs (fluid-filled 'cushions' of cartilage between the vertebrae; Figure 4.1a) burst under the pressure; this is what we call a slipped disc and it causes immobility and pain to the sufferer (Figure 4.1b). As humans evolved from partly bipedal ancestors, the pelvis (hip bone) developed wide 'blades', thereby giving support to the internal organs in the abdomen, such as the intestines, which are pulled downwards by gravity (Figure 4.1c).

Figure 4.1 (a) A normal disc. (b) A 'slipped disc' (a major cause of back pain) pressing against the spinal nerve and spinal cord. (c) The pelvis (hip bone) of a bipedal human. Ilium is the name given to the large flank of the pelvic girdle. The sacrum is formed by the fusion of five vertebrae, which is completed by early childhood.

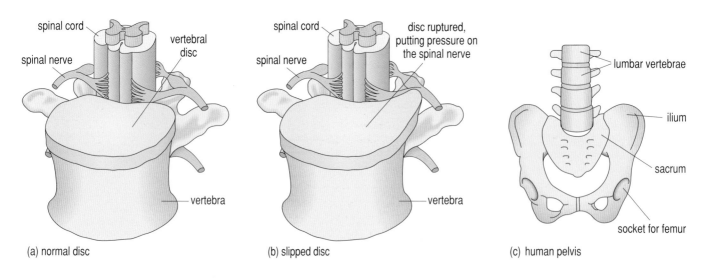

(a) normal disc

(b) slipped disc

(c) human pelvis

Sheets of muscle are wrapped around the abdominal organs, thus holding them in, but occasionally over-exertion can cause these sheets to rupture and part of the intestine can push through them, forming a lump under the skin; this is called a *hernia*.

Changes in pelvis shape, i.e. becoming shorter and more rounded, which facilitated bipedal walking, were balanced with the process of childbirth. The large heads of human babies have to rotate to pass through the birth canal. Childbirth is riskier for both mother and child in humans than in other primates.

Wear and tear in joints such as the hip and knee become more noticeable in later life, as do long-term stresses and strains on the spine. Many of these problems can be lessened by appropriate physical activity throughout life.

The disadvantages of bipedalism are numerous and they tend to accumulate and catch up with us in later life. We carry the 'scars of evolution' resulting from when, for some as yet unknown reason, it became advantageous for our ape-like ancestors to stand on their own two feet.

Summary of Sections 4.1 and 4.2

1   The musculo-skeletal system has five functions: movement, support, protection mineral storage and production of red blood cells.

2   Many health problems, for example spinal injury and varicose veins, arise as a consequence of bipedalism.

4.3 The skeleton

As the words of a well-known song tell us: 'The hip bone's connected to the thigh bone; the thigh bone's connected to the leg bone;…,' and so on. In fact, there are 206 bones all connected together in the human body and they are moved by around 700 muscles.

Human bones are made from an extremely hard substance that resists decay and so are one of the few body structures that remain after long-term burial. Studies of the bones of Ancient Egyptians or those from medieval graveyards have given us many clues about the diseases suffered by individuals in the past, as many diseases and disorders leave their mark on the skeleton, e.g. tuberculosis and arthritis. Recent laboratory techniques have also been developed that extract and examine the DNA present in ancient bones to study the process of human evolution.

The 206 bones in the skeleton are classified into two divisions, the **appendicular** and **axial** skeleton (Figure 4.2). The 126 bones that form the upper and lower limbs, the pelvic (hip) girdle and the pectoral (shoulder) girdle are part of the appendicular skeleton, whilst the 80 bones that form the axis of the body, such as the skull, ribcage and spine are part of the axial skeleton.

Bones are referred to both by their common names and by those derived from Latin names. For example, the collar-bone is also known as the clavicle, from the Latin *clavicula*, meaning 'little key', which this bone resembles. Furthermore, the thigh bone is known as the femur, whilst the shoulder blade is known as the scapula. It is not essential to learn the names of all the bones, but you should

[handwritten margin notes:]
SKELETON (206 bones):
• APPENDICULAR (126 bones)
  ↳ appendages
    ↳ e.g. -limbs,
      - pelvic girdle
      - shoulder girdle

• AXIAL (80 bones):
  ↳ axis
    ↳ e.g. -skull
      - ribcage
      - spine.

become familiar with the Latin names of the major ones, which are labelled in Figure 4.2 and have their common names in brackets.

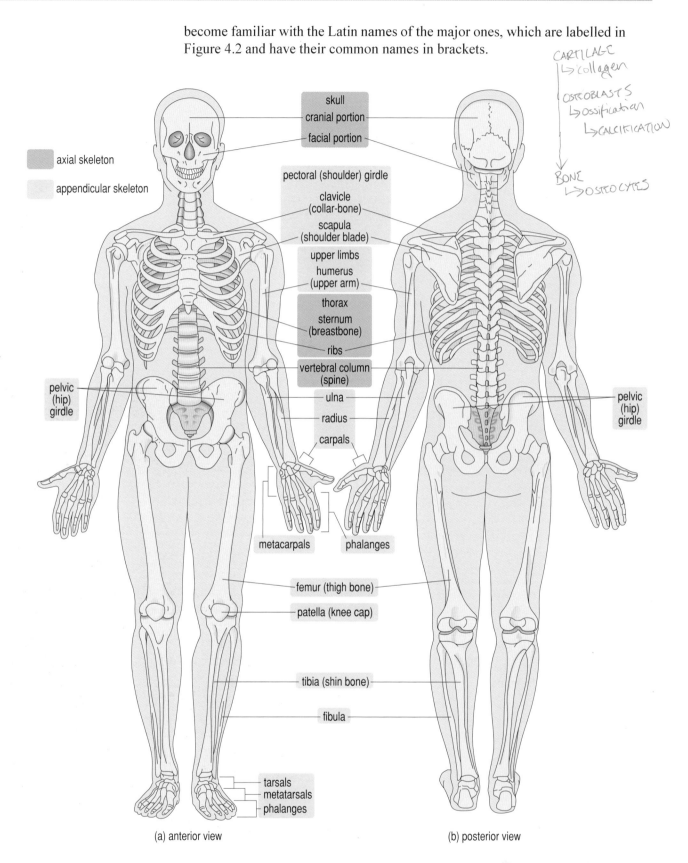

CARTILAGE
↳ collagen

OSTEOBLASTS
↳ ossification
  ↳ CALCIFICATION

↓

BONE
↳ OSTEOCYTES

Figure 4.2 The human skeleton, showing the axial and appendicular divisions. (a) Anterior (front) view; (b) posterior (back) view. Common names are in brackets.

The skeleton of a human embryo is made initially of **cartilage**, a strong and flexible tissue which can withstand considerable mechanical stress. Cartilage is a structural tissue made up of cartilage cells embedded in a matrix of a jelly-like substance that contains various fibrous proteins including collagen (Book 1, Chapter 2). The cartilage cells secrete the fibrous proteins and jelly-like substance.

In the seventh week of the embryo's development, the process of bone formation, known as ossification, begins. Gradually the older cartilage is replaced by hard, bone tissue. Certain cells become specialized to carry out the task of bone formation, and these are called **osteoblasts** (the prefix *os-* means that the word has something to do with bone). Osteoblasts secrete the protein collagen to form a framework of fibres into the spaces of which calcium and magnesium salts, especially phosphates, are deposited. It is these mineral salts that give bone its **hardness** (the tissue is said to have undergone **calcification**), whilst the collagen fibres give bone its ability to bend slightly and to resist stretching forces. Without the collagen framework, bone would be too brittle to perform its functions and would resemble egg shell, while without the mineral salts, bones would be too rubbery. The original osteoblasts get trapped in the newly forming bone and mature into **osteocytes** which are incapable of further cell division. Osteocytes remain in contact with each other in the bone via gap junctions (Book 1, Chapter 2), and these cells maintain the integrity of compact bone tissue by releasing calcium ions which arc incorporated into the tissue.

Flat bones, such as those that make up the skull, ribs and breastbone, go through a similar process of ossification but instead of starting from cartilage, they are formed on or within membranous sheets made from fibrous connective tissue.

If all the bones in the human body were formed from solid mineral material, they would be very heavy and would require considerably more muscle tissue to move them than humans normally possess. In fact, the shafts of the long bones of the skeleton (such as the thigh bone), which are the strongest parts of the bone, are hollow, with the outside of the shafts being made from dense **compact bone** with less dense **spongy bone** in the ends of the bones (Figures 4.3a and b). This structure maximizes strength and minimizes weight.

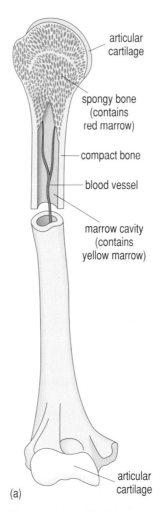

articular cartilage

spongy bone (contains red marrow)

compact bone

blood vessel

marrow cavity (contains yellow marrow)

articular cartilage

(a)

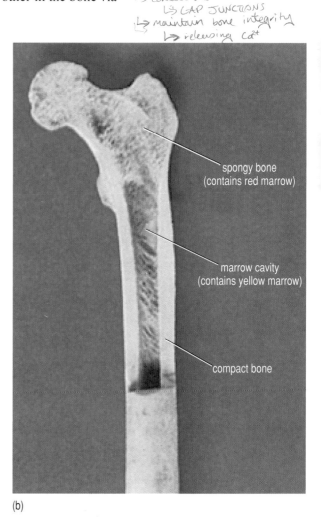

spongy bone (contains red marrow)

marrow cavity (contains yellow marrow)

compact bone

(b)

Figure 4.3 (a) Diagram and (b) photograph of a partially sectioned long bone (femur) showing its internal structure.

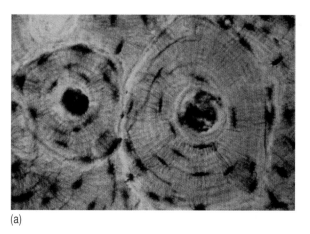
(a)

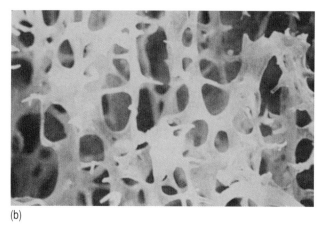
(b)

Figure 4.4   Microscopic structure of (a) compact bone and (b) spongy bone.

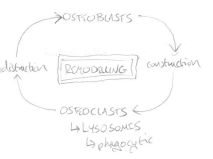

Compact bone is also found on the outside of all other bones and, seen under a microscope, this tissue is shown to be made from concentric rings of dense, calcified tissue within which osteocytes are trapped (Figure 4.4a). Spongy bone is made from a network of thin bony plates called **trabeculae** (Figure 4.4b). Trabeculae act like struts in a building and support the bone along lines of mechanical stress.

The spaces in the spongy bone are often filled with a tissue called red marrow. In adults, red marrow is the site for the production of blood cells. The hollow shafts of the long bones of adults also contain fatty tissue called yellow marrow, which is one of the fat stores of the body.

As humans develop, their skeletal system grows and develops. This growth and development process depends upon the combined activities of osteoblasts, which make new bone, and another cell type, **osteoclasts.**

● Osteoclasts contain many lysosomes and are phagocytic. What clue does this give you about their function? Hint: you met lysosomes first in Book 1, Chapter 2.

◐ Osteoclasts engulf fragments of bone and break them down within the lysosomes. Lysosomes contain protein-digesting enzymes, which enable osteoclasts to break down collagen. Acids present in the lysosomes also help to break down the mineral components of bone. So osteoclasts are involved in the destruction of bone material, whilst osteoblasts build it up.

During growth, bone develops into a hard and rigid material, but it is constantly being broken down by osteoclasts and undergoes **remodelling**. This process allows bones to be reshaped as they grow, so that bone shape and size are appropriate throughout childhood. In adult life too, bone tissue (in common with other tissues) is constantly being broken down and rebuilt. This process of remodelling in adults replaces old, worn-out bone tissue with new, helping to maintain the strength and health of the skeleton.

Healthy bones rely on a delicate, dynamic balance between construction and destruction. This is another example of homeostasis.

● What do you think might happen if either cell type became more active than the other?

○ Too much osteoblast activity would mean more bone tissue would be formed than could be removed and the bones would become thick and heavy. If this material was deposited as lumps and bumps on the bone, then the smooth movement of joints could be affected. If too much tissue was removed, the bones would become thin and brittle. (Imbalances between osteoblast and osteoclast activity occur in some human bone disorders and they have just these effects on bone structure.)

As well as in the remodelling which occurs throughout life, the activities of the osteoblasts and osteoclasts can be readily seen when a bone is broken. Firstly, the fracture leads to the severing of blood vessels around the breakage. A large blood clot forms around the fracture; this is called a **fracture haematoma** (Figure 4.5a).

● What is the function of a blood clot? (If you are unsure, look back at wound healing in Book 1, Section 2.10.)

○ It will prevent continued blood loss.

Case Report 4.1 Fractured neck of femur

Annie is a 78-year-old woman who was widowed 30 years ago and since has lived alone. She has a small council-owned flat on the second floor of a small block of similar flats. Annie likes a 'smoke' and has about 10 cigarettes a day usually whilst watching sport – especially horse racing – on television, though she also keenly follows the news. Annie has three children who live in other towns and who visit infrequently. In the past, Annie has used the train to visit her children and her nine grandchildren. She has guarded her independence fiercely, not wishing to burden her children but also having no desire to live with them. Annie has always prided herself on staying trim, but of recent years her body weight has become low. She now visits the local shops less frequently than she used to, because last winter she fell on her way to the shops. Although she did not sustain anything other than cuts and bruises, Annie felt her confidence in going out of the flat diminishing. This was compounded by her failing eyesight, and in the back of her mind was the fact her own mother had fractured her hip in the later years of her life.

Mindful that she must maintain a healthy diet, Annie went shopping for food and on her return fell very heavily on her left hip as she was climbing up the concrete steps to her flat. A neighbour found Annie, called the ambulance, and Annie was taken to a nearby hospital. On arrival, Annie was examined and her left leg was found to be shortened and externally rotated. An X-ray was taken and Annie was diagnosed as having sustained a fractured neck of femur. Her leg was immobilized and pain relief in the form of morphine plus an anti-emetic (an anti-sickness drug) given. It was explained to Annie that she would need an operation to fix her fracture and that would involve internally fixing the fracture with a dynamic hip screw or a prosthetic replacement (i.e. an artificial hip joint).

To the person with the broken bone, the symptoms are obviously pain, swelling, redness and heat around the site of the break as blood flows into the area. The ends of the bone can be re-aligned manually before the whole area is immobilized. For distal limb regions (i.e. those furthest from the torso), this may involve a plaster cast, but for others, such as the neck of the femur (near the pelvis), the bone will be secured by internal fixation and a plaster cast is

Distal – furthest from torso

impractical. In order to carry out these procedures, the individual is usually given a local or a general anaesthetic. As well as the obvious benefit of pain relief, the anaesthetic is often necessary to prevent the strong, regular muscle spasms that frequently accompany a fracture. The spasms occur in the immediate vicinity of the broken bone and make it impossible to re-set the bone accurately.

Most people think of broken bones as being the result of an accident of some sort (Case Report 4.1). This is indeed the most frequent cause, particularly in young people. The fracture is known as a *simple* (or *closed*) *fracture* if the bone ends are not visible but it is termed a *compound* (or *open*) *fracture* if the bone ends have broken through the skin. Recall that this terminology is used for head injuries too (Section 1.11). It is often the case that a fracture occurs because the bone has been weakened by disease such as cancer or, in older people, osteoporosis; in this case, the fracture is classified as a *pathological fracture*.

Once the person with the broken bone has been treated, they have to rest the area affected. For fractures of the upper arm and clavicle, the treatment may be using a sling. The body as a whole is not resting; various body processes continue around the fracture that actively mend and remodel the broken bone. Phagocytic cells in the blood and osteoclasts remove the cellular and bony debris and new blood vessels grow into the haematoma over the next few weeks (Figure 4.5b). This is a similar process to that found in the healing of skin wounds.

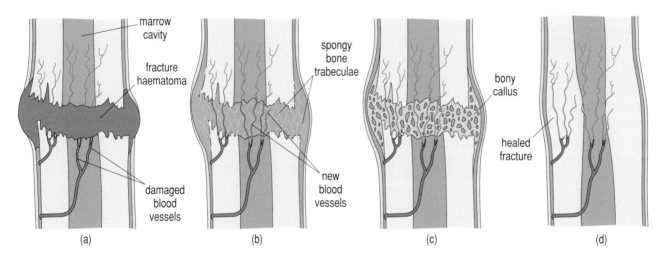

marrow cavity

fracture haematoma

damaged blood vessels

spongy bone trabeculae

new blood vessels

bony callus

healed fracture

(a) (b) (c) (d)

Figure 4.5   (a) A blood clot forms at the site of the fracture, the fracture haematoma. (b) Cells from the blood and from the ends of the broken bone form a bridge of cartilage and spongy bone between the bone ends. (c) Cartilage is replaced by more spongy bone. (d) Compact bone replaces the spongy bone around the edge of the fracture and the bone is remodelled into its original shape.

The haematoma changes into **granulation tissue**. Granulation tissue is important in all cases of tissue healing; remember its function in the healing of skin wounds. Granulation tissue contains many tiny, newly formed blood vessels and is a sign of a rapidly healing wound. Fibroblasts (Book 1, Section 2.9.4) begin to lay down a network of collagen fibres across the fracture, and other cells (called chondroblasts) produce a fibrous cartilage. The ends of the bone are now connected by this fibrous pad of tissue called a **callus**, which lasts for about three weeks. Osteoblasts begin to build a web of spongy bone throughout this pad, gradually changing it into a bony pad in a process lasting three to four months

(Figure 4.5c). Slowly the spongy bone is replaced with compact bone around the shaft of the bone and osteoclasts 'trim' away excess bony callus until the area of broken bone is usually indistinguishable from the surrounding bone, even in an X-ray (Figure 4.5d). If a plaster cast has been used to immobilize the fractured bone until it has healed sufficiently for the person to have regained the use of that part of their body, the area around the fracture often has a 'wasted' look due to lack of use of the surrounding muscles during the healing process. Patients are encouraged to maintain as much activity as they can whilst the healing process is ongoing, so that complications such as stiffness of joints are avoided.

Despite the best of care, complications can still occur. Particularly when a long bone such as the femur is fractured, there may be considerable loss of blood.

● Why might a fracture to the shaft of a femur cause this particular problem?

◐ Aside from the loss of blood which would occur if the fractured bone penetrated adjacent blood vessels, there could be loss of red blood cells from the red marrow of this long bone.

Additionally, after a fracture, bits of the fatty tissues of the yellow marrow can enter the circulatory system as a fat **embolus** (a freely circulating blood clot). Should these then block vessels, the condition is very serious. (More will be said about this in Book 3, Chapter 2.)

In young children, where the bones are not fully calcified, bones break with a *greenstick* fracture; they break just like a green, flexible piece of wood, with just one side of the wood breaking and the other bending (Figure 4.6).

The healing of fractures happens quickly in the young, but occurs more slowly as we get older. The slow healing of fractures in older people can be due to poor blood supply to the affected area, the reduced capacity of tissues for repair, or poor nutrition (see later in Section 4.4.4).

As well as healing rapidly, the bones of the young also grow rapidly. This is the topic of the next section.

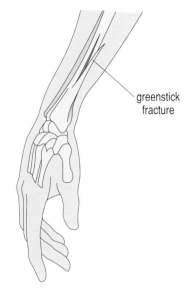

greenstick fracture

Figure 4.6 Children's bones often break with a greenstick fracture as their bones are still fairly flexible and not fully calcified.

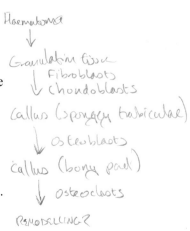

[handwritten margin notes:]
healing ∝ age
time

{ poor blood supply
reduced tissue capacity
poor nutrition

Haematoma
↓
Granulation tissue
  Fibroblasts
↓ chondoblasts
Callus (spongey trabecular)
  ↓ osteoblasts
Callus (bony part)
  ↓ osteoclasts
REMODELLING?

Summary of Section 4.3

1 The 206 adult human bones are made by progressive calcification, i.e. the deposition of calcium and magnesium salts into the embryonic cartilage skeleton, to form an extremely hard and durable material that resists decay.

2 Bony tissue is found in two forms, compact and spongy bone. Compact bone forms the outside of the shafts of long bones whilst spongy bone is found in the ends of these bones. Large bones are hollow, thus reducing their weight and allowing the storage of red and yellow marrow.

3 Bone is a living tissue which is constantly being broken down, built up and remodelled. Osteoblasts build up bone, eventually becoming trapped within the tissue and maturing into osteocytes. Osteoclasts break down bone tissue. Healthy bone relies on a balance between the activities of osteoblasts and osteoclasts.

4 Broken bones are healed by a process involving phagocytic cells, fibroblasts, chondroblasts, osteoblasts and osteoclasts.

4.4 Growth in the musculo-skeletal system

4.4.1 Growth in height

We are all familiar with the rapid growth in height that occurs in children, registered by the frequent measurements made by their parents against the doorposts of the house. Rapid increases in height during childhood and adolescence are due to rapid increases in the growth of bones such as the femur (thigh bone). Long bones like the femur grow in length by the rapid division of a zone of cartilage cells at the ends of each shaft, called **epiphyseal plates** or growth plates (Figure 4.7a and b). New cartilage cells secrete matrix, including collagen, which is subsequently calcified, then broken down and replaced by new bone.

Figure 4.7 X-rays showing epiphyseal or growth plates (arrows) in the lower femur (thigh bone) and the upper tibia (the shin bone) of the knee of a young child. (a) Front view. (b) Lateral view.

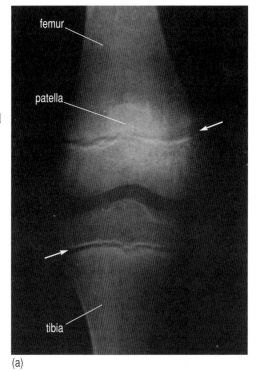
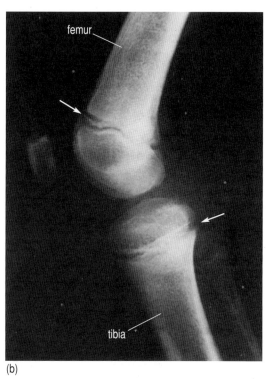

(a) (b)

Humans usually stop growing in height during early adulthood, around 16–18 years of age in females and 18–21 in males. Long bones stop growing as the cartilaginous epiphyseal plates become solid bone; the plates are 'closed'. All of the cartilage that formed the early skeleton is now replaced with bone, except for that found in joints where one bone moves (articulates) against another (see Figure 4.3a).

Testosterone

Height charts (i.e. graphs of height against age) are used by those interested in child health, as growth in height can be influenced by many factors. These charts are constructed from height measurements on large groups of children (1000+) that have been collected in prescribed ways so as to minimize any errors in measurements taken by different people. There is great individual variation in height – even in children of the same age – and to indicate this, a range is shown on the chart (Figure 4.8). Boys and girls show growth spurts at different ages and at different rates, so separate charts are constructed for each sex.

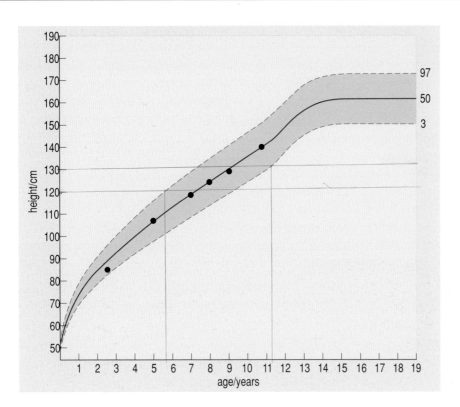

Figure 4.8 A height against age chart for girls, with a number of actual measurements of a child (indicated by the filled circles) included to nearly the age of 11.

The lower end of the range (labelled 3) indicates that only 3% of children in the group used to construct (plot) the chart had heights below that line, whilst the line labelled 97 shows that 97% of the group had heights below that line.

The measurements of the child in Figure 4.8 follow the line marked '50'. This indicates that her growth was near normal in that it followed that of the average height of the group of children used to construct the chart.

Bearing in mind the discussion in Book 1 about variation and evolution, reflect on the use of the word 'normal' in relation to children's growth.

Individual children's growth plots show great variation, as their growth rates can increase and decrease erratically. Many parents worry if their children's growth plots lag behind those of the others around them, but there can be large variations in growth without there being any cause for concern about the health of the child. Using the word 'normal' to indicate the average value gives the false impression that other values must be abnormal.

In our society, there is a social stigma attached to being 'too short' (especially for men) or 'too tall' (especially for women). Anyone deviating from the 'normal' range of heights can find simple life activities such as shopping for clothes or shoes very difficult. Many people equate lack of height with a lack of power or character and people who are shorter than average complain of 'heightism'.

4.4.2 Genetics and height

It is not surprising that genes should influence height. All body cells carry information needed for their proper functioning, in the form of genes (Book 1, Chapter 2). As can be seen by the number of body systems mentioned in this chapter, many cell types are involved in human growth in height and so the interaction of genes in this process will necessarily be complex. Genetic influences on growth interact with many environmental factors, so it is difficult, and perhaps counterproductive, to try to isolate genetic from other influences on growth. Defects in single genes or gene groups can have devastating effects on growth in height, as in *achondroplasia,* a condition caused by a mutation in a single gene. In this condition, the normal process of long bone growth does not occur, there is a disruption in the growth of cartilage and stature is much reduced (adult height reaching only 120–130 cm).

● Why would a disruption in cartilage growth affect long bone growth?

○ The growth of cartilage and its calcification, subsequent destruction and replacement by bone at the epiphyseal plates in long bones is the process that elongates these bones and causes an increase in overall height.

● Use Figure 4.8 to find out over what range of ages girls reach heights of 120–130 cm.

○ There is a large age range. A few girls as young as six are already 120 cm in height; on average, by the age of nine, girls are about 130 cm tall, but a few do not reach this height until around 12 years old.

Furthermore, studies on twins with identical sets of genes (known as **monozygotic twins** because the two individuals have developed in one uterus from a single zygote as a result of the separation of the embryo after the two-cell stage) have shown that differences between individuals in body shape, size, fat deposition and overall growth patterns are strongly influenced by genetic constitution. Twin studies attempt to discriminate between genetic factors and environmental factors when looking at specific aspects of human biology and behaviour, separating the influences of nature and nurture (Book 1, Chapter 1). Identical twins that have been separated at birth and brought up separately are studied to see if they develop similar or different traits. If the two twins share similar characteristics even though they grew up in different environments, then those characteristics are likely to have a strong genetic element. Twin studies into the genetics of height have shown that identical twins (who share the same genes) have similar heights whether brought up together or apart, i.e. whether or not they grew up in different environments. This shows that there is a considerable genetic element determining height in humans.

4.4.3 Hormones and growth

The rapid growth in height and in shoulder and hip girth in adolescents, the 'growth spurt', is due to an increased production of hormones.

● What are the defining characteristics of hormones?

○ Hormones are substances secreted by certain organs into the bloodstream in which they circulate around the body. They are 'chemical messengers' which target and alter the physiology of certain tissues.

● What name do we give to the organs that produce hormones?

● Hormone-producing organs are known as endocrine glands.

These glands, the hormones themselves and the receptors to which the hormones bind are collectively known as the *endocrine system* and were discussed in detail in the previous chapter.

Many of the hormones produced in adolescence promote bone growth. Some hormones also encourage the release or accumulation of minerals from bone tissue.

● What are the two main minerals found in bone?

● Calcium and magnesium salts, particularly phosphates, are found in bone tissue (Section 4.3).

Parathyroid hormone promotes the breakdown of bone by osteoclasts, thereby playing a crucial role in controlling bone remodelling during growth, and also throughout life. By encouraging the breakdown of bone by osteoclasts, parathyroid hormone causes the release of calcium, magnesium and phosphate into the bloodstream. A constant level of calcium in the blood is required by the body, as fluctuations in the blood calcium level can affect breathing and heart rate. (Calcium is also involved in the process of muscle contraction – Section 4.7.)

● What other process requires the participation of calcium ions?

● Neurotransmission at chemical synapses (Section 1.9.2). constant variable

Nerve, muscle and enzyme function depend on a constant calcium blood level as does blood clotting (Book 3, Chapter 2). When too much calcium is detected in the blood, levels of parathyroid hormone drop. This inhibits the activity of osteoclasts and encourages calcium deposition in bone, resulting in a lowering of blood calcium levels. Together with other mechanisms, which you will meet in the chapter on the kidney (Book 3, Chapter 1), this hormone regulates blood calcium levels within tight limits, using the skeletal bone tissue as a mineral reservoir.

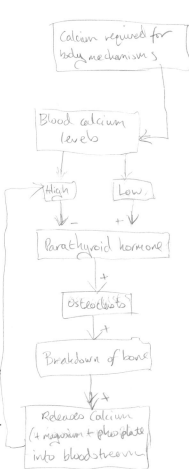

Sketch out two flow charts showing the sequence of events linking the detection of (a) low calcium ion levels and (b) high calcium ion levels in the blood to the production of parathyroid hormone.

(See top of p.148 for answer.)

● This effect of calcium levels on parathyroid hormone secretion is an example of what type of control in the body?

● It is an example of a negative feedback control system. A regulated variable (blood calcium level) is held close to a constant value by actions (initiated here by parathyroid hormone) that tend to eliminate any deviation from that constant value.

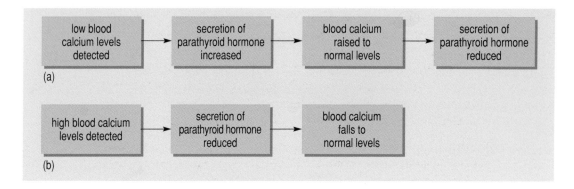

(a)

(b)

During childhood and adolescence, the major hormone involved in controlling bone growth is *growth hormone*, GH. During puberty blood levels of growth hormone and IGF-1 are at their peak. When a child shows continued lack of growth in height, with measurements falling substantially outside the normal range of height for children of comparable age and the same sex, it may become necessary to consider administering GH. This procedure will then increase the rate of growth, if the child is not producing enough hormone naturally.

● Which organ releases GH?

● GH is released from the anterior pituitary gland (see Chapter 3, Table 3.2).

So what are the mechanisms by which GH promotes growth? GH has general effects on most body tissues, causing an increased rate of cell division and stimulating body cells to take up amino acids rapidly from the bloodstream. The cells, particularly those in the bones and muscles, use these amino acids to build proteins and new cells. GH promotes the breakdown of lipids stored in adipose tissue, thereby providing other tissues with fatty acids as an energy source, so conserving carbohydrates and proteins. Many of the effects of GH depend on this hormone stimulating the liver to produce small protein signalling molecules called *insulin-like growth factors* (IGFs), which you met in the previous chapter.

● Where and how does IGF-1 act to affect growth (Section 3.8)?

● IGF-1 stimulates cartilage cell proliferation in epiphyseal growth plates.

● Up to what point in an individual's life can GH be administered?

● GH has to be given to the child before the epiphyseal plates fuse, otherwise no increase in bone length can be achieved.

GH was originally prepared by extracting it from its site of production, the pituitary glands, taken from the brains of human corpses (up to 3000 glands were used for one batch of GH). This unfortunately led to some of the batches of hormone becoming contaminated with an 'infectious protein' (now called a *prion*) that causes a condition called Creutzfeldt–Jakob disease (CJD). CJD is a slow degenerative disease of the brain which has an average incubation time of 15 years, i.e. it takes 15 years or more for symptoms to develop from the initial infection. CJD is incurable and inevitably leads to death. Because of the long incubation time, some of the pituitary glands used to make GH were infected with the causative agent of CJD, without there having been any signs of the disease in the person from whom the gland was taken. The large number of glands needed to provide enough GH for medical uses meant that infected tissue was mixed with uninfected tissue, so many batches of GH were contaminated. This resulted in CJD cases much later on in the life of the treated children.

The extraction of GH from human sources was stopped in 1985, but the long incubation period meant that cases continued to arise. GH is now produced by bacteria into which the gene coding for GH has been introduced by genetic engineering. The bacteria are cheap and easy to grow and can produce large quantities of GH. Thus GH treatment is now safe and easily available. The disadvantage of this type of GH treatment is that it is not now restricted to severely under-height children and the hormone is commonly used in the USA to boost the height of children who would not be medically diagnosed as too short for their age but are deemed by their parents to be suffering from psychosocial disadvantages compared to their taller contemporaries. The long-term effects of treating children who are 'socially' diagnosed as being too short, with GH is unknown but the wide range of effects this hormone has on the body may indicate that many physiological problems might arise in the future due to such GH abuse.

What questions does this over-use of GH by those who can afford the treatment raise in your mind?

There are questions about the ethics of treating children with a hormone that has unknown long-term effects, for a condition that is socially, rather than medically, defined. It also raises issues around what is normal or abnormal height. Where is the dividing line? How does someone's height affect the way others react to them? Under what circumstances should GH be given to a child whose height measurements were not substantially below those of their contemporaries? Should an ability to pay for this hormone mean that treatment can take place? Or should the decision be made on other criteria?

There are no easy answers to these questions. However, intriguingly, studies have found that taller than average men have more children than men of average height (Pawlowski et al., 2000) and a decreased chance (at least in the UK) of going through life without having had a major relationship (Nettle, 2002). The former observation has implications for biological fitness (Book 1, Section 1.4.2) and the latter is relevant because a great many studies have shown that married people tend to live longer than their unmarried peers.

Other hormones involved in the growth of the musculo-skeletal system are those produced by the **thyroid gland**. The thyroid gland is a small, butterfly-shaped gland which sits below the larynx (voice box) at the front of the throat. It produces a number of hormones that are important for growth and development.

● From the previous chapter recall the names of two of these hormones.

● Thyroxin (also known as tetra-iodothyronine) and **tri-iodothyronine** are secreted by the thyroid gland.

These small molecules are derived from the amino acid tyrosine combined with atoms of the element iodine. This element is found in traces in our diets and is essential to the correct functioning of the thyroid gland. In some countries, iodine is lacking in the diet and people's thyroid glands are unable to make thyroid hormones (thyroxin and tri-iodothyronine). As you have read earlier, the anterior pituitary gland, continually stimulates the thyroid by producing thyroid-stimulating hormone (TSH). In response to chronic stimulation by TSH, the thyroid glands of these people enlarge but cannot produce the hormones without an adequate supply of iodine. This condition is known as goitre (shown in the previous chapter, Figure 3.12).

● What is the major effect of thyroid hormones?

● Thyroid hormones raise the metabolic rate of the body and are involved in temperature regulation.

The metabolic effects of thyroid hormones are to increase protein synthesis (e.g. collagen synthesis by osteoblasts in growing bone), the breakdown of storage lipids and the use of glucose to produce ATP, thus aiding the body's growth processes. These varied effects are brought about as a consequence of the hormones stimulating the transcription of genes (Book 1, Chapter 2). Receptors for the hormones may interact directly with the DNA to initiate transcription of a wide variety of genes and thereby increase protein synthesis in cells.

Thyroid hormones are crucial to the development of an infant's brain and lack of them in early life can cause mental retardation and restricted growth. Adults too can suffer from underproduction (hypothyroidism) as well as overproduction (hyperthyroidism) of thyroid hormones.

● What are the symptoms of these two conditions, and how do these symptoms relate to the effects that thyroid hormones have on the body's metabolism?

● Adults with hypothyroidism have a low body temperature, general lethargy and a tendency to put on weight, all of which are the effects of a slowing down of the body's metabolic rate. In cases of hyperthyroidism, the symptoms are those of an increased metabolism, where the cells of the body need an increased supply of oxygen and nutrients, e.g. high body temperature, increased respiration rate, hyperactivity and loss of weight despite a good appetite (Section 3.1 of the previous chapter).

Other hormones that have a major influence on growth and development are the sex hormones. Oestrogens and testosterone increase the activity of osteoblasts and thus promote the rapid bone growth seen at puberty. They also cause the epiphyseal cartilage to calcify, so eventually stopping the elongation of the long bones and further growth in height. People who take anabolic steroids (which mimic testosterone activity) before puberty to enhance muscle growth, e.g. some young weight-lifters and athletes, can develop a premature calcification of their epiphyseal cartilage and their growth is therefore stunted. The horrific effects of long-term usage of anabolic steroids at high dosage were described in the previous chapter in relation to athletes from former communist East Germany (Section 3.1).

4.4.4 Nutrition and growth

If the human body is to grow, develop and function correctly over its life-time, it must have the necessary nutrients with which to produce, maintain and repair the fabric of the body. These nutrients come from the breakdown of food by the digestive system into small molecules, as was described in Book 1, Chapter 4. These small molecules can be used by cells as the building blocks for the synthesis of proteins, nucleic acids, lipids and other large molecules required for growth. Cells also break down molecules such as glucose and fatty acids and convert the energy released into ATP. The energy required for chemical reactions in cells, such as the synthesis of large molecules, is provided in a usable form by ATP.

● Name the six key nutrient groups.

○ Nutrients are classified into six groups: carbohydrates, lipids, proteins, vitamins, minerals and water.

● Which two of these groups are required in small amounts? What collective name is used for them?

○ Vitamins and some minerals are often called micronutrients because they are required by the body in very small amounts.

Elements such as calcium and iron are required in larger amounts than elements such as zinc and iodine, which are called trace elements as only minute quantities are needed in the diet (Tables 3.11 and 3.12 in Book 1, Chapter 3).

Adequate nutrition for growth and maintenance of the body throughout the lifespan is not simply getting enough energy (calories) but obtaining the full range of nutrients outlined in the COMA report (Book 1, Chapter 3). Calories are a measure of the amount of energy that the body can obtain from certain foods, e.g. lipids are high-calorie or energy-dense foods, as they provide the body with a concentrated source of energy. A survey, carried out in 1995, showed that children who were receiving 30% of their daily energy intake solely from sugary drinks had poor appetites, diarrhoea and poor weight gain (Hourihane and Rolles, 1995). These children were obtaining large amounts of calories but only from one source, refined sugar. Their diets lacked many of the other essential ingredients of a healthy diet.

Skeletal growth obviously needs an adequate dietary supply of the mineral constituents of bone tissue, i.e. calcium, magnesium and phosphorus, as well as trace elements which influence osteoblast activity. Vitamins such as vitamin A, C, D and B_{12} are also essential to bone growth. Vitamin A affects the development of the skeletal system in children as it influences the activity of osteoblasts and osteoclasts.

● Under what other conditions is a good diet important for bone growth?

○ A good diet is essential for bone healing. (The link between a good diet and wound healing was first mentioned in Book 1, Section 2.11.)

[handwritten margin note:]
THYROID GLAND
↳ Thyroxin (T4)
↳ Tri-iodotyrinine (T3)
↳ Calcitonin
↳ Parathyroid?

A lack of vitamin D in children's diet causes the bone disorder of rickets. Rickets was commonly seen in the past in children whose diet was inadequate in vitamin D and whose living conditions did not allow them adequate exposure to sunlight, as vitamin D is also formed by the action of sunlight on human skin. This vitamin aids the absorption of calcium from the gut into the bloodstream and influences many other aspects of bone growth. Children who were deficient in vitamin D developed leg bones that were characteristically bowed inwards to give a 'knock-kneed' posture. The leg bones were not rigid enough – due to too little deposition of calcium in the bone tissue – to withstand the weight of the body. In the second half of the 20th century, rickets was an extremely rare condition in the UK due to improved diets and living conditions. However, a survey carried out in the early 1990s, of children aged 1.5 to 4.5 years throughout the UK found that some were deficient in vitamin D, especially in the dark months of winter (MAFF and Department of Health (DoH) Social Survey Division of the Office of Population Censuses and Surveys (OPCS) and Medical Research Council (MRC) Dunn Nutrition Unit, 1995).

● Name a type of diet that would increase the risk of a child developing rickets.

○ There is concern for those on vegetarian diets (which may be low in vitamin D), particularly if they are living in parts of the country with few hours of sunlight (Book 1, Section 3.7.4).

This stresses the importance of a varied and balanced diet for children, as well as outdoor activity to ensure exposure to sunlight. There is a group of children for whom there are particular difficulties, as was revealed by an American study of infants and children with rickets (Kreiter et al., 2000).

● All the patients were African American children living in North Carolina; what particular problem do you suppose they have?

○ They all have dark skin colour but are living outside of the tropics. The skin pigmentation acts as a barrier to the sunlight, and in North Carolina there is insufficient sunlight available for them to be able to manufacture vitamin D.

Bones respond to the mechanical stress of exercise by increasing the amount of collagen produced and the amount of mineral salts deposited onto the collagen fibres, thus increasing overall bone density. Humans who remain inactive for long periods of time or are not subjected to the usual stress of movement against gravity, e.g. astronauts in weightless conditions and some elderly people, lose minerals and collagen from their bones.

● Can you name another group of people who are inactive over prolonged periods?

○ People who are confined to bed. Therefore in cases where fractured bones are involved, early mobilization is be encouraged wherever possible.

Mechanical stress also increases the production of the hormone **calcitonin**.

● Which gland produces calcitonin and what is the role of this hormone?

○ Calcitonin is secreted from the thyroid gland and it acts to keep calcium in the bones.

In fact, calcitonin inhibits bone destruction by osteoclasts by reducing resorption of calcium from bones and so causes more bone to be built up than lost.

Bone mass declines with age in both men and women. This is a result of mineral loss and a reduction of the organic matrix of bone.

● Which element is of greatest importance in providing the strength that we associate with bone?

○ Calcium.

The loss of calcium results in a reduction of bone density. In compact bone, the rate of bone loss exceeds the rate of deposition of new material, so that the outer shell of bone becomes thinner. Trabecular bone loses the horizontal spars of the reinforcing network, thus weakening the bone. A major determinant of bone mass in old age is the amount of bone at maturity. Also, the rate of bone loss with age varies from person to person.

There is tremendous individual variability; in fact, some older people have more bone than younger people. The underlying factor responsible for the loss of calcium from bones seems to be age-related changes in calcium metabolism. Older people absorb less of the calcium that they consume in their diet, owing to age-associated changes in the absorptive cells lining the gut (Book 1, Chapter 4). In addition, they often suffer from vitamin D deficiency.

● Why might an older person suffer from vitamin D deficiency?

○ There are two possible sources of vitamin D. It can be absorbed from food, so changes in the cells lining the gut will result in less efficient uptake of vitamins from the diet. Alternatively, it can be manufactured in the skin using sunlight to activate this synthesis. Many older people spend less time in the open air; as a result of this, and also because of changes in the skin, they could fail to obtain adequate amounts of vitamin D from this source.

● In what way is vitamin D deficiency relevant to a discussion of bone loss?

○ Vitamin D facilitates the transport of calcium through the lining of the small intestine into the blood, and it controls the deposition of calcium in bones. So a reduction in available vitamin D results in the slowing down of new bone growth to replace old bone as it is destroyed.

Reduction in bone mass is much more frequently a problem for women. In general, men have greater bone mass in early adulthood than do women. Relative bone mass decreases faster with age in women than in men, with an abrupt increase in rate of loss at menopause. This fact and the greater longevity of women means that more women than men reach the age at which their skeleton has become very fragile. Changes in calcium metabolism are more pronounced in post-menopausal women than they are in men of the same age. Older women excrete more calcium in their urine than they take in from their diet, because calcium is withdrawn from their bones.

Age-associated changes in bones can pose a serious threat to health, especially in women.

● What is the name of the condition where the level of bone mass falls below a critical point.

● Osteoporosis.

● What susceptibility is associated with osteoporosis?

● People with osteoporosis have an increased risk of fractures.

In some research studies, treatment with oestrogen (hormone replacement therapy, HRT) has had a beneficial effect on calcium balance, and has reduced the rate at which bone density was lost in older women. However, the results are contradicted by other studies and so the use of HRT remains controversial. Half an hour's brisk exercise daily is reported to reduce bone loss in post-menopausal women and ensuring adequate dietary calcium is also a sensible measure. There is no firm consensus over what 'adequate' might be! But as a guide, a pint of skimmed milk contains about 700 mg of calcium which should meet the daily needs of most older people.

To conclude, a good diet – together with exercise and exposure to sunlight – is all essential to healthy bone growth and maintenance, especially in the young and the elderly. However, these environmental conditions are often lacking for children growing up in conditions of material and emotional poverty and may be difficult to achieve in later life too.

4.4.5 Psychological factors and growth

Emotional disturbance can give rise to what is termed 'non-organic failure to thrive'. An organic failure to thrive is due to a physiological problem that inhibits growth, whereas a non-organic failure is due to social or psychological problems. Emotional neglect seems to act by suppressing the production of GH and by stimulating or enhancing the production of hormones that slow down growth. Emotional neglect and abuse may also involve malnutrition of the children involved, which will also affect their growth.

Emotional disturbance can be linked to families living under the conditions of poverty, over-crowding and unemployment. Thompson and Kaplan (1996, p. 144) state that 'Appropriate emotional provision is required for children to reach their full potential for physical growth'.

Psychosocial factors
• Emotional disturbance
↳ poverty, over-crowding etc
• Emotional neglect/abuse
inhibit growth hormone
↳ "Non-organic failure to thrive"
(also malnutrition)

Summary of Section 4.4

1　The rapid growth in height seen in children is due to the progressive elongation of long bones such as the femur. Elongation takes place at the cartilaginous junction, called the **epiphyseal plates**, between the bone shaft and bone ends.

2　Records of a child's height kept over several years can give information about that child's health and development.

3　There is a strong **genetic element** influencing height and overall growth patterns, although **environmental factors** such as nutrition, social class and emotional neglect also influence growth.

4　Various hormones influence growth and development, especially growth hormone. Growth hormone is now more readily available to treat children with reduced growth, whether that is medically or socially defined.

5　Diet and exercise can help reduce bone loss and the associated risk of developing osteoporosis in the elderly. Diet, exercise and various psychosocial factors also influence children's growth.

4.5 Changes in body shape and posture

Just as there are periods of rapid and periods of slow growth in height, the different parts of the body also grow at different rates. This leads to the obvious changes in body shape and posture that occur from birth to adolescence (Figure 4.9).

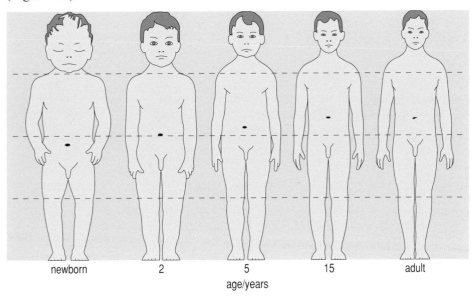

newborn　　　2　　　　5　　　　15　　　　adult

age/years

Figure 4.9　Changes in body proportions with age. The relative size of the head and the position of the midpoint of the body (indicated by the middle line) change dramatically.

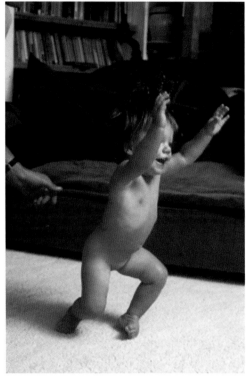

Figure 4.10 Toddlers are top-heavy, causing them to walk unsteadily and fall frequently.

● What are the changes in body proportion shown in Figure 4.9?

◐ The length of the head is a quarter of the length of the body at birth but changes to an eighth of the length of the adult body. The lower limbs are relatively short at birth but grow extensively to contribute nearly half of an adult's height.

A toddler's liver is a relatively large organ and also contributes to the large upper body weight. The bladder is found in the upper abdomen (the area below the lungs and above the pelvis) in infancy but descends into the pelvic area as the pelvis grows. This **upper concentration of weight** due to a large head and upper body means that a toddler is 'top-heavy' (Figure 4.10) and this contributes to their characteristically unstable walking and frequent falls.

The differential rates of bodily growth are seen especially at adolescence where the feet and hands grow in size before the rest of the body, giving the characteristic 'gangly youth' appearance. When the limbs and the rest of the body 'catch up', it is often referred to as 'filling out'.

● What are the most noticeable changes in the skull from birth to adulthood as shown in Figure 4.11?

◐ The jaw bone has grown considerably since birth to accommodate the teeth. The length of the face (y) has increased in the adult relative to that of the cranium (x).

Figure 4.11 (a) Shape of the skull at birth. The pink-coloured areas indicate the fontanelles. (b) The skull of an adult.

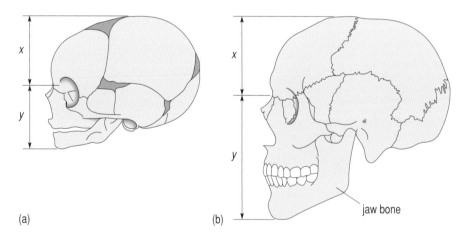

(a)   (b)   jaw bone

The plates of bone which make up the skull of the newborn are not fused together into a solid mass but have fibrous membranes (sheets of tissue) stretched over the spaces between them. These spaces or **fontanelles** allow the skull to deform and squeeze through the birth canal without damage and also allow the rapid growth in brain size seen in infancy; the skull's volume at birth of 400 cm³ increases to 950 cm³ at two years of age when the last of the fontanelles closes up. The fontanelles disappear as the cranial plates fuse together, leaving lines or sutures in the skull bone marking their edges. The more 'upright' adult face appears as the bones of the face and jaw grow rapidly during adolescence. The facial features do not become permanent until about the age of 25.

Sex differences in the skeleton, present from birth, are accentuated in adolescence, with the female pelvis becoming wider and shallower, which facilitates childbirth. In girls who become pregnant at a very young age, this pelvis growth may not have occurred sufficiently to allow a safe birth and this accounts for one of the risks of under-age motherhood.

In males, the shoulders increase in size relative to the pelvis. In females, during adolescence there is also a deposition of fat around the breast and pelvic areas, which changes the body's shape considerably. This fat deposition is under the hormonal control that initiates puberty, a time when there can be great sensitivity to body shape. For young girls, this sensitivity is accentuated by the current Western 'ideal' female body depicted in the media as tall and thin with few natural curves. The clash between the body changes at puberty, called secondary sexual characteristics, and the socially accepted body image can lead to emotional problems which may become manifest as eating problems (Book 1, Section 3.2.2).

Major changes in posture from birth to adulthood are those necessary to enable upright walking on two legs. Newborn babies have only two curves in the spine (Figure 4.12a) and the bones at the base of the spine are still separate; these bones will fuse later into a permanent curve.

BIPEDALISM

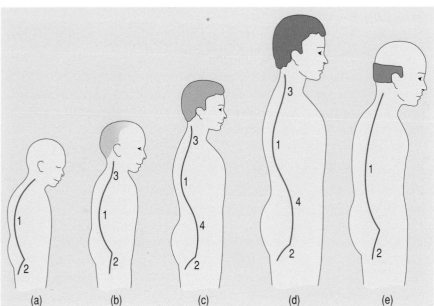

Figure 4.12 Changes in the curvature of the spine over the lifespan, from (a) newborn, (b) three months old, (c) infant, (d) adult, (e) old age. 1–4 indicate the number and appearance of curves in the spine over the lifespan.

When the baby begins to hold up his/her head, another curve forms in the neck or cervical section of the spine (Figure 4.12b). When the baby sits up unaided, a further spinal curve forms in the lower back or lumbar region of the spine (Figure 4.12c). Once walking, the weight of the upper body pushes the bottom of the spine downwards into the pelvis, causing the pelvis to broaden out (Figure 4.12d). The action of walking also deepens the hip socket, making this joint more stable. Eventually the adult posture is achieved (Figure 4.13). Notice that in old age (Figure 4.12e), the number and position of the curves is the same as that in the newborn (Figure 4.12a).

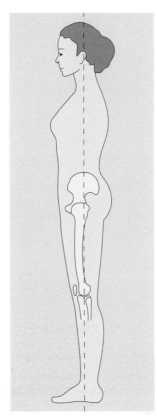

Figure 4.13 Idealized adult standing posture.

If the weight of the body moves too far from the line indicated in Figure 4.13, the proprioceptors and organs of balance in the inner ear (Section 2.7) will detect the changes and the body's position will be adjusted by the muscular system to avoid falling.

Summary of Section 4.5

1   Different parts of the body grow at different rates, leading to the obvious changes in body shape and posture from birth to adolescence, e.g. the 'top-heavy' toddler and the 'gangly' youth.

2   At puberty, males and females show different patterns of growth and development.

3   The number and position of spinal curves change from infancy to old age in response to sitting up unaided and walking.

4.6 Joints

The skeleton must have joints or articulations to allow the human body to perform a vast range of movements. Consider the movements involved in gymnastics, running for a bus or using the hands for sign language. This type of free movement is made possible by the joints such as that in the knee between the thigh bone (femur) and lower leg bones (tibia and fibula).

● The most obvious joints in the body are those in the arms and legs. Where else does bone have to articulate against bone?

◐ The bones in the spine (the vertebrae) have to move against each other as the spine flexes and bends. The bones in the hands and feet articulate to allow a complex range of movements. In the process of breathing, the ribs articulate against the vertebrae.

● What particular problems are posed by breaking a rib?

◐ Broken bones are typically immobilized to allow healing to take place; but immobilizing the ribs would prevent breathing!

In fact, ribs do not need to be immobilized to heal but analgesics (pain-killers) are necessary to enable the patient to breathe deeply. If pain persists, the patient will indulge in shallow breathing to 'protect' their ribs and in so doing will increase the risk of developing a chest infection.

The joints at the knee between the femur and lower leg bones, at the hip between the femur and the pelvis, and at the elbow between the humerus and lower arm bones, are all examples of relatively freely moving joints. These joints are also called **synovial joints**. Figure 4.14 is a simplified diagram of a synovial joint.

There are other points of contact between bones that are less flexible than synovial joints. The teeth fit into sockets in the jaw and form a fairly inflexible joint. (The joint does move slightly to absorb the 'shock' involved in biting and chewing.) The joints between the vertebrae and the intervertebral discs (made

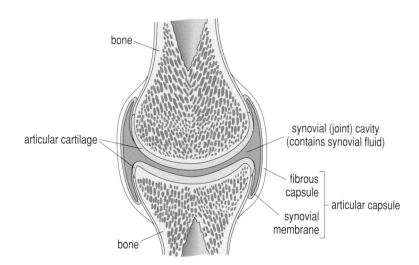

Figure 4.14 A simplified synovial joint. The gap between the bones is exaggerated to show the articular cartilage on the ends of the bones.

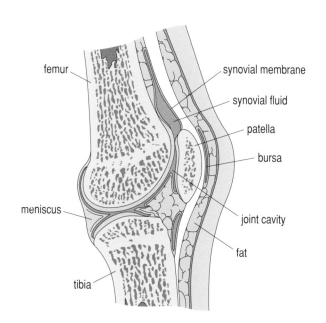

Figure 4.15 A diagrammatic section through the knee joint showing the ends of the thigh bone (femur), one of the lower leg bones (tibia) and the kneecap. The joint is stabilized by pads of cartilage (called menisci; singular meniscus). Friction may occur where the skin runs over the kneecap (patella); a pad of connective tissue filled with synovial fluid (called a bursa) provides protection.

from cartilage) in the spinal column and between the pelvic bones beneath the pubic area are also joints that are capable of only limited movement.

The knee is the largest and most complex synovial joint in the body. It connects three differently shaped bones: the femur (thigh bone) and the two lower leg bones (tibia and fibula). The knee joint must permit bending of the leg without too much side-to-side rotation (Figure 4.15).

The bones of the joint are held together by **ligaments**, which in some joints can form a fibrous capsule around the joint (Figure 4.16). Ligaments comprise bundles of collagen fibres running in parallel, so they can resist recurrent forces pulling on them lengthways, and they form the main structures holding bone to bone.

JOINTS.

○ LIGAMENTS
↳ Join bone to bone
↳ fibrous capsule...?
↳ collagen fibres in parallel
  ↳ high strength in 1 dimension.

○ ARTICULAR CARTILAGE
↳ reduces friction - wear
  ↳ OSTEOARTHRITIS

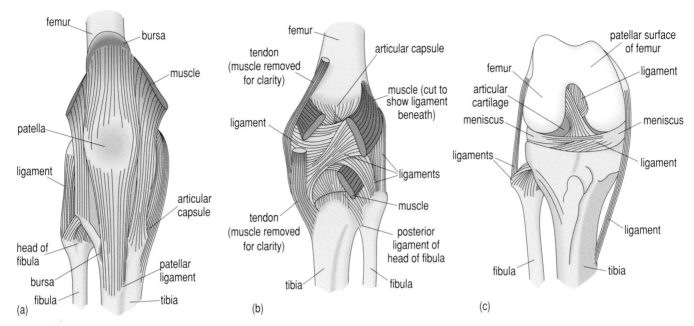

Figure 4.16 The bones in the knee joint are held together by ligaments (and the surrounding muscles). The figure shows the knee ligaments, looking at the knee (a) from the front, (b) from behind and (c) from the front with the knee flexed and the kneecap 'removed' to show the ligaments between the tibia and femur.

The ends of the bones are covered with cartilage, called **articular cartilage** (Figures 4.3 and 4.16), which allows the bones to move smoothly against each other. It is this cartilage that breaks down in people suffering from osteoarthritis and leads to the painful rubbing of bone against bone (see Case Report 4.2).

The small space between the bones is filled with a fluid similar in appearance and texture to uncooked egg white, called **synovial fluid** (Figure 4.14). The knee joint typically contains 3–4 cm³ of synovial fluid. This fluid is produced by the inner layer of the capsule around the joint and helps facilitate movement within the joint. It also provides nutrients for the cells in the articular cartilage, which do not have access to blood (which would normally supply nutrients and remove waste products from cells). The fluid also contains phagocytic cells that scavenge and remove debris that is formed as the joint moves and tissue is thereby worn away. Pads of connective tissue filled with synovial fluid (called bursae; singular bursa) are found in many synovial joints and help to reduce friction between moving tissue, e.g. where the skin passes over the kneecap or where muscle passes over bone. The complex knee joint is also stabilized by pads of cartilage called menisci. These pads of cartilage can become damaged during vigorous exercise (referred to as a 'torn' cartilage) and may have to be removed surgically.

A joint is **sprained** when it is forced to move in a way that exceeds the capacity of its attachments – muscles, tendons and ligaments are over-stretched and damaged. A joint suffers **dislocation** when the bones are forced out of connection with each other in the joint and there may be considerable damage to ligaments and the surrounding capsule. Such musculo-skeletal damage results in pain and inflammation, symptoms that persist until the repair processes are well underway.

Joints stand up well to a great deal of use throughout life and it is remarkable that they can perform their function for well over 70 years without breaking down. If joints do begin to break down, movement becomes more and more restricted and painful. Eventually the joint may be surgically removed and replaced with an artificial one.

● From your general knowledge, which joints are most frequently replaced?

○ Hips and knees.

Despite these possibilities for intervention, many older people suffer considerable pain: joints that are stiff in the mornings and ache when the weather is damp, stiff and swollen fingers and back pain. All of these are symptoms reported by many in the over-60 age group (and quite a few who are younger!). Not every old person experiences these problems but they are common, and we know that joints are susceptible to particular kinds of damage as they age, simply because of the job that they do. Cartilage undergoes constant wear and repair, and tendons are subjected to regular mechanical stresses.

The ability to maintain tissues in the joints alters with age, but it is often difficult to identify intrinsic age-related biological changes, and distinguish them from the results of repairs following minor injuries or reactions to persistent mechanical stresses, such as poor posture or repetitive actions. The thinning of joint cartilage that occurs with age may be due in part to wear and tear, rather than to any underlying age-related changes in the cells that produce new cartilage. However, one exceedingly common age-related trait is the appearance of bone cells in cartilage. This is not necessarily associated with any observable disability, but it can make joints less mobile. The deposition of bone in the costal cartilage (this is the cartilage joining the ribs and breastbone) makes these joints more rigid.

● What function will be affected by increased rigidity of the joints of the ribcage?

○ Breathing.

If there is less mobility between the ribs and the breastbone, rib movements will be restricted during breathing. This will be most noticeable when greater physical exertion is attempted or when the respiratory system is stressed, for example when suffering from a cold, bronchitis or similar respiratory tract infection.

Loss of water from the fibrous cartilage of the shock-absorbing discs between the vertebrae of the backbone is another problem, which can lead to a reduced ability to bear or lift weight. (It is also responsible for the 'shrinking' of older people.)

The catalogue of possible changes in the structural fabric of the body does not in itself represent inevitable disabilities, but it does make the individual more susceptible to diseases of the muscles, joints and skeleton and less able to recover from accidents and injury.

Loss or reduction of mobility and failing strength bring very real distress. The frustration of not being able to participate in sporting activities or even to keep pace with others when out walking can lead to a downward spiral where, eventually, the condition is exacerbated by a failure to take any exercise at all. At the same time, social contact will be reduced, with further negative effects in terms of emotional well-being. In a similar way, hobbies may be harder to pursue, particularly those that require manual dexterity, e.g. embroidery, woodwork, drawing and painting – even card games may present difficulties. Just when there is more time for hobbies, they may become less accessible.

Case Report 4.2   Osteoarthritis

Jimmy is a 72-year-old retired farm worker. He has lived and worked all his life in a small village, working long hours involving heavy lifting and handling of everything on the farm from bales of hay to small lambs. He retired at 65 but occasionally still helps out around the farm he's worked on for much of his life. During his last few years working on the farm, Jimmy experienced some pain and stiffness in his joints, especially his hips. In the early days, the pain was usually felt after a day of hard physical labour, and after a good night's sleep it usually disappeared. But since retirement, the pain has become more frequent and Jimmy can sometimes hear a grating sound when he stands up. Jimmy looked forward to retirement, but now finds his mobility increasingly restricted and affecting his capacity to do the things he wants to do. He finds it increasingly difficult to walk the half-mile to the local village and after much prompting from his wife, Jimmy decided to visit his GP to see if help was available.

The GP examined Jimmy, performed a series of tests to determine if he had arthritis and, if so, what type. X-rays were ordered to see if the bone and cartilage had been damaged, and blood tests were also ordered to rule out other types of disease. When the results of the X-rays and blood tests were available, Jimmy returned to his GP and was told he had osteoarthritis. The GP explained that osteoarthritis develops when cartilage wears out and bone rubs against bone. It was also explained to Jimmy that exercise, rest, weight loss and good nutrition are very helpful in treating the disease, and that non-steroidal anti-inflammatory drugs (NSAIDs) can be used to relieve the pain. Jimmy asked about operations and was informed that total joint replacement surgery, called arthroplasty, has helped many people to regain independence and reduce pain. But in Jimmy's case, pain relief combined with an exercise programme would be tried first. His diet was also checked to ensure that he was eating sensibly. If medicines, exercise and physical therapy fail to provide the needed relief, he will talk to his GP again, about the pros and cons of joint replacement.

Summary of Section 4.6

1   Joints allow the skeleton to move or articulate via the action of skeletal muscles.

2   Synovial joints such as the knee allow relatively free movement. The bones in synovial joints are held together by ligaments and stabilized by pads of cartilage and fluid-filled pads of connective tissue.

3   Joints have to withstand a great deal of wear and tear over the 70+ years of human life.

4.7 Muscles

Joints allow the bones of the skeleton to articulate, but it is the muscles attached to the skeleton that provide the body with movement. Muscle tissue can be of three types: that making up the structure of the heart (**cardiac muscle**); that found in hollow organs like the bladder, intestine and uterus (**smooth muscle**); and that attached to bones (**skeletal muscle**). We shall concentrate on skeletal muscle here, but it is worth noting that all muscle tissue has four common characteristics:

- it responds to stimuli and is *excitable* like nervous tissue;

- it *contracts* in response to a stimulus;

- it can be *stretched* without damaging its structure (although muscles can suffer a **strain** when they become over-stretched);

- it is *elastic*, i.e. the muscle tissue returns to its original shape after contraction or extension.

Skeletal muscles are attached to bones via extensions of collagen fibres from the connective tissue found in muscles. These extensions are called **tendons**. Like ligaments, tendons comprise mainly extracellular material and are stiff but elastic (Figure 4.16 shows both tendons and ligaments). The *origin* of the muscle is where it is attached via a tendon to a stationary bone; the attachment at the other end of the muscle is to a moveable bone and this is called the *insertion* of the muscle (Figure 4.17).

Probably the most well-known tendon in the body is the Achilles tendon, which is found at the back of the heel and connects muscles in the calf with the heel bone. Most of our skeletal muscles are under conscious control; for example, we can choose whether to stand on our toes or not. Cardiac and smooth muscle activities are not under our conscious control; we do not have to think about making our heart beat or about moving food through our intestines.

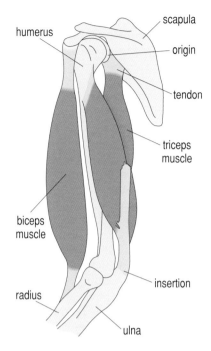

Figure 4.17 The attachment of skeletal muscle to the bones of the upper arm and scapula (shoulder blade).

4.7.1 Functions of skeletal muscle

Muscle tissue is made from a collection of highly specialized cells known as **muscle fibres**. The muscle tissue is surrounded by supporting and protecting fibrous connective tissue (called *fascia*, meaning a bandage), in which are located the plentiful nerve and blood supplies which an active muscle needs (Figure 4.18).

Muscle activity makes heavy demands on the body to supply enough oxygen and nutrients to the muscle cells so that they can produce a steady supply of ATP. This important molecule was

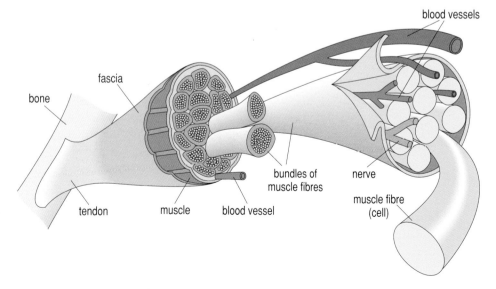

Figure 4.18 The internal structure of skeletal muscle, showing a magnified view of a single bundle containing muscle fibres, blood vessels and a nerve.

Figure 4.19 (a) The internal structure of skeletal muscle, showing a further magnified view of a single muscle fibre (cell) containing sarcoplasmic (endoplasmic) reticulum, mitochondria (singular mitochondrion) and the myofibrils. The dots at the cut end of the enlarged myofibril denote individual actin and myosin filaments, the arrangement of which is shown later in Figure 4.22a. (b) An electron micrograph of a section of skeletal muscle tissue, showing the characteristic banding pattern caused by partial overlapping of actin and myosin filaments within a myofibril. The mitochondria between the myofibrils are also visible.

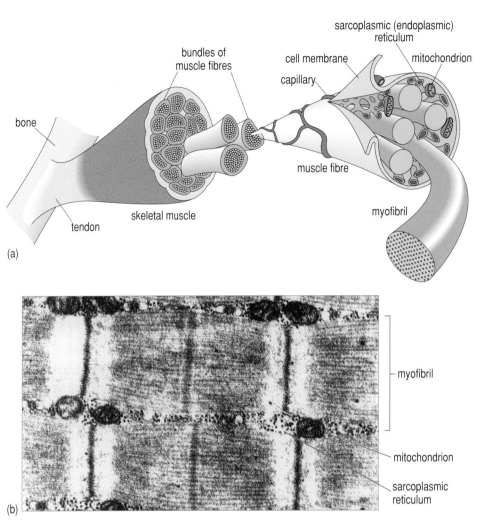

described in Book 1, Section 2.5.2; it is the cell's energy 'currency'. Muscle fibres are large, elongated and highly specialized cells containing numerous mitochondria which make ATP immediately available for the cells to use to power contraction. (Each muscle fibre is a single cell containing several nuclei, which was formed during differentiation by the fusion of adjacent cells.) Running the length of these cells are fibrils made from filaments of two types of protein, actin and myosin. These fibrils give skeletal muscle tissue its characteristic striped appearance under the microscope (Figure 4.19b). The muscle fibres and the connective tissue are the main structural components of muscle. In some parts of the body, the tendons are very long, which means that the muscle is some distance away from the part of the body that it moves. For example, it is muscles located in the forearm that actually move the fingers.

Put in very simple terms, muscle contraction occurs when the actin and myosin filaments slide past each other, thus shortening and contracting the muscle. This process requires energy (ATP) and will be described in the next section.

The role of skeletal muscle in human movement is immediately obvious, but it is not the only function of skeletal muscle.

What other functions does skeletal muscle perform? Even in a relaxed muscle, a few muscle fibres are sometimes contracted to give the muscle some firmness

SKELETAL MUSCLE:
* ORIGIN - attached to static bone
* INSERTION - attached to mov bone
  → by tendons
    → extracellular tissue
    → connective tissue
      → mainly collagen fibres
        → extensions
          → from muscle
* FASCIA (bandage) - surrounds it
  → support + protection
  → nerves
  → blood supply
    → ATP ≈ energy
* composition:
  → Muscle Fibre
    → single cell
    → several nuclei
      → fusion during differentiation
  → fibrils
    → protein filaments
      → ACTIN & MYOSIN
      → striped/banded appear.
* Mechanism:
  → Actin & myosin layers
    → slide between each other
      → req. calcium.

164

or **tone**. This is important in maintaining the posture of the body. For example, the muscles in the neck which are keeping your head upright whilst you are reading this page are not involved in movement or extreme contraction, which would pull the head backwards, but are holding the head steady in one position.

An involuntary increase in muscle tone is triggered when the body feels cold, and we call this **shivering**. The use of energy by muscles in alternately contracting and relaxing not only produces the shivering movement but also releases heat which is transferred to the blood and carried around the body, thereby warming it.

Skeletal muscles also play a part in returning blood to the **heart** from the rest of the body. Veins that run through muscle are squeezed when these muscles contract and the blood in them is pushed towards the heart. Blood is stopped from flowing backwards by flaps or **valves** in the vein (see Figure 4.20).

[handwritten margin notes:]
function:
↳ contraction
↳ movement
↳ tension/firmness
↳ posture
↳ involuntary shivering
↳ warmth
↳ compressing veins + lymph vessels
↳ circulation
↳ e.g. varicose veins

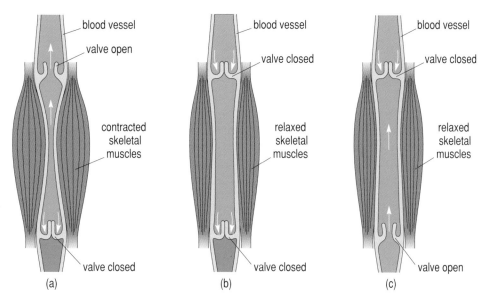

Figure 4.20 Skeletal muscle surrounding a vein pushes blood towards the heart. Blood is stopped from flowing back down the vein by closed valves during the different stages of contraction and relaxation (a–c).

If the person is inactive for too long, as in those who have to stay in bed or stand, or sit in an aircraft for long periods of time, this muscle action does not occur. Some people have weak valves in their veins and if they spend long periods of time on their feet, gravity can cause blood to flow back down the vein. This accumulation of blood eventually stretches the wall of the vein and it loses some of its elasticity. These stretched veins are called varicose veins.

Muscle action is also important in moving a fluid called lymph around the body, as this system of circulating fluid does not have a central pump as in blood circulation (Book 1, Section 1.6). Lymph is important in the body's immune system and is described in Chapter 4 of Book 3.

Clearly, the muscles have many vital functions beyond the obvious one of movement, but it is to movement that we turn in the final section of this chapter.

Summary of Section 4.7

1   Skeletal muscles are attached to the bones via tendons and, by contracting, muscles facilitate movement.

2   Skeletal muscle contraction also maintains body posture, raises body temperature via shivering and helps in returning blood to the heart.

4.8 Muscles and movement

4.8.1 Motor neurons

We return now to the scenario encountered at the beginning of this chapter, namely running away from danger. In Chapter 1 of this book we said that the somatic (voluntary) nervous system controls the muscles that change the position of the parts of the body (Section 1.8.2). Whether the movement is a simple reflex, such as the knee-jerk or pulling your hand away from a hot stove, or a complex carefully coordinated act, such as threading a needle, the way that the muscle is activated by the motor neuron is identical.

● What characteristic do muscle cells share with neurons?

○ They are both excitable cells.

In other words, they are both capable of propagating an action potential. The occurrence of an action potential in a muscle fibre is initiated by an action potential in the motor neuron that innervates the muscle fibre.

● Where do you find motor neurons?

○ The cell bodies of motor neurons are located in the brain stem and in the ventral part of the spinal cord (Section 1.8) They are associated with the cranial nerves, which run between the brain and the regions of the head, and with the peripheral spinal nerves, respectively.

Motor neurons are myelinated; the presence of myelin, formed by glial cells (Section 1.9), increases the speed of conduction of the action potential. A relatively high speed of conduction is important in that it allows a rapid communication of commands to the muscle. A disease such as Guillain–Barré syndrome, which involves loss of myelin from motor neurons, disrupts motor function, leading to paralysis. This disease is an acute inflammatory response following infection of the upper respiratory tract, and if patients survive the acute phase, they usually make a complete recovery.

4.8.2 Motor units

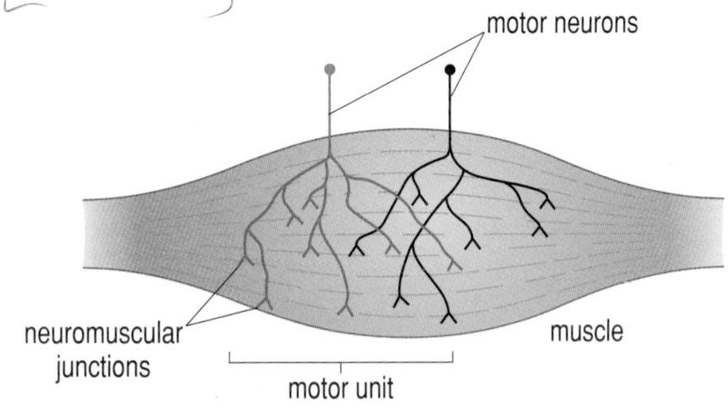

motor neurons

neuromuscular junctions

muscle

motor unit

Figure 4.21 A motor unit branches when it reaches the muscle it innervates, and synapses with many individual muscle fibres. The neuron together with the muscle fibres it innervates is termed a motor unit.

Motor neurons branch within a muscle, each of the branches terminating on a single muscle fibre. The term **motor unit** is used to describe a single motor neuron and the muscle fibres that it innervates. In Figure 4.21, note that in the formation of a **neuromuscular system** from motor units, there is an intermingling of fibres from different motor units. An action potential in a given motor neuron will trigger activity in all of the muscle fibres that make up a motor unit. Motor units vary in size: in some cases, one motor neuron will innervate as few as ten muscle fibres, but in other cases it will innervate hundreds.

One motor unit is activated by action potentials within a single motor neuron arriving at the synapses between the motor neuron and each muscle fibre; such a synapse is called a **neuromuscular junction**.

- How then is the **strength** of contraction in a muscle increased? (You should be able to answer this from what you learned in Chapter 1.)

- The answer is, in part, by increasing the **frequency** of generation of action potentials in a given motor neuron.

In addition, activation of a muscle can be increased by increasing the **number** of motor units that are simultaneously activated, a process termed *recruitment*.

recruitment

- How is this achieved?

- By increasing the number of motor neurons that are active.

Thus increased muscular contraction corresponds to increased excitatory input to motor neurons. The increased excitation of the motor neurons arises as a result of increased input to them from, for example, the **corticospinal pathway** (Section 1.10).

4.8.3 The neuromuscular junction

also ANS

The **neurotransmitter** released at the neuromuscular junction is **acetylcholine** (**ACh**); effective functioning of the motor system requires that acetylcholine is able to be released and then broken down enzymatically (Section 1.9.2). In this way, changes in the activation of the muscle can follow closely changes in motor neuron activity.

i.e immediate breakdown = stimulation stopped (quickly) rapid muscle relaxation

There are various ways in which interference with such transmission can occur. For example, curare (a substance that South American Indians put on the end of arrows to paralyse their prey) binds to the receptors for ACh at the muscle fibre membrane but does not activate the muscle fibres. The result is paralysis of the muscles. Another way in which interference can occur is as a result of infection with the bacterium *Clostridium botulinum*. This bacterium produces botulinus toxin which prevents the **release** of ACh from the terminals of motor neurons.

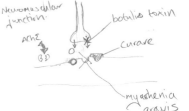

Neuromuscular junction.
AChE
BD
botulin toxin
curare
myasthenia gravis

The disease myasthenia gravis is characterized by symptoms of muscular fatigue. It is the result of a reduction in the effectiveness of ACh-mediated transmission at neuromuscular junctions and is associated with loss of motor function.

- From your understanding of transmission at synapses, can you speculate as to what might be responsible?

- In principle, it could be:

  1 a failure of motor neurons to release sufficient ACh at their terminals;

  2 an abnormally high rate of enzymatic breakdown of ACh;

  3 a loss of receptors for ACh on the muscle membrane.

It could also be any combination of 1–3.

In fact, the evidence suggests that the disorder is caused by a loss of ACh receptors. A therapy that is used for the disorder is to boost the levels of ACh that are available at the neuromuscular junction.

down regulation .

- How, in theory, might this be achieved?

- By preventing the enzymatic breakdown of ACh. *[similar to re-uptake blockers]*

ACh is broken down, shortly after binding to its receptor, by the enzyme
acetylcholinesterase (AChE). Treatment for myasthenia gravis consists of
administering drugs that block the action of AChE. Thereby more ACh is available to
the diminished population of receptors on the muscle cell postsynaptic membrane.

So much for the details of how activating signals reach the individual muscle fibres
via motor neurons. We shall now see how their arrival brings about muscle
contraction.

4.8.4 Muscle contraction

In the previous section, we spoke of the 'activation' of a muscle. Now we need to
look more carefully at what this term means. Activation of an individual fibre
means that a mechanical force is generated within it. The trigger for the generation
of this mechanical force is the occurrence of an **action potential** within the
individual muscle fibre, analogous to that which occurs in a neuron (Section 1.9.1).
As more muscle fibres are triggered into activity, so the force generated by the
muscle increases. This force is caused by the protein filaments of actin and myosin
moving past each other and overlapping, as illustrated diagrammatically in Figure
4.22a. Notice that the filaments do not change in length. Sliding together produces
the state of **contraction** (shortening) and sliding apart produces relaxation
(lengthening) of the muscle. By analogy, muscle contraction is like alternate cards
in a pack sliding past each other as the pack is reassembled after shuffling (Figure
4.22b). The energy to drive the sliding together of muscle protein filaments comes
from ATP, but the process cannot begin until calcium ions are released from
storage in the **sarcoplasmic (endoplasmic) reticulum**, an event that is triggered by
the depolarization of the muscle fibre postsynaptic membrane.

Each individual action potential is said to cause a 'twitch' (i.e. a small contraction)
in the muscle. When the frequency of action potentials increases, so the twitches
tend to merge; this is termed **tetanus**. (This *natural* state of a muscle is distinct
from the pathological condition of the same name.)

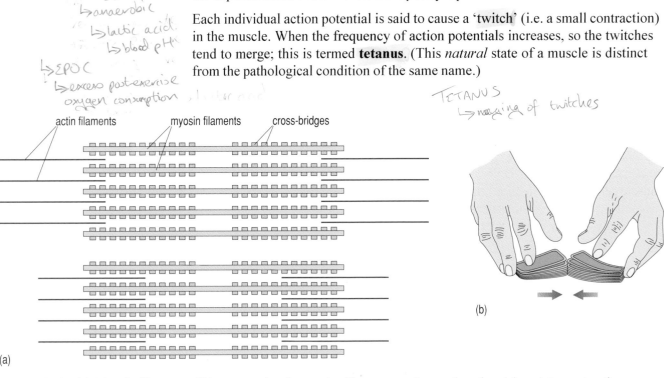

actin filaments   myosin filaments   cross-bridges

(a)

(b)

Figure 4.22 (a) Muscle filaments slide past each other as the fibre moves from relaxation (above) to contraction
(below). (b) Analogy of two sets of cards being interleaved.

When racing away from the bull, your leg muscles will be using a lot of ATP and there is an immediate problem of supply. Even muscle cells have quite limited supplies of ATP. However, they have stores of two other substances that can provide energy (as ATP). One is **creatine phosphate**, which is stored in muscle and can react with ADP to yield ATP and creatine. This ATP source is usually only needed for a few seconds after which the rate of ATP formation is increased to match the demands of the muscle cell. However, if muscle activity is intense and long lasting, a new obstacle is encountered – shortage of oxygen. As you race away from the bull your breathing becomes deeper, but soon this increased ventilation fails to meet the demands for oxygen and the cell cannot supply enough ATP using this limited oxygen supply. At this point, the muscle cell switches to its other energy store, the polysaccharide **glycogen**, which it breaks down **anaerobically** (i.e. without consuming oxygen) to generate more ATP. But in doing so, there is a build-up of two by-products, lactate and hydrogen ions. These lead to a lowering of blood pH (i.e. the blood becomes more acidic). Such activity can only be sustained in short bursts. (If you don't out-pace the bull in a 100 m sprint you've probably 'had it'!) The accumulation of lactate causes aching and heaviness of the limbs, which contributes to muscle fatigue. The lactate must be metabolized (which occurs mostly in the liver) and the muscle creatine phosphate reserves must be replenished. Both these processes are oxygen-requiring. Thus there is an increased demand for oxygen after exercise. This **excess post-exercise oxygen consumption (EPOC)** is the reason why we continue to breathe heavily for some time after intense exercise – which answers one of the questions we asked at the very start of the course.

[handwritten margin note: $H^+ + lactate^- = lactic acid.$]

4.8.5 Muscle and exercise

When considering sporting performance, we should note that not all muscle fibres have the same properties. Of interest to sprinters are the **fast-fatiguing muscle fibres** that produce large contractile forces, although they tire relatively quickly. They contain few mitochondria and rely on *anaerobic* breakdown of glucose for synthesis of ATP. To be a sprinter, you need a high proportion of these fibres in your muscles. By contrast, a marathon runner has a high proportion of **fatigue-resistant muscle fibres** in their leg muscles. Fatigue-resistant fibres contain high levels of enzymes involved in *aerobic* (oxygen-using) catabolism of glucose and fatty acids. Your genes determine the proportion of different types of muscle fibres, but you can increase the efficiency of your muscles through use. When muscle cells are stretched maximally, they respond by synthesizing more of the proteins actin and myosin, thereby increasing their size. On the other hand, cells lose their contractile proteins through lack of use, and atrophy.

Of course, there are some people who build up muscle, not by exercise, but by using drugs. This was mentioned at the beginning of the previous chapter. As you now know from Section 4.4.3, growth hormone and IGF-1 control bone growth. So you might have guessed that they also affect muscle growth; because as bones grow, muscles also must grow or they would be ripped apart! Growth hormone, via IGF-1 secreted by the liver, stimulates muscle growth by increasing protein synthesis and also division of cells that develop into muscle fibres. However, you will also be aware of the adolescent growth spurt (Figure 4.8). It is the surge of **testosterone** secretion during puberty in boys that stimulates increased length and

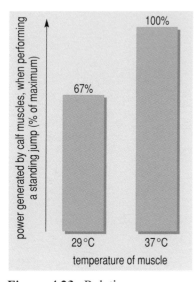

Figure 4.23 Relative power output of human calf muscles at different temperatures.

width of muscle fibres and hence greater muscle mass in men than in women. Testosterone can be manufactured and used medicinally, but it can also be abused.

● To which chemical group of hormones does testosterone belong?

○ It is a steroid, specifically an **anabolic steroid**.

The taking of **performance-enhancing drugs** has become a major problem in competitive sports. Testing for drug misuse is tricky when the substance being used is one that occurs naturally in our bodies. Part of the problem is that the amount that is found in the bloodstream or excreted in the urine will obviously vary from individual to individual as well as over an individual's lifetime. In the case of testosterone, it has been found that as **laboratory synthesis** is from **plant sources** there *is* a way of differentiating between the naturally occurring and the synthetic chemical. Testosterone contains atoms of carbon. The atomic structure of carbon is 6 electrons, 6 protons and 6 neutrons (see Figure 2.2 in Book 1, Section 2.2.1). However, some carbon atoms have an **extra neutron**, which increases their mass; these 'heavy' carbon atoms can therefore be detected. The carbon compounds in plants have a different proportion of 'heavy' to 'light' carbon atoms. Thus testosterone manufactured from plant material can be distinguished from the testosterone that is naturally produced by the human body. So now these particular performance drugs can be **incontrovertibly identified**.

The previous chapter highlighted the successful use of anabolic steroids to treat muscle-wasting diseases. But there is evidence that **muscle fibres** are actually lost as we age. This is believed to be a consequence of the loss of the **motor neurons** that innervate them. Up to 30% of our muscle fibres may disappear between the ages of 30 and 80. Once lost, these cells cannot be replaced. With the loss of muscle fibres comes a diminution of strength. This means that older people may be unable to perform quite ordinary tasks such as opening heavy swing-doors, carrying heavy packages, opening screw-top bottles and jars. This affects well-being and confidence, but the good news is that these changes are not inevitable or irreversible; muscle *performance* can be improved through exercise at any age and this can compensate for loss of muscle fibres that has already been sustained.

● Can you suggest what difficulties might prevent an older person from taking sufficient exercise?

○ There are many factors that inhibit older people's access to enjoyable exercise, e.g. lack of transport, not being able to afford to pay to use leisure or sporting facilities and embarrassment.

● Look at Figure 4.23 and suggest what else should be done to ensure the full use of available muscle power.

○ Keep warm!

This may partially explain the popularity, amongst the well-off, retired citizens of the British Isles, of spending the winter in warmer climes. But we should not forget that there are many older people for whom keeping warm, and therefore keeping their muscles in peak condition, presents real problems.

Summary of Section 4.8

1 A muscle is composed of specialized multinucleate cells, **muscle fibres**, which are activated by action potentials within the fibre.

2 Activity in motor neurons triggers activity in muscle fibres.

3 A motor unit consists of a motor neuron and the muscle fibres that it innervates.

4 Substances that interfere with the neuromuscular junction disrupt movement.

5 Muscle contraction uses large amounts of ATP and oxygen but creatine phosphate and glycogen can replenish muscle ATP levels.

6 Exercise builds up muscle at any age.

4.9 Conclusion

Our musculo-skeletal systems often go unnoticed throughout our lives, until the free, painless movement we take for granted is affected. Most disorders are caused or aggravated by humans' bipedal posture and the subsequent pull of gravity on the musculo-skeletal system. Human **health** is closely related to this body system and the close monitoring of children's musculo-skeletal development provides information on their overall health. Throughout life, muscle shows great plasticity. Muscle tissue shrinks during immobilization but regenerates once mobility is restored. Although muscle fibres are lost during **ageing**, muscles mass and function can be maintained by exercise. In contrast, bone is often regarded as an inert, hard substance but it is a living, changing tissue which responds to environmental stresses as well as to changes within the body. More than any other system, we can use the health of the musculo-skeletal system as a measure of our overall bio-psychological health.

[handwritten annotation: symptoms – pain, swelling, redness + heat ↓ phagocytes – remove cellular/phagocytose debris ↓ haematoma – blood loss (+ blood vessels) ↓ granulation tissue (+ blood vessels) ↓ fibroblasts → collagen fibres ↓ Tissue remodelled to same as surrounding tissue.]

Questions for Chapter 4

[handwritten annotation: • Protection of internal organs (esp ribcage) • Red + yellow marrow – blood cell production + lipid storage • attachment points for muscles • mineral storage (calcium + magnesium, esp phosphates)]

Question 4.1 (LO 4.1)

What functions does the skeleton perform apart from providing support for the body?

Question 4.2 (LO 4.2)

How is the healing of bone fractures similar to wound healing in soft tissue (Book 1, Chapter 2)?

[handwritten annotation: Vit D nec for Ca²⁺ absorption (S.I.) & deposition (bones)]

Question 4.3 (LO 4.3)

Identify the following statements as true or false and justify your answers.

(a) Lack of vitamin D is only a problem in young children, as it affects growth.

(b) Elderly people shrink because they do not eat enough.

(c) You are genetically programmed to reach a particular height.

(d) Lack of thyroid hormone in infancy can be a cause of mental retardation.

[handwritten annotation: due to gravity? Shrinkage due to loss of fluid (water) in lumbosacral discs → spine shortens. Also thinning of cartilage w age (wear'n'tear)]

[handwritten annotation: Maximum potential determined by genotype (twin studies) but environmental factors affect whether this is reached or not, e.g. nutrition + emotional provision (non-organic failure to thrive).]

[handwritten annotation: Thyroid hormones crucial to development of infant's brain.]

If skeleton to remain immobile then joints must be kept rigid. This means muscles (esp. antagonistic) must have tone (firmness). Proprioceptors + organs of balance give feedback on positional/postural changes of body.

If line of postural balance exceeded action potential propagated down motor neurons to neuromuscular junctions at muscle (motor unit) Excites muscle to cause contraction appropriate to movement needed to bring body back into alignment (req. ATP + Ca²⁺ for contraction).

• Varicose veins – blood pooling in legs as circulation insufficient to compensate for gravity.

• Shorter in evenings and as we age. – compression of spine by weight of body + organs

• 'Slipped disk' – uneven pressure on vertebral disks

• Hernias – organs held in vertical alignment by sheets of muscle to compensate for gravity. Over-exertion can rupture and pressure on intestine forces them through this.

• Pelvis shape has changed to compensate for bipedalism, this makes childbirth riskier than for other primates.

Question 4.4 (LO 4.4)

Explain how muscles and joints act to stabilize the skeleton when a person is standing and immobile.

Question 4.5 (LO 4.5)

What is the evidence that bipedalism has adverse effects on human health?

References

BUPA website: http://hcd2.bupa.co.uk (Accessed November 2004)

Clinical Standards Advisory Group. (1994) *Back Pain: Report of a CSAG Committee on Back Pain*, HMSO, London.

Committee on the Medical Aspects of Food Policy (COMA) (1991) *Dietary Reference Values for Food, Energy and Nutrients for the United Kingdom*, Department of Health, HMSO, London.

Hourihane, J. O'B. and Rolles, C. J. (1995) Morbidity from excess intake of high energy fluids: the squash drinking syndrome, *Archives of Diseases in Children*, **72**, 141–143.

Health and Safety Executive website: www.hse.gov.uk/msd/backpain (Accessed October 2004)

Kreiter, S. R., Schwartz, R. P., Kirkman, H. N., Charlton, P. A., Calikoglu, A. S. and Davenport, M. L. (2000) Nutritional rickets in African American breast-fed infants, *Journal of Pediatrics*, **137**, 153–157.

Ministry of Agriculture, Fisheries and Food and Department of Health Social Survey Division of the Office of Population Censuses and Surveys and Medical Research Council Dunn Nutrition Unit (1995) *Report of the National Diet and Nutrition Survey: Children Aged 1.5–4.5*, HMSO, London.

Nettle, D. (2002) Height and reproductive success in a cohort of British men, *Human Nature*, **13**, 473–491.

Pawlowski, B., Dunbar, R. I. M. and Lipowicz, A. (2000) Tall men have more reproductive success, *Nature*, **403**, 156.

Thompson, A. E. and Kaplan, C. A. (1996) Childhood emotional abuse, *British Journal of Psychiatry*, **168**, 143–148.

CONCLUSION

By now you should be getting a feel for the way that the nervous and endocrine systems interact with other body systems to control and coordinate our lifetime development (i.e. the changes that occur from birth to old age) as well as our day-to-day activities. We have painted a couple of rather dramatic scenarios in this book – being chased by a bull and being bitten by an unidentified tropical insect. But I am sure you can think of stomach-churning moments in your life, and undoubtedly the first intimation of trouble will have been captured by sensory receptors and conveyed from sensory afferent neurons to primary sensory areas of the cerebral cortex. Or, put more prosaically, your senses will have made you aware of the potential danger. Of course, we like to think of ourselves as rational beings, the information passing to the frontal lobes for careful conscious consideration and reflection, then planning for deliberate action based on past experience. Yet we are often accused of reacting without thinking first and we are occasionally in a situation where, for our survival, we need to do just that. In truth, we do not have much conscious control over our response when we have been caught off guard. We saw how the senses employ multiple pathways, sending information not just to the cortex of the cerebral hemispheres but to other brain structures such as the reticular formation in the brainstem. In the brainstem there are many interneurons (often packed together into discernible nuclei), and synaptic connections are made with neurons of the autonomic nervous system. You should now recognize that the body's internal homeostasis is maintained by a fine balance between the activities of the sympathetic and parasympathetic systems of the ANS. But this equilibrium is rapidly lost when danger looms. Then it is the sympathetic nervous system that dominates and activation of this system has widespread effects. For example, it speeds up the heart rate and dilates air passages in the lungs. This makes it possible to increase supplies of oxygen and nutrients to rapidly metabolizing tissues such as leg muscles (or arm muscles should we decide to hit out at whatever it is that has scared us). Furthermore, sympathetic neurons also innervate the adrenal glands and cause the release of the hormones, adrenalin and noradrenalin from the adrenal medulla into the bloodstream. Amongst other effects adrenalin mobilizes glucose from the liver. And thus the sympathetic system will have brought about a physiological response before the rational planning has been completed.

As we have just seen that the ANS does not function on its own; instead there is close interaction between nervous and endocrine systems. If the danger persists the hypothalamic-pituitary-adrenal (HPA) axis is mobilized. The hypothalamus releases CRH, which in turn stimulates release of ACTH from the anterior pituitary. This is quickly followed by increased secretion of cortisol from the adrenal cortex. The amount of cortisol secreted varies throughout the day (Figure 3.15) but at moments of intense stress the levels can begin to shoot up very rapidly within tens of seconds, setting in train several metabolic pathways, all of which result in more glucose being made available.

Once the danger is perceived to be past, the parasympathetic branch of the ANS takes over and counterbalances the effects of the sympathetic ANS, gradually returning the body to a more relaxed state. Often we use learned techniques to accelerate this process to achieve a calm disposition, such as deliberately breathing deeply and slowly, a strategy that is available after being bitten by a potentially deadly insect but not after running away from a bull! In the next book we will be studying the workings of the respiratory system and noticing the way that somatic, autonomic and endocrine systems interact to regulate this body system.

You will have noticed not just the interactions but the overlap between the two control systems; an example being the way that they sometimes use the same signalling molecules such as adrenalin. When we study mechanisms at this molecular level it is often not helpful to worry about the 'classical' definitions of hormone, neurotransmitter or cytokine. The interesting questions are about how the molecule works, not how it is classified. In many instances we have good information knowing, for example, the structure of the receptors embedded in cellular membranes with which these molecules interact and the metabolic pathways that they influence, but as scientists we would not claim that we always have the whole story. You may have noticed how many different, important molecules can be made from a single starting point; the monoamine neurotransmitters are all derived from the amino acid tyrosine; the steroids are all derived from cholesterol. (Biology is very economical!) Given that the enzymes that drive these metabolic processes are themselves the products of gene expression and that we are genetically very diverse we must expect to find that there will be variation between individuals at these molecular levels. This translates through to an issue that we have mentioned before; namely the problem of prescribing drug treatments. We use our understanding of physiological processes to prescribe treatment when things go wrong. However, all we can do is prescribe for a 'normal' metabolism, and by now you will be well aware that almost no-one is 'normal'. In 2003, Allen Roses, world-wide vice-president of genetics at GlaxoSmithKline (a well-known pharmaceutical company) suggested that his drugs were only helpful to a minority of patients because they were not tailored to reflect the individual's **genotype** (genetic make-up). Further work in this direction must be a priority for the 21st century, as should monitoring to ensure that this new approach to drug development doesn't result in sidelining groups or individuals based on their genetic variance.

If you have previously studied biology and been exposed to the 'classic' picture of the 'fast' nervous response and the 'slow' hormonal response you probably found yourself questioning this dichotomy. 'Slow' is obviously a relative term! For example, the kidney releases the hormone aldosterone in response to a fall in blood pressure as we stand up and aldosterone causes a compensatory rise in blood pressure that prevents us from fainting. This is a rapid response; however, it should also be said that it does not achieve this single-handedly. Other mechanisms are at work, as you will discover on reading Chapter 1 of Book 3.

The final section of Chapter 4 demonstrated conclusively that neither body systems nor individuals function in isolation. We discovered that in later years, loss of motor neurons leads to loss of muscle cells. The consequential loss of function can be compensated for but only if the individual is able to exercise the remaining muscle tissues appropriately. In turn this requires a supportive social and economic environment. In the next book we add to this picture by a more complete study of the systems that have often been mentioned in this book; the cardiovascular, respiratory and renal system. We also study the immune system, a system that works to protect us from various threats and dangers to our health and wellbeing and could be set alongside the nervous and endocrine systems as having an over-arching role in the regulation and control of body systems.

Answers to Questions

Question 1.1

The missing terms are: (a) grey matter; (b) axons; (c) myelin.

Question 1.2

Sensory nerves have afferent fibres only. Motor nerves have efferent fibres, whilst both cranial and spinal nerves can be mixed.

Question 1.3

The brain and spinal cord are organs of the central nervous system, CNS.

Question 1.4

(a) Loss of sensory function corresponding to one half of the body at a particular dermatome; (b) Loss of motor function corresponding to one half of the body at a particular dermatome; (c) Loss of both sensory and motor function corresponding to one half of the body at a particular dermatome.

Question 1.5

Cardiac muscle is *excited* by neurons of the *sympathetic nervous system* which use the neurotransmitter, noradrenalin. Therefore the drug might act as an antagonist to noradrenalin. Conversely, neurons of the *parasympathetic nervous* system *inhibit* the activity of cardiac muscles, through releasing the neurotransmitter acetylcholine. Therefore the drug in question could act as an *agonist* with similar actions as acetylcholine. With the information available, it is not possible to determine which mode of action the drug effects.

Question 2.1

False. Taste buds are a collection of oval sensory structures found on the tongue, embedded in specialized epithelium that forms structures called papillae. Papillae contain several taste buds.

Question 2.2

(a) False. Although phantom limb pain is 'in the mind' to the extent that it is 'felt' as pain coming from an area that no longer exists, currently it is believed that what is being detected is activity in damaged nociceptors and the activity in tensed up muscles in the stump area of the missing limb. Pathways from this area may also be overly sensitive to stimulation (hyperexcitable).

(b) Partially true. A key point here is where the tracts cross the midline of the spinal cord. The injury (lesion) will cut through all tracts on the right side of the spinal cord. The right dorsal columns receive input from the right leg, where there will be a loss of touch, but pain sense in the right leg will be unaffected. The right spinothalamic tract contains the axons of neurons in the left dorsal horn, and so there will be a loss of pain sense in the left leg. Touch sense in the left leg will be normal. Award yourself a bonus mark if you also mentioned that there will be paralysis of the muscles in the right leg, due to damage to motor nerves in the spinocortical tract on the right side of the spinal cord!

Question 2.3

Light first encounters the cornea, where it is focused, then the lens which adjusts the focal length (the process called accommodation). The shape of the lens can be altered by ciliary smooth muscle fibres – the lens is pulled taught and is elongated and flat for distant vision, and adopts a more rounded shape for near vision. The focal length is too short (i.e. falls short of the retina) in nearsighted (or *myopic*) eyes. This is corrected by placing a *concave* (divergent) lens in front of the eye. Conversely, the focal length is too long (i.e. falls beyond the retina) in farsighted (or *hypermetropic*) eyes. This is corrected by placing a *convex* (convergent) lens in front of the eye.

Question 2.4

(a) We can detect colours using specialized cells within the retina called 'cones', which are located in highest density within the fovea. They contain one of three photopigments, which allow them to detect either red colours (L-cones), green colours (M-cones) or blue colours (S-cones).

(b) Alterations in the photopigments contained within these cells lead to 'colour blindness' – a deficiency in the ability to detect one or more wavelengths of light. Colour blindness is hereditary and predominantly affects males. True colour blindness (where the world is seen in black, white and shades of grey) is very rare.

(c) The most common form of colour blindness is *anomalous trichromacy*, or a shift in the spectral sensitivity (sensitivity to a particular wavelength of visible light) of one type of cone. It usually manifests as a confusion between red and green (i.e. affecting L-cones and M-cones).

Question 2.5

(a) Diabetic eye disease, cataracts, macular degeneration, glaucoma.

(b) Glaucoma.

(c) In glaucoma, a rise in pressure within the eye (intraocular pressure) may arise as a result of inadequate drainage of aqueous humour which bathes internal structures within the eye. This rise in pressure progressively distorts and causes damage to the optic nerve. The condition may also develop secondary to other eye diseases, and in patients with a family history of glaucoma. The common effective treatment is to reduce intraocular pressure with medicated eye-drops or using laser treatment and surgery.

intraoccular pressure.

Question 2.6

The eardrum vibrates in response to different frequencies (or wavelengths) of sound. These vibrations are transferred to the ossicles (the three smallest bones in the body – the malleus, incus and stapes) within the middle ear, which in turn amplify and convey the vibrations to the cochlea in the inner ear via the oval window. Vibrations transferred via the stapes to the oval window are conducted as pressure changes in the fluid (perilymph) within the outer channels (scala vestibuli and scala tympani) of the cochlea, to the round window, where the pressure dissipates. Hair cells located on the basilar membrane that lies within the middle channel (scala media) of the cochlea translate vibrations into electrical neural signals. At the larger end of the cochlea hair cells respond to very high-pitched sounds, while those towards the smaller end respond to progressively lower-pitched sounds. Electrical currents triggered within the hair cells cause the release of glutamate at the base of these cells. This triggers action potentials in axons of the auditory nerve, and conveys information via nuclei in the pons, brainstem, medulla and thalamus to the primary and secondary auditory cortex located in the temporal lobe of the brain. Vibrations at different locations on the basilar membrane are relayed through to specific regions of the auditory cortex, where they are mapped point for point creating a tonotopic map.

Question 2.7

(a) The three main types of hearing impairment are conductive, sensorineural or central. Conductive hearing loss is caused by an obstruction (such as the build up of ear wax, fusion of ossicles or by disease such as an ear infection affecting the outer or middle ear) that usually affects all frequencies of hearing. Sensorineural hearing loss results from damage to the inner ear (for example, the hair cells in the cochlea, or to parts of the vestibulocochlear nerve) and can often affect specific frequencies more than others. A common cause of sensorineural hearing loss is repeated exposure to very loud noises. Central hearing loss is relatively rare and results from damage to the auditory pathways linking the cochlea with other auditory sites within the nervous system (for example, lesions in brainstem structures, thalamus and primary or secondary auditory cortex).

(b) Repeated middle-ear infections (especially following upper respiratory tract infections) are a common cause of conductive hearing loss in childhood. Middle-ear infections often clear up without a specific course of treatment. Antibiotics are found to be effective in 15–20% of cases. Any fluid that persists within the Eustachian tube for more than a couple of months and causes significant loss of hearing can be surgically drained.

Question 3.1

(a) False; high concentrations of thyroxin in the blood, typical of Graves' disease, inhibit secretion of TSH from the anterior pituitary gland.

(b) True; growth-hormone secretion by the anterior pituitary is controlled by inhibition and stimulation by somatostatin and GRH respectively, both secreted by the hypothalamus.

(c) Partly true; levels of blood glucose are not controlled by positive feedback. Levels of glucose in the blood are controlled by negative feedback mechanisms involving the hormones insulin and glucagon.

(d) True. Hypothalamic nuclei consist of cell bodies of neurosecretory neurons, which have axonal endings that release neurohormones into the capillary networks supplying the pituitary gland.

(e) False; these hormones are secreted by the anterior pituitary gland.

(f) False; some cytokines, e.g. IGF-1, are released into the bloodstream.

Question 3.2

(a) GnRH is produced by hypothalamic neurons and is secreted into the bloodstream of the anterior pituitary. GnRH stimulates secretion of FSH and LH, which in turn stimulate secretion of oestrogens (and progesterone) in the ovary. Hence GnRH administration to women who have hypothalamic malfunction, restores ovarian function and increases the likelihood of pregnancy.

(b) Hypothalamic neurohormones are released in a pulsatile manner and can only function as signalling molecules when released in pulses. Therefore single daily injections of GnRH have little stimulatory effect on the anterior pituitary.

Question 3.3

Cortisol facilitates breakdown of glycogen, fat and protein. Muscle wastage observed in Sarah's arms and legs can be attributed to breakdown of muscle proteins stimulated by excessive cortisol. Skin is made of protein too, so degeneration of skin structure would explain the striae observed on her abdomen, and the diminished quality of the skin on Sarah's face. Cortisol facilitates fat metabolism but there is no clear link between increased cortisol levels and excessive deposition of fat around the abdomen and at the back of the neck. Glucose in the urine reflects high blood glucose levels derived from continual synthesis of glucose from protein, and reduced inflow of blood glucose into muscle and adipose tissue, facilitated by the action of excessive cortisol.

Question 3.4

(i) Leptin signals a replete state for adipose tissue. When adipose tissue is well-loaded with stored lipids, adipocytes secrete leptin into the bloodstream.

(ii) Receptors in the hypothalamus and other regions of the brain detect high leptin levels in the blood and inhibit secretion of neuropeptide Y, an appetite stimulant.

Question 3.5

There are a number of ways of drawing the flow chart and Figure 3.30 demonstrates one way of doing so.

Question 3.6

(a) At time zero, blood glucose level for participant A is about 4.5 mmol l^{-1}, and levels peak at 30 minutes reaching 6.5 mmol l^{-1} (as glucose enters the bloodstream from the stomach). Blood insulin levels increase from 10 μ units ml^{-1} at time zero, to 100 μ units ml^{-1} at 30 minutes after the glucose drink. From 30 minutes to 2 hours blood glucose declines to about 4.5 mmol l^{-1}, as does insulin, dropping to 10 μ units ml^{-1}.

In contrast, B initially has a higher blood glucose level, around 7 mmol l^{-1} and insulin at about 80 μ units ml^{-1}. B's blood glucose levels rise sharply after the drink, reaching 11 mmol l^{-1} at 30 minutes and peaking at 13.75 mmol l^{-1} at 1.5 hours. Removal of glucose from the blood is minimal at 2 hours post glucose drink. Insulin levels in B climb to about 340 μ units ml^{-1} at 30 minutes, peaking at 400 μ units ml^{-1} 2 hours after the glucose drink. Therefore from time zero to 2 hours after the glucose drink, both glucose and insulin levels are much higher in B.

(b) A has a normal blood glucose level at time zero and by 2 hours after the glucose drink, blood glucose has dropped to normal again after peaking at 6.5 mmol l^{-1}.

B is diabetic as levels of blood glucose are elevated from time zero to 2 hours. There is little sign of clearance of glucose from the blood by 2 hours after the drink. However levels of blood insulin are elevated, even at time zero and peak at 2 hours after the drink. As B has elevated insulin levels but does not show clearance of blood glucose, there must be target cell insensitivity to insulin due to down regulation of receptors. It is likely that B has type 2 diabetes (non-insulin dependent).

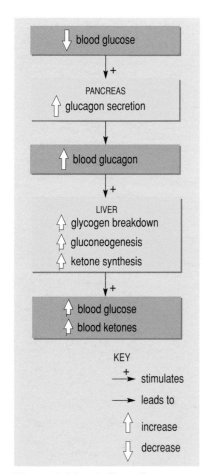

Figure 3.30 A flow diagram that shows the factors that affect the release of glucagon and the effects of the hormone on blood glucose and ketone levels.

Question 3.7

The four factors are:

(i) the presence of suitable receptors at target cells;

(ii) the rate at which the hormone is released into the bloodstream;

(iii) the rate at which the hormone is broken down in the liver and in the target cells;

(iv) the rate at which the hormone is excreted via the kidney.

Factors (ii) and (iv) control the concentration of the hormone in the bloodstream.

Question 4.1

There are several other functions:

1   The skeleton also provides protection for soft internal structures, such as the lungs and the brain.

2   Muscles pulling on the bones allow movement to occur around the joints.

3   Bone tissue is made from calcium and magnesium salts (mainly phosphates) and so serves as a store of these minerals.

4   Within the cavities of long bones (such as the femur) red bone marrow produces blood cells and yellow marrow acts as a lipid store.

Question 4.2

The first symptoms of both soft tissue damage and bone fracture are pain, redness, swelling and increased heat at the site of the injury (the typical inflammation response).

The broken ends of a bone are usually immobilized in a plaster cast. In the case of large wounds to soft tissue (such as the skin and underlying muscle) stitches are used to bring together the wound edges and thus close the wound.

Blood clots form in both types of wound and phagocytic cells remove cell debris and any infecting microbes. Fibroblast cells are attracted into the wound area and gradually the haematoma changes into granulation tissue.

The final stage of wound healing in both cases is remodelling. In bone, osteoblasts turn the fibrous pad into spongy bone and then into compact bone; osteoclasts then trim away any excess bony tissue, leaving the healed bone almost identical in appearance to its pre-fracture state. In skin, collagen fibres are reorientated in the direction of the tension lines of the skin and the epidermal cells form into the hexagonal stacked units. Traumatic wounds to soft tissue may leave visible scarring; in the case of a healed fracture, a thickening around the fracture site may be seen in X-rays.

Question 4.3

(a) False. Lack of vitamin D certainly is a problem in young children and can lead to the development of rickets but older people can also suffer vitamin D deficiency. This results in a reduction in bone mass because the vitamin is needed to facilitate uptake of calcium from the gut. With inadequate uptake of calcium, new bone growth is slowed and bone is lost faster than it is replaced.

(b) False. Old people shrink when vertebrae become more and more compressed, due to the effects of gravity.

(c) Partially true, in that there is a considerable genetic influence on height. However, other factors, such as nutrition are of importance too. A child who is malnourished will not achieve his/her height potential.

(d) True (see Section 4.4.3).

Question 4.4

The muscles maintain the body's posture by being in tone even when the person is relaxed, and they work with ligaments, pads of cartilage (menisci) and fluid-filled pads of connective tissue (bursae) to stabilize joints.

Question 4.5

Health problems associated with the musculo-skeletal system are very common, especially as we bipedal humans age. Stresses on the spine are greater in bipedal mode than they would be if we were quadripedal, giving rise to associated back, joint and muscle problems. In addition, the development of varicose veins in adults, particularly those who stand for long periods of time, is in part attributable to bipedalism – gravity causes the blood to pool in the lower extremities, stretching the veins and so damaging the valves and impairing the return flow of blood to the heart.

ACKNOWLEDGEMENTS

Grateful acknowledgement is made to the following sources for permission to reproduce material within this product.

Figures

Figure 1.1a: Sovereign/Science Photo Library; *Figure 1.1b*: Scott Camazine/ Science Photo Library; *Figure 1.1c*: Tim Beddow/Science Photo Library; *Figure 1.2*: Science Photo Library; *Figure 1.4*: Gray, H. (1918) *Anatomy of the Human Body*, Lea and Febiger; *Figure 1.7*: Courtesy of Professor Mark Dupin; *Figure 1.12*: Fried, I. (1998) Electric current stimulates laughter, *Nature*, **391**, 12 February 1998. Used with permission of Nature Publishing Group; *Figures 1.13 and 1.26*: Vander, A. J., Sherman, J. H. and Luciano, D. S. (2001) *Human Physiology, The Mechanisms of Body Function*, 8th international edition, copyright © 2001, 1998, 1994, 1990, 1985, 1980, 1975, 1970 by McGraw-Hill, Inc., with permission of The McGraw-Hill Companies; *Figure 1.14*: Carola, R., Harley, J. P. and Noback, C. R. (1990) *Human Anatomy and Physiology*, 6th international edn, The McGraw-Hill Companies; *Figure 1.19*: Gray, E. G. (1976) The synapse, *Science Journal*, IPC/New Scientist Magazines.

Figure 2.6: Adapted from the website of the Department of Anatomy, University of Bristol; *Figures 2.9 and 2.11*: Adapted from the website of Cullen Lab Research, McGill Faculty of Medicine; *Figure 2.12*: http://transportation.ky.gov/ drlic/eye_test.htm; *Figure 2.19*: Courtesy of Advanced Bionics UK Ltd.

Figure 3.5: Biophoto Associates/Science Photo Library; *Figure 3.12*: John Paul Kay, Peter Arnold/Science Photo Library; *Figure 3.13*: Dr P. Marazzi/Science Photo Library; *Figure 3.15*: Krieger, D. T., Allen, W., Rizzo, F. and Krieger, H. P. (1971) Characterization of the normal temporal pattern of plasma corticosteroid levels, *J. Clin. Endocrinol. Metab.*, **32**, 266–284. Copyright © Williams and Wilkins, Publishers; *Figure 3.19*: Unger, R. H., Raskin, P., Srikant, C. B. and Orci, L. (1977) Glucagon and the A cells, *Recent Progress in Hormone Research*, **33**. Copyright © Academic Press Ltd.

Figure 4.1a and b: Redrawn from Vander, A. J., Sherman, J. H. and Luciano, D. S. (2001) *Human Physiology, The Mechanisms of Body Function*, 8th international edition, copyright © 2001, 1998, 1994, 1990, 1985, 1980, 1975, 1970 by McGraw-Hill, Inc., with permission of The McGraw-Hill Companies; *Figure 4.1c*: Martin, R. D. (1992) Primate locomotion and posture, in Jones, S., Martin, R., Pilbeam, D. and Bunney, S. (eds), *The Cambridge Encyclopaedia of Human Evolution*, Cambridge University Press; *Figures 4.3, 4.5, 4.16 and 4.20*: Tortora, G. J. and Grabowski, S. R. (1993) *Physiology*, 7th edn, HarperCollins Publishers Ltd; *Figure 4.4a*: Ed Reschke; *Figure 4.4b, 4.15, 4.18 and 4.19a*: Gottfried, S. (1994) *Human Biology*, Mosby Publications – Year Book, Inc.; *Figure 4.19b*: Biophoto Associates; *Figure 4.7, 4.9, 4.11 and 4.13*: Sinclair, D. (1989) *Human Growth After Birth*, 5th edn, by permission of Oxford University Press; *Figure 4.10*: Courtesy of Sally and Richard Greenhill.

Every effort has been made to contact copyright holders. If any have been inadvertently overlooked the publishers will be pleased to make the necessary arrangements at the first opportunity.

INDEX

Entries and page numbers in **bold type** refer to key words which are printed in **bold** in the text. Page numbers in italics are for items mainly or wholly in a figure or table.

A

accommodation 63

acetylcholine (ACh) 29, 119
  in muscle activation 167–8
  role in disorders 36

Achilles tendon 163

achondroplasia 146

acoustic tumours 79, 81

ACTH (adrenocorticotropic hormone) *99, 104*, 109, 128

actin 164, 168

action potentials 31–4
  generation 166–7, 168

acute pain 59

Addison's disease 109

ADH (antidiuretic hormone) 90
  secretion 100–1
  synthesis *99*

adipose tissue hormones 112–14

adolescents
  body shape and posture *155, 156, 157*
  bone growth 144, 146–8

adrenal glands 88, **93**–4
  damage to 109

adrenalin, secretion of 93–4, *124*, 126

adrenocorticotropic hormone (ACTH) *99, 104*, 109, 128

adrenocorticotropic hormone-releasing hormone (CRH) 103, *104*, 109, 128

adults, body shape and posture *155*, 156–7

aetiology 107

afferent fibres 11

ageing
  bone growth and 153
  curvature of the spine *157*
  hearing 78
  joint damage and 161–2
  muscle fibre loss 169–70
  musculo-skeletal disorders 134
  taste and smell 52, 54
  vision 65, 70

agonist 36

AIDS, use of anabolic steroids 87

alcohol
  drug interactions 44
  effect on cerebellum 20
  effect on eyes 67

aldosterone 88
  secretion of 94, 136

Alzheimers' disease
  neuron loss 8
  neurotransmitters and 36
  sensory ability 52, 54

amacrine cells *64*, 65

Amadori product 120

amputation, phantom limb pain 60

amygdala 17

anabolic steroids 86–7, 150
  testing for 170
  see also testosterone

anaerobic 169

androgen 95

aneurysm 46

anomalous trichromacy 69

anosmia 54

antagonist 36

anterior pituitary gland 95, 101–10

anti-inflammatory response, control of 88, 122

antibodies 97

antidepressants 36–7

antidiuretic hormone (ADH) *see* **ADH**

appendicular skeleton **137**, *138*

aqueous humour 63, 71

arachnoid mater 12

arthroplasty 162

articular cartilage *139, 159*, 160

aspartame 55

asthma, treatment of 86

astigmatism 65

astrocytes 31

ataxia 20

athletes
  drug abuse 86–7, 170
  injuries 134

ATP, in muscle activity 163–4, 169

audiometry 81

auditory agnosia 77

auditory cortex *15*, 17, 75
  damage to 77

auditory nerve 75

auditory system 73–7

autocrine action **122**

autoimmune responses 97

autonomic ganglion 28, *29*

autonomic nervous system 28–9
  see also enteric nervous system; parasympathetic nervous system; sympathetic nervous system

axial skeleton **137**, *138*

axons *30*, 31
  action potential 34
  in the corticospinal pathway 42
  damage to 46
  in nerves 10–11
  in retinal cells 68

B

babies
  body shape and posture *155, 156, 157*
  sensory ability 51–2

back pain 134–5, 136

balance 78
  control of 42–3
  loss of 78, 80, 81
  see also posture

basal ganglia *14*, **17**
  in movement 41

basilar membrane 75, *76*

behavioural disturbances 12, 16, 20
  see also psychological problems

benzodiazepine 45

betahistine 81

bipedalism 135–7

bipolar cells *64*, 65
blind spot *63*, **65**, 71
blindness 70, 71
blood calcium levels 147, *148*
blood cells
    production site 140
    synthesis 95
blood clots, in fractures 141, *142*, 143
blood corticosteroid levels 108, *109*
blood flow and gravity 135–6, 165
blood glucose levels
    regulation of 115–21
    in stress 94
body shape, changes in 155–8
body-water volume 89, 90, 91, 100
bone mass, reduction in 153–4
bones
    formation 139–41
    growth of 151–4
    human body 137, *138*
brain 13–20
    auditory pathways 75, *77*
    gustatory centres 56, *57*
    imaging 8–10
    lateralization 22–3
    olfactory pathways *55*
    pain centres 60, *61*
    response to tissue damage 38–42
    size 13
    visual areas 68
brain injury 45–6, 47
brainstem 19, 38
breast cancer, levels 86
breastfeeding, hormonal role in *100*, 101
Broca's area *15*, 22
Brodmann areas *15*
bursae *159*, 160

C

calcification 139
calcitonin 95, 153
calcium 35, 53, 95
    blood levels 147, *148*
    in bones 139, 147
    in healthy diets 152
    loss in bones 153, 154
callotomy 18
callus 142

calories 151
cameras, mode of action *63*
camouflage 69
cannabinoids 47
carbamazepine 44, 45
cardiac muscle 163
cartilage 139, *142*
    in growth 144, 146, 148
case reports
    Cushing's syndrome 111
    epilepsy 44
    fractured femur 142
    glaucoma 71
    Graves' disease 107
    head injury 48
    laughter 23–4
    Ménière's disease 81
    Phineas Gage 16
cataracts 70
catecholamines 34
    secretion *124*, 126
cell bodies *see* nucleus
cell membrane, electrical changes 32–4, 53
central loss of hearing 79
central nervous system (CNS) 10–11
    environment 12
    see also brain; spinal cord
cerebellum *16*, *19*, **20**
cerebral cortex 7
    areas and functions 15–17
    somatosensory 39
    thinning of 14–15
cerebral haemorrhage 46
cerebral hemispheres *9*, **14**–18
    lateralization 22–3
cerebrospinal fluid (CSF) 12, 14–15
childbirth
    riskiness 137
    role of oxytocin 91, *92*
childhood
    body shape and posture *155*, *157*
    growth hormone 148–9
    growth in 144–5, 146
cholesterol 88, 127, 128
choroid plexi *9*, 12
chromaffin cells 126
chronic pain 59
chyme, hormone secretion 91, 112

circumvallate papillae 54, *56*
CJD (Creutzfeldt-Jakob disease) 148–9
closed head injuries 46
Clostridium botulinum 167
CNS *see* central nervous system
cocaine 36, 67
cochlea 73, 74, 75, 80
cochlear implant 79
collagen, in skeleton development 139
collateral branch 38–9
colour blindness 69–70
colour vision 68–70
    in babies 51–2
coma 19, 47
compact bone 139–40
    formation *142*, 143
compound fracture 141
computerized angiography 8
computerized tomography (CT)
    scanning 8, *9*, 14
concave lenses *65*
concussion 47
conductive loss of hearing 79
cones 64, 69
congenital 54
consciousness
    levels of 47
    loss of 45–6
contact lenses 65
convex lenses *65*
cornea 63
corpus callosum 14, 18, 23
cortex *see* cerebral cortex
cortical association areas 16
cortical deafness 77
corticospinal pathway *41*, **42**, 60
corticosteroids 86, 88
    blood levels 108, 109
    secretion of 93, 94
    see also cortisol
cortisol 88, *127*
    binding 124
    effect on hepatocytes 96
    levels of 94
    secretion regulation 108–10
    synthesis 128
cortisone *127*
cranial nerves 21

cranium 15

creatine 169

Creutzfeldt-Jakob disease (CJD) 148–9

CRH (adrenocorticotropic hormone-releasing hormone) 103, *104*, 109, 128

cribriform plate 53, *54*

crushing injuries 46

CSF (cerebrospinal fluid) 12, 14–15

CT scanning 8, *9*, 14

curare 167

curvature of the spine 157

Cushing's syndrome 109–10, 111

cytokines 121–3

D

deafness 77

demyelination 31

dendrites 30

depolarization 33

depression, and neurotransmitter release 36

depth perception 51, 68

dermatomes *26*, 39

dermis 58, *59*

detectors, in physiological response 89

diabetes 119–20

and eye disease 68, 70, 71

diazepam 45, 80, 81

dichromacy 69

diffuse axonal injury 46

digestive hormones 112

discriminative touch 58

dislocation 160

diuretics 47, 80, 81, 90

diurnal rhythm **108**

dizziness 80, 81

dogs, sense of smell 52–3

dopamine 103, *104*

receptors 36

secretion *124*, 126

dorsal column–medial lemniscal tract 60, *61*

dorsal root ganglion 25

downregulation 114

drugs

anti-epileptic 44, 45

ear disorders 80, 81

effect on eyes 67, 68

psychotic 36

thyroid conditions 107

see also illegal drugs

dry eye syndrome 68

duodenum, hormone secretion 87, 91, 112

dura mater 12

E

eardrum 73

perforation 79

ears 73–5, *76*

infections 79–81

see also hearing

earwax 78, 79

effector organs *27*, *29*

efferent fibres 11

Einstein, Albert 8, 13

electrical potential, neurons 32–3, 53

electrical stimulation, brain 18, 24

electrocochleography 81

electromagnetic spectrum *62*

electronystagmography 81

embolus 143

emotions

and smell 52–3

tears 68

endocrine gland 87

endocrine system 85–8

organization of 93–7

role of 89–92

signalling in *98*, *100*

see also hormones

endogenous compounds **47**

endolymph 74, *75*, 78

endothelial cells 31

enteric nervous system 28, 29, 112

epidemiology

epilepsy 43

obesity 113

epidermis 58, 59

epilepsy 43–5

surgery for 18, 23, 24

epiphyseal plates 144, 148

erythropoietin 95

Eustachian tube *73*, *74*

excitatory synapses 35

exercise

effect on bones 152, 154

and muscles 169–70

see also athletes

exocrine glands 87

exocytosis 35

extradural haemorrhage 46

eyes 62–5

reflex response 66–8

refractive errors 65–6

eyesight *see* vision

F

facial nerve 54, 56, *57*

farsightedness 65–6

fascia 163

fear, smell of 52–3

feedback control

cortisol secretion *108*, *110*

insulin secretion *116*

lipid stores *113*

parathyroid secretion 147, *148*

and regulation 90–2

secretin secretion 91

thyroid secretion *106*

feedforward mechanisms 117

femur *138*, *139*

fractured 142, 143

growth in 144, 146

'fight or flight' 29

filiform papillae 54

Flourens, Marie-Jean-Pierre 7

fMRI (functional MRI) 10

focal point 63, 65–6

focal seizures 18, 43

foliate papillae 54, 56

follicle-stimulating hormone (FSH) *99*, *104*

fontanelles 156

food

control of intake 113–14

taste and smell 52, 54–6

see also nutrition

fovea 64, 69

fracture haematoma 141, *142*

fractures 141, 142, 143

frequency of sound 73

frontal lobes **16**

electrical stimulation 24

FSH (follicle-stimulating hormone) *99*, *104*

functional MRI (fMRI) 10

fungiform papillae 54, *56*

G

Gage, Phineas 16

ganglion 25, 28

gastric inhibitory peptide (GIP) 117

gastrin 112

genetics, and height 145–6

genotype 174

glabrous skin *59*

Glasgow Coma Scale 47

glasses 65

glaucoma 71

glial cells 31

glossopharyngeal nerve 54, *57*

glucagon 116

    breakdown 118–19

glucocorticoids 88

    see also cortisol

gluconeogenesis 94, 118–19

glucose 115

    see also blood glucose levels

glucose transport molecules 117

glycation 120

glycogen 117, 118

    in muscle activity 169

glycogen synthase 117–18

goitre 86, 106

gonadotropin-releasing hormone (GnRH) 103, *104*

gonads 95

    see also ovaries

grand mal 43

granulation tissue 142

Graves' disease 106, 107

gravity, and bipedalism 135–6

greenstick fracture 143

grey matter 25

growth

    genetics and 145–6

    in height 144–5

    hormones and 146–50

    nutrition and 151–4

    psychological factors and 154

growth factors 121–3

growth hormone

    effect on hepatocytes 96

    release of *99*, *104*

    treatment with 148–9

growth hormone-releasing hormone (GRH) 103, *104*

Guillain-Barré syndrome 166

gustation 52

    see also taste

gustatory cortex 56, *57*

gustatory pathway *57*

H

haematoma 46, 47

haematopoietic stem cells 95

haemorrhage, cerebral 46

hair cells 74, 75, *76*

hair follicle *58*, *59*

half-life of a hormone **123**–4, 128

hand-eye coordination 52

Harlow, John 16

head injuries 45–8, 54

healthy diet 151

hearing 73–5

    auditory pathways 77

    in babies 52

    impaired 78–9

hearing aids 79

heart, neural influences on 28

'heavy' carbon atoms 170

height

    and genetics 145–6

    growth in 144–5

    'normal' 145, 149

height charts 144–5

hemispheres *see* cerebral hemispheres

hepatocytes

    hormone secretion 96

    insulin signalling 117 18

    target cells 06

hernia 137

hippocampus 17

histologically identifiable **17**

homeostasis 28, 89, 91

    in bones 140

horizontal cells *64*, 65

hormone deficiencies, treatment 86

hormone replacement therapy (HRT) 86, 154

hormones

    adipose tissue 112–14

    digestive 112

    and growth 146–50

    life of 123–9

    production and generation 19

    regulation and control 90–2

    secretory sites *93*

    target cell interaction 96–7

    see also pancreatic hormones; steroids; thyroid hormones

human development

    body shape and posture 155–7

    height 144–5

    musculo-skeletal system 134, 139–40

humour *see* laughter

Huntington's disease 17

hydrocephalus 14–15

hydrocortisone 88

hyperglycaemia *115*, **119**–20

hypermetropia 65–6

hyperpolarization *33*, *34*

hyperthyroidism 85–6, 106–7, 150

hypoglycaemia *115*, **118**

hypothalamic-anterior pituitary axis 101–10

hypothalamic-pituitary axis 98–101

hypothalamus 10, *93*

    hormone secretion 95, *103*, *104*

    oxytocin secretion 91, *92*

    thyroid hormone secretion 105

hypothyroidism 85–6, 150

I

ICP (intracranial pressure) 46, 48

idiopathic epilepsy **43**, 44

IGF-1 *see* insulin-like growth factor

IL-2 (interleukin-2) 122

illegal drugs

    action at synapses 36

    effect on eyes 67

    in sports 86–7, 170

immune response, control of 122

infections

    ear 78, 79, 80–1

    fighting 122

inhibitory synapses 35

injuries *see* tissue damage

insulin

    injections 120

    secretion 116–18, 125

insulin-like growth factor (IGF-1) 95, 96, 122–3

    and bone growth 148

interleukins 122

interneurons 11

intracranial pressure (ICP) 46, 48

intraocular pressure 71

involuntary activities 28

iodine 86, 105, 106, *126*

iris 63

islets of Langerhans 116, *125*

J

joints 158–62

    pain detection 58, 59

ketone bodies 119

kidneys, hormone secretion 88, 94, 95

knee *159*, *160*

L

L-cones 69

labyrinthitis, acute 81

lactate accumulation 169

language *see* speech

laser treatment for eyes 70, 71

Lashley, Karl 7

lateral geniculate nucleus (LGN) 68

laughter, neuroanatomy of 23–4

lens 63

leptin 113–14

lesions 10

    to cerebellum 20

LGN (lateral geniculate nucleus) 68

LH (luteinizing hormone) *99*, *104*

ligaments 159, *160*

ligands 96–7

light *62*, 63–4

light reflex 66–7

limbic system 17, 18

    in gustatory pathway *57*

    in olfactory pathways 52, *55*

    see also amygdala; hippocampus

limbs, phantom pain 60

liver cells *see* hepatocytes

localization of function 13

luteinizing hormone (LH) *99*, *104*

lymph, movement of 165

lymphocytes 122

lysosomes 140

M

M-cones 69

macular degeneration 70

magnesium, in bones 139, 147

magnetic resonance imaging (MRI) 8, *9*, *24*, 81

    scanner *10*

mannitol 47, 48

marrow 140, 143

mechanical ventilation 47, 48

mechanoreceptors 58, 74

media, and neuroscience research 8

medial geniculate nucleus (MGN) 75

medulla 19

    auditory processing 75

    gustatory pathway 56, *57*

Meissner's corpuscles 58, *59*

melanocytes 109

melanoma, treatment of 122

membrane potential 32–3, 53

memory, hippocampus role in 17

Ménière's disease 80, 81

meninges 12

meningitis 12

menisci *159*, *160*

menopause

    osteoporosis and 154

    side effects 86, 95

Merkel's discs 58, *59*

MGN (medial geniculate nucleus) 75

microglia 31

micronutrients 151

midbrain 19

mineral salts

    for bone growth 151

    in bones 139, 147

mineralocorticoids 88

monozygotic twins 146

motor cortex *39*, 40, 41–2

    primary *15*, *16*

motor homunculus *39*

motor neurons 10, *30*, 166

    role in movement 27, 40–2

    in the somatic nervous system 28

    in the spinal cord 25

motor units 166–7

movement

    ageing and 161–2

    basal ganglia and 17

    brain regions involved in *39*, 40–1

    cerebellum and 20

    control of 42–3

    muscles and 166–70

    musculo-skeletal role in 133–4

    vestibular system and 78

MRI scanning **8**, *9*, *10*, *24*, 81

mucous membrane

    and smell 53, *54*

    and tear production 67

multiple sclerosis 31

muscle contraction 168–9

muscle fibres 163–4

    types of 169

muscles 163–5

    exercise and 169–70

    innervation 40, *41*

    movement and 166–70

    pain detection 58, 59

    reflex action 27–8, 29

musculo-skeletal system 133

    damage to 134–5, 160

    functions of 134

    growth in 144–54

    see also joints; muscles; skeleton

myasthenia 167–8

myelin 14, 25, *30*, 31, 166

    and transmission rates 34, 42

myelination 31, 42

myofibrils *164*

myopia 65–6

myosin 164, 168

N

nasal cavity, smell receptors 53, *54*

nearsightedness 65–6

negative feedback *see* feedback control

nerve cells *see* nucleus

nerve fibres *see* axons

nerve impulse *see* action potential

nerves 10–11

nervous system *11*
  signalling in *98, 100*
    see also central nervous system; peripheral nervous system
neurohormones 95, 98, *99*
  secretion of 102, *103*
neuromuscular junction 31, *32*, **166**, 167–8
neuronal cell bodies *see* nucleus
neurons
  action potentials 31–4
  loss in Alzheimers' disease 8
  in the nervous system 30–1
  neurosecretory 98, *99*
  in the peripheral nervous system 28
  see also interneurons; motor neurons; nociceptors; sensory neurons
neuropathic pain 59
neuropeptide Y 95, 113
neurosecretory neurons 98, *99*
neurosis, obsessional 36
neurotransmitters 29, 34–7, 56
night-time vision 64
nociceptors 27, 31, 39
  pain detection 59, 60
nodes of Ranvier *30*, 34
non-corticospinal pathway 42
non-steroidal anti-inflammatory drugs (NSAIDS) 162
noradrenalin 29
  secretion of 93–4, *124*, 126
norepinephrine 29
NSAIDS (non-steroidal anti-inflammatory drugs) 162
nucleus 17, *30*, 31, 95
  neurohormone secretion 98, *99*, 102
nutrition
  and growth 151–4
  see also food

O

obesity, clinical 113–14
obsessional neurosis 36
occipital lobes **16**
odours *see* smell
oedema 46
oestrogen 86
  and growth 150
old age *see* ageing

olfaction 52
  see also smell
olfactory bulb 53, 54, *55*
olfactory nerve 54
olfactory pathways 52, *55*
olfactory receptor neurons 53, 54, *55*
oligodendrocytes 31
open head injuries 46
opsin 64
optic chiasm *68*
optic nerve 65, 68
  damage to 71
orbitofrontal cortex *55*
organ of Corti 75, *76*
ossicles 73
ossification 139
osteoarthritis 160, 162
osteoblasts 139, 140–1
osteoclasts 140–1
osteocytes 139
osteoporosis 134, 141, 154
otitis media 80
otolith organs 78
oval window 73, *74*
ovaries, hormone synthesis 86, 95
oxygen consumption, post-exercise 169
oxytocin
  role of 91, *92*, 100–1
  synthesis *99*

P

pacemakers 8
Pacinian corpuscles 58, *59*
pain
  nervous system response 27, 29, 38–42
  sense of 59–61
pancreatic hormones 87, 91, 95
  role of 116–19
papillae 54, *56*
paracrine action **122**
parasympathetic nervous system 28–9
  eye reflex 67
  insulin secretion 116–17, *118*
parathyroid hormone, in bone growth 147
parietal lobes **16**
Parkinson's disease 17, 41
partial seizures 18, 43

pathological fracture 141
pelvis 136–7
peptides, secretion 95, *124*, 125
perilymph 74, *75*
peripheral nerves 25, *26*
peripheral nervous system (PNS) 10–11, 27–9
  see also autonomic nervous system
permeability, cell membrane 32–3
permissive role **108**
personality changes *see* behavioural disturbances
PET scanning **8**, *9*
petit mal 43
pH, feedback control of 91
phagocytes 140, 141
  in joints 160
phantom limb pain 60
phenytoin 45
phosphates, in bones 139, 147
photopigment 64, 69
photopupillary reflex 66–7
photoreceptors 64, 65
  damage to 67
phrenology 7
physiological variables, regulation and control 89–90
PIF *see* dopamine
pituitary gland
  anterior 95, 101–10
  endocrine cells in 95
  growth hormone from 148–9
  hormone secretion *103*
  hypothalamus and 98–101
  posterior 90, 100–1
PNS (peripheral nervous system) 10–11, 27–9
  see also autonomic nervous system
polypeptides, secretion *124*, 125
pons 19
portal veins 101–2
positive feedback 91–2
positron emission tomography (PET) 8, *9*
post-traumatic amnesia (PTA) 47
posterior pituitary gland, ADH secretion 90, 100–1
posture

changes in 155–8
control of 42–3
see also balance
potassium ions 33, 88, 94
pre-pro-hormones 125
presbyopia 65
primary auditory cortex *15*, **17**, 75
damage to 77
primary gustatory cortex 56, *57*
primary motor cortex *15*, **16**
primary olfactory cortex 53, *55*
primary somatosensory cortex *15*,
17, 39
primary visual cortex *15*, **17**, 68
pro-hormones 125, 126
progesterone 86, *127*
progestin 86
prolactin *99*, *100*, 101
proprioception 58
protein hormones, half-life 128–9
psychoactive drugs 36
psychological problems
and growth 154
see also behavioural disturbances
PTA (post-traumatic amnesia) 47
pupil 63
damage to 67
pure word deafness 77

R

receptor proteins, function of 96–7
red marrow 140
referred pain 60
reflex 27–8, 29, 40
refractive errors 65–6
refractory period 34
regulation
blood glucose levels 115–21
feedback in 90–2
physiological variables 89–90
rehabilitation centres 48
release-inhibiting factors 103, *104*
releasing hormones 103, *104*
remodelling of bone **140**–1
renal cell carcinoma 122
repolarization 33
resting potential 32–3
reticular formation 38–9

retina 63, 64
retinal ganglion cells *64*, **65**, 68
retinene 64
ribs
breaking of 158
breathing difficulties 161
rickets 152
rods 64
round window 74, *75*
Ruffini endings 58, *59*

S

S-cones 69
saccharin 55
saccule *74*, **78**
salt, dietary 80, 81, 87
saltatory conduction 34
salty taste 55
scalae 74, *75*
Schwann cells 31
SCN (suprachiasmatic nuclei) 68
second messenger 54
secretin 87, 91, 92
role in digestion 112
secretion 90
seizures
in epilepsy 43, 45
partial 18, 43
semicircular canals 74, **78**, 80
sensorineural loss of hearing 79
sensory homunculus 39
sensory neurons 10
in the spinal cord 25
sensory receptors *58*
serotonin 36–7
sex hormones 86, 88
and growth 150
production 95
see also oestrogen; progesterone;
testosterone
shivering 165
SIF (somatostatin) 103, *104*
sight *see* vision
signalling, in the nervous and
endocrine systems 98, *100*
signalling molecules 121–3
binding sites 96–7
hormones as *87*
simple fracture 141

skeletal muscle 163–5
skeleton 137, *138*, 139–43
see also bones; femur; vertebrae
skin, receptors in 58, *59*
skull, changes to 156
slipped disc *136*
small intestine, hormone secretion
87, 91, 112
smell 52–4, *55*
smiling 23–4
smooth muscle 163
activity 28
in the eye 63
Snellen letter chart 66
sodium ions 33, 53, 80, 94
sodium valproate 45
somatic nervous system 27, 28, *29*
somatosensory cortex *15*, 17, 39
pain pathways 60, *61*
somatostatin (SIF) 103, *104*
sound *see* hearing
sour taste 54, 55
speech
brain processing of 75
left brain link *15*, 22, 23
see also laughter
spinal cord 25, *26*
corticospinal pathway *41*
spinal nerves 25, *26*
spine *138*
curvature of 157
see also vertebrae
spinothalamic tract 60, *61*
'split-brain' patients 18, 23
spongy bone 139–40
formation *142*
sports *see* athletes; exercise
sprained joint **160**
standing up 136
stapedius 73–4
starvation 118–19
steroids 88
mode of action 108
secretion *124*, 127–8
treatment with 86
see also anabolic steroids;
corticosteroids
stomach, hormone secretion 112

strain **163**
stress, cortisol levels 94, 108–9
stroke 12
sub-arachnoid haemorrhage 46
sub-dural haemorrhage 46, 47
substantia nigra *14*, 41
sugars 55–6
sulcus 15
sunglasses 67
sunlight, and bone growth 152, 153, 154
suprachiasmatic nuclei (SCN) 68
surgery
    amputation 60
    brain 18, 23, 24
    eye 70, 71
    thyroidectomy 107
sweet taste 55, 56
sympathetic nervous system 28–9
    eye reflex 67
    glucagon secretion 119
synapses 31, *32*
    in neurotransmission 35–7
    in the tongue *56*
synaptic cleft 31, *32*, 56
synaptic vesicles 35, *56*
synesthesia 82
synovial fluid *159*, **160**
synovial joints 158–9

T

T lymphocytes 122
tachistoscope 23
target cells
    hormone interaction 87, 96–7
    for leptin 113
    neurohormones *103*
taste 54–7
taste buds 54, *56*
taste cells 54
TBI (traumatic brain injury) 45–6, 47
tears 67–8
temperature
    and muscle power *170*
    and thyroid hormone levels 89–90
temporal lobes **16**, 17
tendons *160*, **163**
tensor tympani 73–4
testosterone 86–7, *127*

and growth 150
tetanus in muscles **168**
thalamus 18–19, 38
    in gustatory pathway *57*
    in olfactory pathways *55*
    in visual pathways 68
thermoreceptors 58
thyroglobulin 127
thyroid gland 86, 95, 149
thyroid hormones 85
    in growth 149–50
    regulation 89–90
    secretion *104*, *105*–7, *124*, *126*–7
thyroidectomy 107
thyroxin *103*, *104*, 105
    in growth 149–50
    synthesis 126
tinnitus 80, 81
tissue damage
    detection 59
    healing of 142–3
    in joints 161
    nervous system response 27, 29, 38–42
tone in muscles 164, **165**
tongue *56*, *57*
    taste buds 54
tonotopic map 75, *77*
touch 58, *59*
trabeculae 140
trace elements 151
traumatic brain injury (TBI) 45–6, 47
traumatic head injuries 45–8, 54
TRH (thyroid-stimulating hormone-releasing hormone) 103, *104*, 105–6
tri-iodothyronine *103*, 105
    in growth 149–50
    synthesis 126
TSH (thyroid-stimulating hormone) 99, *103*, *104*, 105–6, 150
tunnel vision 71
twins, studies on 146
'twitch' 168
tympanic membrane 73
tyrosine, reactions 126–7

U

ultraviolet radiation, eye damage 67
under-reporting of disorders 135

urine production 90, 100
uterine muscle contractions, oxytocin role 91, *92*
utricle *74*, **78**

V

vagus nerve 112
varicose veins 136, 165
veins, blood flow 165
ventricles *9*, **12**, 14
vertebrae 25, *26*
    pressure on 136
vertigo 78, 80, 81
vestibular nerve 78
vestibular system *73*, **78**, 80
vestibule 74
visible light *see* light
vision
    and ageing 65, 70
    babies 51–2
    impaired 70–1
    night-time 64
    refractive errors 65–6
    see also colour vision
visual acuity 51, 66
visual cortex *15*, 17, 68
visual system 62–8
vitamin A 64, 151
vitamin D 152, 153
vitamins, for bone growth 151–2
vitreous humour 70
voluntary nervous system 27, 28, *29*

W

wavelengths 62, 69
Wernicke–Korsakoff syndrome 20
Wernicke's area *15*, 22
white adipose tissue *112*
white matter 25
work-related disorders 134–5, 162
wounds *see* tissue damage

Y

yellow marrow 140, 143